The Politics of Sentiment

The Politics of Sentiment

Imagining and Remembering Guayaquil

BY O. HUGO BENAVIDES

University of Texas Press ◀▼▶ *Austin*

First edition, 2006

Requests for permission to reproduce material from this work should be sent to:
Permissions, University of Texas Press, P.O. Box 7819, Austin, TX 78713-7819.
www.utexas.edu/utpress/about/bpermission.html

∞ The paper used in this book meets the minimum requirements of ANSI/NISO
Z39.48-1992 (R1997) (Permanence of Paper).

Library of Congress Cataloging-in-Publication Data

Benavides, O. Hugo (Oswald Hugo), 1968–
  Power and sensibility : the translocation of Guayaquilean modernity / by
O. Hugo Benavides. — 1st ed.
     p.   cm.
  Includes bibliographical references and index.

   ISBN: 0292713363

   1. Ethnology—Ecuador—Guayaquil.   2. Ecuador in literature.   3. National
characteristics, Ecuadorian.   4. Silva, Medardo Angel, 1898–1919—Criticism
and interpretation.   5. Guayaquil (Ecuador)—Social conditions.   6. Guayaquil
(Ecuador)—Race relations.   7. Guayaquil (Ecuador)—Politics and government.
I. Title.
  GN564.E2B46 2006
  306.09866'32—dc22
                                                              2006003103

To Gregory Lamont Allen,

Sin ti la cama es
ancha, sin ti no
entiendo el despertar

To G. Melissa García,

Por el esmero . . . ,
y la amistad, a pesar
de los pesares.

Volver a los 17 es como descifrar signos sin ser sabio competente.
—MERCEDES SOSA, *ORO*

It is like balancing books at a business college. And all history books are balanced, as balanced as books in a business college.
—RICHARD RODRÍGUEZ, *BROWN: THE LAST DISCOVERY OF AMERICA*

Por lo demás, nada tan contaminado de ficción como la historia de la Compañía . . . Desvarío laborioso y empobrecedor el de componer varios libros; el de explayar en quinientas páginas una idea cuya perfecta exposición oral cabe en pocos minutos.
—JORGE LUIS BORGES, *FICCIONES*

Contents

Preface
The Politics of Sentiment
and the Nature of the Real

This book is an ethnographic exploration of the politics of sentiment at the turn of the twentieth century in Guayaquil, Ecuador. I have used two theoretical constructs—Raymond Williams' (1977) notion of "structures of feeling" and Jacques Lacan's (1977) use of the nature of the Real—to assess the hegemonic ambiguity that develops within historically specific postcolonial contexts such as Guayaquilean identity in Ecuador.

The book is quite ambitious in scope, dealing as it does with issues of identity, politics, sentiment, history, and hegemony. In this sense, it is, above all, a study of the nature of hegemonic production and domination in Ecuador but always maintains a Latin American comparative perspective. The book is thus also a logical extension of my first book, which deals with the role of history in the hegemonic domination of the Latin American nation-state, again using Ecuador as a specific case study. My main objective here is to assess the role of sentiment in its historical production as essential to normative domination in which cultural production is implied and constantly operationalized.

Williams' (1977) structures of feeling are perfectly positioned to assess the political nature of the production of feeling. Like Williams, I am very much preoccupied with how hegemony works at the level of the particular, not because national hegemonic forms are unimportant but because we know less about how hegemony gets reproduced on a local, day-to-day scale. At the same time, even national discourse depends on localized production of culture, since, without daily cultural acts, there would be no ideological or material discourses through which to build political projects. The book thus asks how it is that hegemony is operationalized in people's lives. How is it that personal concerns of livelihood, survival, or simply existence are tied to larger historical discursive constraints and larger national discourses of domination? Using this line of inquiry, I envision, in a profoundly respectful way, this book as an ethnographic test of Williams' model of structures of feeling.

The evasive issue of life itself is also present in the book, and in my entire research endeavor. This research was fueled by my, and several colleagues', nostalgic figuration of postcolonial Guayaquilean identity. In a social gathering, like many before, between drinks, music, and tears, it became unbearably clear that this form of collective memorialization had to do as much with postcolonial politics as with looking for personal spaces in which to live a bit less burdened and limited by life's beautiful, but chaotic, reality. As a result of this experience, the political nature of sentiment became all the more apparent as well as a socially relevant issue to explore. Admittedly, one of my biggest challenges was to carry out the research in a manner that was conscious of the political dimension of sentiment and yet did not deny the unfathomability and unbearableness of those same feelings, and through them, of life.

It was at this crux that Jacques Lacan's (1977) discourse of the nature of the Real became not only useful but also central in my thinking through the political dimensions of sentiment and their ultimate success as repositories of hegemonic ambiguity. Lacan's idea of the Real allowed me to explore social reality as reality and fiction at one and the same time. According to Lacan, social realities (almost infinite in productive possibilities) are always produced by a profound internal process. The Real is, by its very nature, inaccessible to human knowledge and therefore to social analysis, precisely, perhaps, or even when the Real is implied in a historically informed manner through which particular social realities develop, as in the case of Guayaquilean identity.

I have used primarily Žižek's (1989, 1996, 2002; Žižek, Butler, Laclau 2000) understanding of Lacan's concept of the Real as a central void that occupies the core from which human experience can be understood, since, without this empty center, one would descend into insanity (it is precisely the absence of this void that marks schizophrenia). It is significant, to some degree, that, instead of using Antonio Gramsci's (1971) and Jacques Lacan's (1977) original formulations, I have decided to use two other theorists who, I believe, have reworked the concepts of hegemony and the Real to bring them closer to our postmodern understanding of the world. Thus, Williams' (1977) and Žižek's (2002) work contribute to rather than merely borrow from Gramsci's and Lacan's original theoretical proposals. These theoretical concerns are made more explicit in the first two chapters.

I hope that the book will serve as an ethnographic mirror that problematizes sentimental historical production in the articulation of hegemonic domination. I also hope to successfully exemplify domination without destroying or eliminating the ambiguous nature of all cultural (i.e., hegemonic) projects, all the while recognizing the centrality of life in all our social effects as complex and ambiguous human beings.

Acknowledgments

*A subsidiary question, not without general relevance: how to account
for the fact that all my life I've been the child who says the Emperor
is naked, while my brother never, not once, doubted or criticized
authority?*

*Mind you, a talent for seeing the Emperor's nakedness can mean his
other qualities are not noticed.*

*I am trying to write this book honestly. But were I to write it aged
eighty-five, how different would it be?*

—DORIS LESSING, UNDER MY SKIN

First of all, I would like to thank the grantors and institutions that made
this research possible. Primary among them is the Career Enhancement
Fellowship for Junior Faculty from Underrepresented Groups (Woodrow
Wilson National Foundation and Mellon Foundation), which allowed me
a yearlong sabbatical in which to finish the book. This time away from
teaching and administrative duties proved invaluable in allowing me to
think through my arguments and put the last touches on the manuscript.
I also must acknowledge the support of both a Fordham University Faculty
Fellowship and a Summer Grant that provided key support to carry
out the research.

As always, Fordham University has continued to provide a nurturing
environment for my scholarly pursuits. Primary among my supporters
has been the university chaplain, Father Gerald Balszczak, who, with
incomparable wisdom, humility, and humanity, contributed to making
the university setting the intellectually challenging and compassionate
place it should be. Thanks to the Department of Sociology and Anthropology,
which has been nothing less than supportive and welcoming of
my anthropological agenda. Special recognition to Profs. Allan Gilbert,
Mark Naison, and Orlando Rodríguez for helping me maneuver the intricate
world of academia and for shrugging off more than one frustrating
circumstance. Also my sincere gratitude to my colleagues Profs. Jeanne

Flavin and Jacquie Johnson for their generous friendship and support, again making this intellectual pursuit much more gratifying and meaningful than it otherwise would have been. Again my thanks and recognition to Rosa Giglio and Paula Genova for keeping the fort functioning, time after time, even under the most trying of circumstances.

To Prof. Leith Mullings, for her support over the years way above and beyond the call of duty. I continue to learn from her professional commitment to intellectual production for social transformation and a more just society. I only hope that I support and advise students with the same wisdom and generosity that she has shown me.

I also want to recognize the continued support of Profs. Juan Flores and Thomas Patterson, who have helped me since my graduate days at City University of New York. They have also made academic life that much easier and provided me with actual models for a socially committed and generous intellectual production.

A special recognition to my family, Gregory Allen, Melissa García, and Elissa West:

> To Gregory Allen, my partner and life, who has been there through good and bad times with the encouraging support that has always been beyond that of my wildest imagination. The last two years during which this book was coming to fruition may have been the hardest of our lives, only confirming my decision that there is nobody else with whom I would rather travel this rocky road of life.
>
> To Melissa García, sister and friend, who also has shared this project and my constant doubt with incredible tenacity and love. She, more than anybody else, has been the recipient of middle-of-the-night calls and intellectual doubts that over and over again she managed to convert into precious moments of insight and camaraderie. I also must recognize her important intellectual contribution to the book in multiple ways: as my assistant during the fieldwork stage of the project; carrying out and transcribing interviews, providing photographs; and tracking down books and facts on the Web, a task that would easily have overwhelmed me.
>
> To Elissa West, for her assistance in helping me to get to know whom I really have always wanted to be.

As always, to my friends Aseel Sawalha, Bernice Kurchin, Jeannete Bramlett, Murphy Halliburton, Molly Doane, Arlene Dávila, and Beverlee Bruce, who have also helped me traverse the complicated roadway these last couple of years. There is no way Greg and I could have done it without you, and there is no way to repay that gift.

To the staff at the University of Texas Press for its support and labor in seeing this project through. Particular thanks to Allison Faust, Nancy Bryan, and Leslie Tingle for attending to the review process and answering all my inquiries, and above all to Theresa May for believing in this project with her characteristic creative buoyancy and intellectual honesty. Her support made the project a much more exciting and tenable adventure than I had initially dreamed it could be. To all at the Press, including the reviewers, my sincere thanks for making this book possible.

My gratitude to Kathy Bork for her work, cultural awareness, and powerful editing skills as well. Her labor and commitment have made this book and my previous one (*Making Ecuadorian Histories: Four Centuries of Defining Power*) more coherent and readable than they were originally. I am happy to have found somebody as competent, meticulous, and responsible as she to share the editing process of these projects with.

As always, to Julio Jaramillo, Olimpo Cárdenas, José Feliciano, Charlie Zaá, Joan Manuel Serrat, Simply Red, Diana Krall, Seal, among many others, who provided the music that continually fed life into the project.

A special thanks to a group of writers, all women, who in the last two years have provided me with significant faith and excitement in believing in the power of words: Doris Lessing, Marguerite Yourcenar, Elena Poniatowska, Jamaica Kincaid, and Alma Guillermoprieto. My sincere gratitude, also, to Marguerite Duras, to whom the Conclusion is particularly indebted. In many ways, the last chapter is an expression of my continuing struggle to understand the full dimensions of her masterpiece, *The Lover* (1997).

Again, my heart and love to Gregory. There are no words to describe the beauty and struggle which his presence has brought to my life. The courage of the last two years only makes me yearn for more and contemplate in awe the path already traveled.

And finally, to Medardo Ángel Silva. This book is definitely his and dedicated to his memory in more ways than one, but, perhaps above all, in recognition of his courage and struggle to maintain hope and love in a context that was very close to being hopeless. For that momentous effort, which clearly afforded me and countless other Guayaquileans a place of solace when we felt we had none, mis más sinceros agradecimientos.

The Politics of Sentiment

Introduction
Medardo Ángel Silva and Guayaquil Antiguo at the Turn of the Twentieth Century

The Hegemonic and Cultural Implications of a Guayaquilean Romance

> Perdona que no tenga palabras con que pueda
> decirte la inefable pasión que me devora
> para expresar mi amor solamente me queda
> rasgarme el pecho, Amada, y en tu mano de
> seda; ¡dejar mi palpitante corazón que te
> adora!
>
> —MEDARDO ÁNGEL SILVA, "EL ALMA EN LOS LABIOS"

These last lines of Medardo Ángel Silva's influential poem, "El alma en los labios," have provided Guayaquileans a productive tool for self- and communal identification over the last century. (See Vallejo's novel about Silva [2003].) The poem, sung by legendary Guayaquilean artists such as Julio Jaramillo and Olimpo Cárdenas, has become an emotional outlet not only for love-torn individuals but also for those who, at different times, have faced the tragedy of not obtaining the ultimate object of their desire, whatever that desire might be. In this manner, Silva's life and work have provided a succinct form of national identification within the prohibitive nature of desire in the postcolonial setting of the city of Guayaquil. A century after his death Silva's poetry is sung, memorized, and studied with a keenness that betrays the central place it holds in the development of the city's national identity ("El arte se junta con la medicina" 2001). This is a phenomenon of remembrance that was already evolving only twenty-six years after his death ("Página literaria de 'El Telégrafo'" 1945).

The fact that Silva's production (in which category I include his life as well as his literary work) has assumed such a hegemonic stance in contemporary discourse is surprising precisely because he lived only twenty-one years, and his existence was fraught with unbearable emotional and social contradictions. Yet it is these same contradictions that, although directly contributing to Silva's death, also enabled him to become the dominant and iconic figure that he is today.

The importance of sentiment in the production of a national Guayaquilean identity was made explicit to me at a small gathering of friends as we listened to Silva's poem transformed into *pasillo* (a traditional Ecuadorian musical genre). As we shared drinks and nostalgic memories of our lives and the city, it became painfully obvious that these "individual memories" and "sentiments" were neither merely individual nor devoid of larger social significance. Rather, they were the most social of our effects and provided for our singular identification as Guayaquileans, marking us, naturally, as lifelong friends. In this manner, our feelings' explicitly individual markers—far from denying their social importance—allowed our nostalgia- and desire-driven sentiments to fulfill their nationalizing and political goal of fusing and providing for our geographical and cultural identification. It was this normalizing feature of sentiment that was most salient, due to its provocative silence.

This drinking episode (*chupa* in Guayaquilean parlance) fueled my research and made me decide to interview Guayaquileans, in both Guayaquil and the United States, regarding the national elements of the production of sentiment. Raymond Williams' (1977) work on the consolidation of hegemony through the structures of feeling was particularly helpful in organizing the research project. I carried out in-depth interviews and collected life histories of Guayaquileans. I asked them questions about national and regional identification, nostalgia for the city, *pasillos,* alcohol, motherly love, and other effusive sentiments. My research was supported by my own Guayaquilean identity and by my having lived in the city throughout my adolescence and early adulthood.

Almost at the outset, I was extremely intrigued by the ambiguous iconization of the Afro-Ecuadorian poet Medardo Ángel Silva. Everybody I spoke with knew who he was; many of them shared tears, alcohol, and memories with me as we listened to Silva's poetry and music as performed by Julio Jaramillo. However, what people said about Silva seemed always to be contradictory: they heralded him as representative of Guayaquilean pride but glossed over the more transgressive details of his character, such as his being expelled from high school (for refusing to cut his hair, *melena*) and, of course, his un-Catholic decision to commit suicide (if he in fact did). At the same time, most people's comments only vaguely related to the official version of Silva's life as expressed in the compulsory teaching of his work and in all the city's high school textbooks.

Therefore, even though he was almost exclusively the only Ecuadorian or Guayaquilean poet anybody could name, only a couple knew Silva was black, and even fewer had any inkling of the disturbing social (and sexual) contradictions that might have led to his early death. For example, everybody I interviewed was willing to emphasize his longing for his pubescent girlfriend but not his acknowledged despair over the death of his closest male friend just a couple of months before his probable suicide. Perhaps even more telling was that few if any of my informants wondered why or, even better, how a poor young black man who lived over a hundred years ago could provide such a significant means of identification and reaffirm our national Guayaquilean identity in such contemporary terms.

Tellingly and in this same vein, none of my informants were able to place Silva and his work within the politically troubled turn of the twentieth century. During Silva's life (1898–1919), Guayaquil lived through what is arguably its most violent period and the consolidation of Ecuador's Liberal Revolution (1895–1912). The Liberal Revolution would catapult Gen. Eloy Alfaro to power and allow the coastal bourgeoisie to challenge the highland *hacendado* elites' claim to national government while producing an enormous impact in terms of national restructuring of economic and race relations. Silva's lifetime would also include the vast mobilization of workers, many of whom would perish in the massacre of November 15, 1922, which ultimately resulted in the founding of socialist and leftist political parties. However, these two processes, Silva's intense poetic images, and his troubled social surroundings are never integrated but, rather, function as two totally different sources of effusively sentimental identification. On the one hand, one has a nostalgic image of a representational Guayaquil Antiguo (Old Guayaquil) as a paradisiacal and ephemeral tropical fantasy city at the turn of the century; on the other hand, we have a troubled Silva feeling love-torn emotions that led to his early death. These are the similar individual emotions that Guayaquileans share in their continual engagement with their past while drinking and listening to *pasillos* with enormous feelings of sadness and nostalgia.

This book focuses on these two seemingly contradictory, if romantic, images and assesses how is it that they not only coexist but also are actively invested in the production of a Guayaquilean identity and the image of the city as we know it today. In this book I question, using Williams' structures of feeling, the cultural amnesia essential for the nostalgic production of the past that enables the city's contemporary political structure of domination and oppression. In this manner, I am investing Silva's memory with the romantic memorialization of a Guayaquil Antiguo and the troubled historical period that this metonymic image so effectively and ambiguously represents and conceals (see Chapters 1 and 2). At the same time, I use Silva's memory, life, and work as a hermeneutical tool for assessing the cultural, gender, and racial problematics that a Guayaquilean identity necessarily affords (see Chapters 3, 4, and 5). Ultimately, I use Silva and Guayaquil Antiguo as cultural forms that engage Guayaquilean modernity and assess how they came to serve the present political project while necessarily providing an effusive form of social agency for Guayaquileans. It is this same social agency that continues to attract most of the national migrants from throughout the country to Guayaquil. This is why I have interviewed Guayaquileans living in the United States, specifically, New York City. These diasporic interviews provide a way of assessing the migration of Guayaquilean modernity as well as the reoccurring disruption of Guayaquilean identity as an essential constitution of its dynamic, modern rearticulation.

The Soul on Medardo Ángel's Lips

Silva's early death is described with unbearable horror in the newspaper reports of the period ("Medardo Ángel Silva" 1919; see also Gómez Iturralde 1998), and even a century later it is shocking to his fellow Guayaquileans ("El arte se junta con la medicina" 2001; "Medardo A. Silva: Le fueron duros sus años" 1999). As I argue throughout the book, however, the emotions, ideas, and intimate pain reflected in his writing and in his tragic life are not shocking to the same Guayaquilean population that seems unwilling to legitimate his suicide as a valid cultural act. Silva's poetry is an integral part of the cultural composition of Guayaquil, Ecuador's largest urban center and port. Silva is unarguably the most influential poet in the city's modern history. His relevance is expressed in the monuments erected to his memory, his poems' transformation into popular *pasillos,* and the requirement that his poetry be read in all of the city's high schools.

The Liberal Revolution and the workers' (i.e., the socialist) movement (1910–1930) were central formative experiences for the still-emerging Ecuadorian nation, and therefore were vital to Silva's preoccupation with race, sexuality, and class. This preoccupation could not but problematize the European (i.e., white) and elite modernist ideal that pervaded the young Ecuadorian republic and its intellectuals during Silva's lifetime. His oeuvre thus came to ambiguously represent the popular strands of daily sentiment inherent in the city's vibrant street life as well as the refined tastes of the city's elite and most powerful cultural circles. It is this hegemonic ambiguity that makes Silva's life a useful source for assessing the dynamics of cultural power and the production of popular culture.

I question how sentiments both determine and are determined by the social milieu that they embody and explore how feelings are intimately woven into and produced within the social tapestry of racial, ethnic, class, gender, sexual, and age differentiation. Thus, rather than assessing them as independent subjective elements, I judge emotions as essential in the production and maintenance of social hierarchies (see Davis 1998; McCarthy and Franks 1989; Shank 2000; Wexler 2000).

There is little doubt that Silva's use of romantic distance and a pseudoautobiographical approach afforded him poetic license. It would seem that these literary concealments were warranted by the hostile social environment in which he lived. There is also little doubt that this harsh social environment was central in providing him the (painful) inspiration and motivation for the ambiguous emotions and feelings that are traditionally kept in check by the normative Guayaquilean cultural order. In this respect, Silva's writing is very much in keeping with a postcolonial legacy harbored between ingrained and internalized forms of domination and less-explicit mechanisms of external oppression (Fanon 1970; Kincaid 1997; Memmi 1991).

As Williams (1977) and other scholars (Butler 1997b; Foucault 1980; Taussig 1992), note, cultural hegemony works in subtle yet powerful ways. Feelings, emotions, and sentiments as powerful cultural markers are interwoven into more structural constraints that define one's way of acting and, most important, of being. Silva, almost alone, carved out a particular semantic structure that expressed the different class, racial, and sexual inhibitions that he experienced in the early part of the twentieth century in Guayaquil. It has been argued that Silva's early suicide symbolizes the failure of his life, yet his iconic popularity and semantic power would seem to denote the contrary. Silva's inability to connect to his surroundings, his family, and, ultimately, himself has struck a "popular" chord in generations of Guayaquileans who have faced similar postcolonial forms of social restraint and repressive environment (see Kincaid [1997] and Fanon [1970] for similar discussions). Therefore, far from making him a failure, Silva's poetic license may have cost him dearly but still enabled him to enunciate the stark social identities that Guayaquileans have struggled with and against in the dynamic self-definition of their modern cultural identity.

It is not a coincidence that Silva's ambiguity and personal anguish, more so than that of any other cultural icon, marks the most realistic form of social identification for the country's largest metropolis. Through his life's work Silva crystallized structures of feeling that slowly became hegemonic and defined a dominant social formation which was only just beginning to emerge during his lifetime. As Williams (1977) claims, it is only now that this hegemonic social formation is locked into place, which is demonstrated by Guayaquileans being able to publicly weep for their love, their lost youth, or, ultimately, for all that these translate into: an identity of loss, in other words, an identity based on the rejection of oneself and constituted of what one does not have or is not. In essence, Silva's structures of feeling comprise a way of being constituted by the anguish and pain that come from not belonging, of not fitting in.

Today these sentiments are no longer preemergent, as they were in Silva's time, but are a way of being for most Guayaquileans, that is, of being Guayaquilean, which has been seductively hegemonized into position. It is this identity of postcolonial rejection, I argue, that makes Guayaquileans identify with Silva and that, at the same time, allows us, through Silva's writing, to start assessing the socially constitutive nature of these sentiments more fully.

This colonial-identity mode of rejection, translated into a postcolonial setting, is marked by its no longer exclusively, or even mostly, being sustained by official empirical constraints, since those have been triumphantly internalized into the subject's constitution. It is because of this postcolonial turn of events, in which the dominated dominate themselves, that Silva's writing and life are useful tools for assessing cultural hegemonic articulation. In a broad sense, understanding how the postcolonial subject is constituted as such and formulates its future as a free agent in which it subjects itself without a colonial empire to blame is also the essence of the postcolonial debate (see Butler 1997a, 1997b; McClintock, Mufti, and Shohat 1997).

Analyzing Silva as an Ecuadorian cultural icon enriches our understanding of hegemony and how it works at a much more daily, local level (see Martillo Monserrate 1999) without allowing us to lose sight of its influence on the larger, national scene. Hegemony's power lies not only in its grand ideological manipulation but also in its subtle forms of articulation in the daily sentiments of a community's history. Hegemony works not because it is monolithically sustained and advocated but, rather, because it relies on people's living contradictory lives, or what they on some conscious level know to be an outright denial of reality (Sayer 1994), what Taussig (1997: 114) refers to as "the duper being duped" (see also Nelson 2001; Žižek 1989). Hegemony, therefore, is articulated through the subtle classification of the chaos that is life into artificial categories and concepts (Foucault 1993; see also Baldwin 1984; Duras 1986; Lessing 1987). In similar fashion, Silva's ambivalent articulation of structures of feeling expresses how essentializing sentiments are formulated and classified into normative behavior. Ultimately, analysis of Silva's life and work contributes to the understanding of the hegemonic relationship between the development of popular icons/semantic figures, the officialization of memory, and the daily construction of people's livelihood.

The fact that a century after his death Silva's writing is still a powerful cultural marker of Guayaquilean identity testifies to the underlining hegemonic agents with which he wrestled. Even though his poetry has been consistently portrayed as individualistic, melancholic, nostalgic, and sentimental (Cueva 1986), it has greatly echoed among the city's passing generations. It is Silva's popularity that makes one question an individualistic interpretation of his work; instead, it reflects the communal ramifications of these "individualistic" feelings, since they are shared by the majority of Guayaquileans. However, even though most Guayaquileans feel and understand what Silva is talking about, that is, an intimate anguish in the face of social upheaval and hierarchical constraints, these sentiments are still defined as individual feelings (which all know to be a lie) rather than as structures of feeling that are intimately tied to a normative and exploitative social hegemonic structure. This denial betrays the fact that an assessment of these particular structures of feeling, which began to emerge almost a century ago, would question not only the reigning moral order and the oligarchic stronghold of Guayaquil's wealthiest families but also the official representation of the city's past and reconstructed cultural identity (Benavides 2002; see also Kraniauskas in Monsiváis 1997).

In the remaining sections of this introductory chapter, I focus on both the theoretical framework of the book and the complex and subtle autobiographical approaches Silva used. I argue that Silva's life was afforded such a degree of hegemonic positionality that a century later his approaches are part of the main tenets of Guayaquil's and Ecuador's national cultural vitality, precisely because they reflect the physical and emotional impossibility of his life. To this end, I use Silva's writing to assess the consolidation of sentiments as "pure" feelings and culturally neutral acts at the turn of the twentieth century in Ecuador.

There is no question that Silva's life and sentiments have achieved a hegemonic position in the city's reified historical imagery. It is a remarkable form of revenge that it was Silva, one of the city's most economically oppressed, racially discriminated against, and sexually ambivalent inhabitants, who expressed what feeling and being from Guayaquil is all about. When Silva says (N.d.: 88),

Madre: la vida enferma y triste que me has dado
no vale los dolores que ha costado;
no vale tu sufrir intenso, madre mía,
ese brote de llanto y de melancolía,[1]

Guayaquileans know exactly what he is talking about, and cultural hegemony is seductively locked into position.

Structures of Feeling and Cultural Hegemony

Since the 1980s, hegemony, and particularly cultural hegemony, has become a focus of scholarly concern (Joseph and Nugent 1994; Mallon 1995; Popular Memory Group 1982; Scott 1985; Sider and Smith 1997; Silverblatt 1988). Gramsci's (1971) original proposal, written, significantly, from a prison cell to explain communities' self-imposed domination, has been continually revisited by Marxist thinkers wishing to analyze the articulation of political domination and power (see Crehan 2002). Two of the most original contributions to the reassessment of Gramsci's concept of hegemony have been offered by Louis Althusser (1971) and Michel Foucault (1988, 1990, 1994, 1995). Althusser's widely influential analysis of political domination freed the discussion of power from both the economic and the dialectical determination of traditional Marxist class analyses. He placed the formative elements of ideological power in the cultural production of material processes that constrain and define political domination. His examples of state education and religious indoctrination furthered the exploration of ideology not as a mere epiphenomenon of economic production but as a quasi-independent element of cultural interaction. Despite struggling to maintain a more orthodox Marxist perspective, and significantly distancing himself from his own problematic conclusions, Althusser opened the way for assessing the independent productive power of domination instead of assessing it only in negative and repressive terms (see also Merleau-Ponty 1963).

This is precisely where Michel Foucault's work is most enlightening. Some of his main contributions are located within his studies of social institutions—prisons, asylums, hospitals—as normalizing agents as well as the elaboration of social discourse as a useful analytical tool. For Foucault, hegemony works not because it is actively operationalized from the outside but, quite the opposite, because domination is actually connected to our own center, making us the most active imposers of our own constraints:

> What makes power hold good, what makes it accepted, is simply the fact that it doesn't only weigh on us as a force that says no, but that it traverses and produces things, it induces pleasure, forms knowledge, produces discourse. It needs to be considered as a productive network which runs through the whole social body, much more than as a negative instance whose function is repression. (Foucault 1980: 119)

> In thinking of the mechanism of power, I am thinking rather of its capillary form of existence, the point where power reaches into the very grain of individuals, touches their bodies and inserts itself into their actions and attitudes, their discourses, learning processes and everyday lives. (Foucault 1980: 39)

In a similar vein, Raymond Williams was also actively concerned with the articulation of hegemony and cultural production. In his influential *Marxism and Literature* (1977), Williams develops elements that, according to him, serve to assess hegemony and offer a better understanding of how it is deployed. "Structures of feeling" are such an element and, according to Williams, help bridge the gap between a static understanding of class formation lodged in its own formative institutions and corresponding ideology and the daily life of individuals and the production of popular culture. Williams proposes his structures of feeling as a "cultural hypothesis" for understanding the relationship between structural constraints and the dynamic elements of everyday life (1977: 132): "[Structures of feeling are] concerned with meanings and values as they are actively lived and felt, and the relations between these and formal or systematic beliefs. A social experience which is still in process, often indeed not yet recognized as social but taken to be private, idiosyncratic and even isolating but which in analysis (though rarely otherwise) has its emergent, connecting and dominant characteristics, indeed its specific hierarchies."

Far from abandoning a formal class analysis, Williams is interested in thinking through the problem of class formation. He is aware that social analysis is incredibly adept at defining class formation in static periodizations of historical production but has a much harder time assessing societies' dynamic and constant class reproduction. In other words, social analysis is equipped to assess society in descriptive historical terms but is almost incapable of addressing historical life in its daily possibilities and impossibilities.

A similar theoretical constraint has become central in the debates of contemporary historiography, particularly in postcolonial contexts (see McClintock, Mufti, and Shohat 1997; Mignolo 2000; Spivak 1999). These postcolonial texts critique social analyses that are content to describe discrete periods of cultural and social reproduction but seem unable to describe societies' dynamic cultural life. It would seem that these moments of social analysis always translate into the death of the social subject, and that the subject's death is essential to making the subject known, or "real," and vice versa (see Butler 1997a, 1997b; McClintock, Mufti, and Shohat 1997; Murray 1997; Salecl and Žižek 1996).

A varied number of writers, from Herman Hesse (1994) to Marcela Serrano (1997), have expressed the personal and political depth of this problematic: that the written representation implies the subject's death; and that only a dynamic nonrepresentational approach could actually provide a way of assessing life in its multiple incongruencies. This humanistic debate, unfortunately trivialized by many social scientists, not only is essential to our understanding of cultural behavior but also has slowly become an intricate part of the debates over human rights and native communities' struggle. For example, it is precisely this point that is at the heart of 1992 Nobel Peace Prize laureate Rigoberta Menchú's final account of her struggle for indigenous rights in Guatemala (1985: 247): "Nevertheless, I'm still keeping my Indian identity a secret. I'm still keeping secret what I think no-one should know. Not even anthropologists or intellectuals, no matter how many books they have, can find out all our secrets." This "secret" (and the ravaging controversy over Menchú's historical accuracy—see Arias 2001; Nelson 2001; and Stoll 1999) is what seems to be at the heart of all these scholars' and writers' concern. Ana Castillo has captured this historical disjuncture, complete with the engendered problematic also critically articulated in Gayatri Spivak's (1999) writing (1996: 119; my emphasis): "One had to be convinced that there was merit in recording history since that was the purpose of writing, after all. It might be history that everyone agreed with or history that got you hanged for writing it but for which your name was revered in the future and then read to revise history. But it was all history and it was all myth, since history is myth. Starting with one's own story. More specifically, her story, which was a myth which she resisted to make into *history*."

In this problematic context, Williams' structures of feeling provide a sophisticated manner in which, if not to solve, then at least to broach the specific disjuncture between historical and cultural representation. This is evident in the fact that he refers to "thought as felt and feeling as thought (1977: 132): practical consciousness of a present kind, in a living and interrelating community." As Williams states, he is interested in the actual, lived-in relationship of people in their daily life and not simply in a model or abstraction of their social processes (1977: 130): "in relationships that are more than systematic exchanges between fixed units." For Williams (1977: 131), "it [structure of feeling] is a kind of feeling and thinking which is indeed social and material, but each in an embryonic phase before it can become fully articulate and defined exchange."

Williams also distances himself from orthodox Marxist thought and explicitly states that "structures of feeling" are not mere "epiphenomena of changed institutions, formations and beliefs, or merely secondary evidence of changed social and economic relations between and within classes." However, in this same regard, he is quite careful to not equate all artistic expressions with "structures of feeling" (1977: 131). He believes that there always will be, and that even the majority of artistic ventures are, a direct manifestation of dominant or residual social formations. Meanwhile, structures of feeling do not respond to either kind of social formation but, rather, represent and express an emerging social formation still unidentifiable in an explicit manner (1977: 134):

It is a structured formation which, because it is at the very edge of semantic availability, has many of the characteristics of a pre-formation, until specific articulations—new semantic figures—are discovered in material practice: often, as it happens, in relatively isolated ways, which are only later seen to compose a significant (often in fact minority) generation; this often, in turn, the generation that substantially connects to its successors. It is thus a specific structure of particular linkages, particular emphases and suppressions, and, in what are often its most recognizable forms, particular deep starting-point and conclusions.

Because of their unique internal dynamic, structures of feeling are very much a "cultural hypothesis" that always needs to be reassessed. Strongly within a Marxist tradition, Williams proposes structures of feeling as both an empirical historical and cultural question of "detailed substantiation" (1977: 135). Because of the nature of social life in general, it is impossible (beyond a mere informed guessing game) to define structures of feeling in the present. Rather, all we are capable of doing is concretely informed historiographical work to understand how particular structures of feeling, undetectable at their time of origin, managed to contribute to the solidification of a contemporary dominant social formation. Far from falling into the trap of present-day cultural representations (see Rosaldo 1989, for a similar critique), Williams is acutely aware of the need for a critical historiography. Unlike many social scientists, he is not interested in describing or analyzing contemporary social life as much as in assessing how contemporary social life came into existence and achieved its hegemonic stance (1977: 132): "These [structures of feeling] are often more recognizable at a later stage, once they have been formalized, classified, built into institutions and formations. By that time the case is different; a new structure of feeling will usually already have begun to form, in the true social present."

Taking into account Williams' contribution, I question the representation of sentiments as neutral, personal, and individual elements precisely because they are so closely tied to the social milieu in which they are produced. By questioning their neutral representation, I also see the articulation of sentiments as a cultural manifestation of power dynamics, since it is exactly this assumed neutrality that makes sentiments essential in the enabling of any reformulation of power (see Butler 1997a; Foucault 1993; Stoler 1996; Taussig 1992).

Silva's literary and historical figure within the mythical representation of Guayaquil Antiguo (see next section) clearly provides a valuable opportunity for assessing Williams' structures of feeling as a cultural hypothesis and their relationship to the normalizing of social life and the enabling of hegemonic articulation. Silva expresses an effusive level of sentiment (structures of feeling) that resonated within a wider cultural context of social power and normative agents throughout the twentieth century. Not surprisingly, his work traditionally has been seen as private, subjective, and individualistic (Cueva 1981, 1986) instead of as offering an opportunity to assess social experience in the making, within its specific formulations of power and set hierarchies. My main objective is understanding the particular process by which his poetry and life, and their sentiments, achieved a hegemonic stance (Alonso 1995).

Ultimately, Silva allows us to assess the formative hegemonic construction of sentiments that were normalized racially, sexually, and in terms of class initially almost a century ago in Guayaquil. Today these define what being from Guayaquil is all about. It is also at this crossroads that the use of structures of feeling proves quite advantageous in defining the contours of the production of a vibrant Guayaquilean past (Guayaquil Antiguo) and popular national cultural heritage.

Guayaquil Antiguo: Guayaquil at the Turn of the Century (1895–1930)

The images of Guayaquil at the turn of the twentieth century have forever been captured in etchings and photographs (Figures 1–4). These turn-of-the-century drawings and pictures have provided the city with the reification of its past commonly referred to as Guayaquil Antiguo. Like all reconstructions, this one is an artifice for rebuilding a past we wish might have been (Abu-El Haj 2001; Alonso 1988; Castañeda 1995,

Figure 1. Colegio Vicente Rocafuerte, where the present-day post office is located. Archivo Histórico del Guayas (http://www.guayaquilhistorico.org.ec/webpages/fundacion.htm).

Figure 2. Calle Villamil. Archivo Histórico del Guayas
(http://www.guayaquilhistorico.org.ec/webpages/fundacion.htm).

1996; Handler and Gable 1997; Kohl and Fawcett 1995; Patterson and
Schmidt 1995; Trouillot 1995). The name Guayaquil Antiguo itself offers antiquity and, through it, authority and authenticity tied to a past
that is less than a century old. But more important, the black-and-white
representations of grand wooden houses, lumberyards, and empty central
avenues depict a setting devoid of the class conflict, racial tension, and
sexual repression which permeated the city at the turn of the century.
These idealized representations of Guayaquil also provided a romantic
fantasy of peace and tranquillity for the largely white and white/mestizo
landholding elite. The lack of evidence for the urban chaos in these pictures speaks volumes about the representation of two of the city's largest
social movements (the Liberal Revolution and the workers' movement)
and about the city's worst modern massacre, which occurred during this
period.

Particularly telling in this regard is how Silva's life, tumultuous and
tragic as it was, is continually described as denying his coexistence with
either of these two social revolutions. Even Silva's main biographer, Abel
Romero Castillo (1970), ignores both of these events in his detailed
narrative of Silva's life. Considering Silva's emerging literary and journalistic importance; his attendance at Guayaquil's most important schools,

La Filantrópica and Vicente Rocafuerte; and the known participation of students in street skirmishes and social uprisings, this absence becomes quite significant.

There is no doubt, however, that this absence is not exclusively a construction of Silva's biographer or of later analyses of Silva's work. Silva himself carved out a unique isolation from these two major social movements, both of which would dramatically affect the political and artistic scene of Ecuador's then-emerging national identity. In his singular way, Silva seems to have been working against the grain in creating a fantasy world of escape, love, and death that successfully and systematically blocked out the major social concerns that preoccupied the majority of his contemporaries.

Because of the depth of the social transformations that these revolutions afforded in terms of shifting class relationships, consolidating new social formations, restructuring old ethnic and racial categorizations, establishing new forms of economic alliances, and realigning global alliances and cultural identifications, it seems highly improbable that Silva was unaware of the movements or of their national implications. On the contrary, it is most likely that he made conscious choices to efface himself from his social-political surroundings, all the while managing to produce

Figure 3. The urban train. Archivo Histórico del Guayas
(http://www.guayaquilhistorico.org.ec/webpages/fundacion.htm).

Figure 4. The Plaza Colón. Archivo Histórico del Guayas
(http://www.guayaquilhistorico.org.ec/webpages/fundacion.htm).

a rich body of work in which he placed himself and his feelings, and not the social setting, as the central and exclusive protagonist. It is also through this process of essential and internalized consumption that he was able subtly to erase any supposed impact of the social surroundings on his work. This was also partly carried out by allowing himself to be celebrated by the city's cultural elite and integrating himself into the country's modernist literary movement, of which he would be the only member not from the upper class.

It is this particular form of "antisocial" writing that strongly contributed to Silva's image as a morose poet in battle against the world and devoid of any major political agenda. At the same time, this representation of an apolitical Silva seems to contradict his increasing popularity over time. His poetic contribution continues to capture the imagination of Guayaquileans generations after the greatest representatives of the Liberal and Socialist revolutions have lost their central importance. A visible sign in this respect is that the Liberal and Socialist parties have both lost any significant electoral support in Guayaquil and the coast (and the whole country, for that matter), with the possible exception of the northern province of Esmeraldas, which, tellingly, has the country's highest concentration of Afro-Ecuadorians.

It is this ambivalent identification that affords Guayaquileans such a powerful icon in Silva, what Williams refers to as a "semantic figure," a mirror of their own ambiguous identity. It would make more sense to see Silva actively invested in protecting himself and his work from the seemingly dangerous social maelstrom throughout his life than to consider him immune to his social surroundings. Once again, this is not an unimaginable scenario for the situation in which Guayaquil's impoverished population finds itself today. But perhaps most significant is that writing against the backdrop of his social setting must have taken an enormous amount of effort and energy—strenuous effort belied by the fact that it is barely visible in any of his work or even in posthumous biographical attempts.

Toni Morrison (1993) addresses a similar issue in her analysis of U.S. literature. According to her, a repeated effort to deny an African presence within the United States' literary borders requires much more work, emotional drive, and energy than is humanly possible to maintain. This is an interesting strategy, since, according to Morrison, it would have been more economical to accept the complex social and racial reality than to deny it (see Butler 1997b for a similar analysis). Therefore, one could ask, What was the price Silva paid (his life?) in his denial of his society's ventures? And is this perhaps the "price of the ticket" (see James Baldwin in Leeming 1994), which still captures Silva's city dwellers' imagination as they continue to invest in the production of similar forms of cultural survival and denial?

First, we must analyze how both the Liberal and the Socialist revolutions were invested in social and cultural transformations quite central to Silva's work. Although both revolutions primarily targeted economic relationships, each of them imbued different sections of the struggling population with transformative types of cultural identity and political empowerment. The Liberal Revolution, even though most clearly demarcating new regional and productive economic relationships, transformed the traditional racial/ethnic hierarchy of the nation. With support from the newly emancipated Afro-Ecuadorian population, including the first officially recognized black generals, the Liberal Revolution empowered this traditionally oppressed and exploited coastal community. The placing of Afro-Ecuadorians at the forefront of social revolt provided an escape valve for this group's oppressive reality but, in many ways, also reinstated many of the fears of mainstream white and white/mestizo Ecuadorian society. Silva's outward conflict with his own blackness makes his ambivalent reaction to the Liberal Revolution's social and racial/ethnic transformations that much more understandable. It is not unrealistic to recognize his probable fear of the black population's uprising and its negative portrayal of him, as expressed in the following excerpt from a letter to a friend:

> I despair in poverty and I am offended by blackness. It is curious: I am a man of pure white race. My grandfather was Spanish. It is useless to explain a freak phenomenon of nature. But you must know that in me harbors a pure Iberian heritage. However, I look like a black Moor. And this physical reality, in my country, is a source of shame. But I would not mind as much being the black member of my family, if, in addition I also were not poor. This is what is most horrible. To have been born to be a sojourner in a fatuous palace, and to be obligated to have nothing to eat in a hole of misery. (In Romero Castillo 1970: 323)

In this fashion, his constant need to redefine himself in normative (i.e., white/Spanish and upper-class) terms could have only suffered as he watched the national order being overturned around him by "low-class" Afro-Ecuadorians and former Indians turned mestizos and *cholos* at the vanguard of the Liberal political scene (see Chapter 2). Because of the period's dramatic impact on Silva, rather than ignore his larger social surroundings, it seems useful and even essential to look at the cultural impact of the Liberal and Social revolutions.

The Liberal Revolution's greatest leader was Gen. Eloy Alfaro, who, in league with a contingency of rebel leaders, such as his brother Flavio Alfaro, and the coastal populace, represented a regional uprising against the conservative interests of the highland hacienda-holding elite. The Liberal Revolution brought into power a whole new coastal bourgeoisie that, unlike the traditional latifundistas (large landholders) and cattle ranchers, represented a new agro-export model that would return to power to neutralize the Liberal Revolution's most progressive objectives. The movement articulated the demise of feudal forms of labor production and introduced Ecuador to modern global capital relations of wage earning and transnational interests. While in power, Pres. Eloy Alfaro (1895–1901, 1906–1911) wrought drastic changes by constructing a national railroad system, secularizing education, and providing for separation of church and state. These secular policies, including the introduction of legal divorce and his Freemasonry, further contributed to a great animosity on the part of the highland Catholic population and political elite and contributed to his death by public lynching and the burning of his body in El Ejido Park, together with those of his closest allies, on January 28, 1912.

By the time of Alfaro's death, however, the Liberal movement had already created a whole new set of agents on the national scene, such as mestizos, *cholos,* and the black population, particularly from Esmeraldas, which, since emancipation in the late 1880s, had been largely ignored and continued to be discriminated against (Ayala Mora 1993, 1995).

Silva did not have to contend only with this Liberal transformation of class and racial/ethnic relations, however, but also with an emerging socialist movement, which had slowly increased its power and visibility in workers' unions and guilds throughout Guayaquil. If the Liberal turn of events had managed to affect the problematics of an oppressed black identity, the socialist movement only increased the rebellions against the traditional feudal/colonial class structure still prevalent in the country. Once again, Silva's constant preoccupation with social status, particularly that of the upper-class Spanish kind, could only have been significantly shaken and questioned at its core by this communal protest from the city's impoverished masses. For Silva it could no longer be simply an issue of obtaining greater status and wealth but of seeing his whole social structure being upturned in a chaos of mass protests and police/military repression precisely at the moment when he seemed to be gaining entrance to the elite circles and hierarchical structure under attack. This chaotic social situation must have created great angst in Silva, even though its most explicitly tragic resolution occurred three years after his death: the massacre of hundreds of workers in November of 1922 (see Maiguashca 1994; Quintero and Silva 1991).

The socialist-influenced workers' movement gained enormous momentum from the city's large migrant population. Like today, at the turn of the century, Guayaquil constituted the largest migratory center in the whole country. In many respects, the workers' movement was the natural progression of the Liberal ideals already abandoned by the Partido Liberal (Liberal Party) in the 1920s, which had taken on a more conservative bent. The workers' movement and the creation of *sindicatos* (unions) represented a new understanding of the relationship between capital and labor that seriously subverted the traditionally racist colonial relations of hacienda production and latifundios that had survived the institution of the republic in 1830. This new economic organization transformed the traditionally racialized peasants into new urban workers and proletarians. At the same time, within this global economy, the drop in cacao prices, the First World War, and the Mexican and Soviet revolutions, in

1910 and 1917, respectively, contributed to the demand for better social conditions (Quintero and Silva 1991).

The movement (in which the bakers' guild played a key role) reached its tragic climax on November 15, 1922. The police and the army, with the approval of the national government, massacred over fifteen hundred persons for demonstrating in favor of union rights, better wages, and better working conditions and threw the victims' bodies into the Guayas River. This massacre would be immortalized by Joaquín Gallegos Lara in *Las cruces sobre el agua* (The Crosses on the River) [1980(1944)] and in other literary works such as the Afro-Ecuadorian Adalberto Ortiz' *El espejo y la ventana* (The Mirror and the Window) (1983) and would also contribute to the left-leaning military coup of July 9, 1925.

Both titles are quite meaningful. *Las cruces sobre el agua* refers to the practice of depositing floating wreaths on the Guayas River every year where the bodies of the massacred workers were discarded with official approval. *El espejo y la ventana* uses a dualistic literary technique in each chapter to describe the main character looking at himself in the mirror while watching the uprising, the massacre, and the official discarding (and denial) of the workers' bodies from his window. In many regards, the mirror and the window also seem to represent the two media that Silva had to contend with in his life.

The workers' movement would finally see part of its struggle realized in the creation of the Socialist Party (1926), the Communist Party (1929), and a new era of social consciousness marked by the publication of Lara's novel and the groundbreaking collection of short stories, *Los que se van* (Those Who Leave) (Gallegos Lara, Aguilera Malta, and Gil Gilbert 1973 [1933]). It is in this period of conflict that Medardo Ángel Silva lived his brief life and struggled to make sense of a national scene whose chaos was directly related to shifting international power. It is this world that most probably contributed to his premature death in 1919 and that would forever be denied in the successful historical representation of a Guayaquil Antiguo devoid of conflict, violence, and social unrest.

Medardo Ángel Silva and the Hegemonic Power of an Ambivalent Representation

Silva's fantasy-filled poetic images, for many, evidence a lack of social concern (Cueva 1986; Handelsman 1987; "Medardo A. Silva" 1999; Romero Castillo 1970). However, a closer look reveals a much more problematic figure who was clearly concerned with social conventions and hierarchies. Silva (1898–1919) was deeply troubled by both the darkness of his skin and his quite limited socioeconomic standing. His concern about his race was so apparent that his own mother publicly acknowledged the "unfortunate" circumstance of his "blackness" (Romero Castillo 1970). Silva's poetic imagery, as this excerpt from "Aniversario" (Birthday) shows, is full of exquisite images, Middle Eastern symbolism, and sensual representations of whiteness (i.e., blondness and gold) that are contrary to his undervalued national, class, and racial identity (Silva N.d. : 107):

Pero, ¿quién atendía a las explicaciones? . . .
¡Hay tanto que observar en los negros rincones!
y, además, es mejor contemplar los gorriones
en los hilos; seguir el áureo derrotero
de un rayito de sol o el girar bullanguero
de un insecto vestido de seda rubia o una
mosca de vellos de oros y alas color de luna.

¡El sol es el amigo más bueno de la infancia!
¡Nos miente tantas cosas bellas la distancia!
¡Tiene un brillar tan lindo de onza nueva! ¡Reparte
tan bien su oro que nadie se queda sin su parte!
Y por él no atendíamos a las explicaciones;
ese brujo Aladino evocaba visiones
de las Mil y una Noches, de las Mil Maravillas
y beodas de sueños, nuestras almas sencillas
sin pensar, extendían las manos suplicantes
como quien busca a tientas puñados de brillantes.[2]

Silva was born in Guayaquil in 1898 and died under mysterious circumstances at the age of twenty-one, while visiting his fifteen-year-old girlfriend in *el centro* (downtown). It is postulated that he was murdered because of a love triangle or that he committed suicide. Although both hypotheses satisfy the romantic ideal of his life, the second is given most credence, especially since he refers to his future suicide in many of his poems. His idealization of death and suicide is paramount, for example, in his *pasillo* "El alma en los labios." Death is so central that his sole biographer describes Silva as sitting at home on Avenida Quito enthralled at a very early age by funeral processions making their way to the cemetery (Romero Castillo 1970), processions that continue to this day.

Why is death so dominant in a poet who by the age of nineteen had already published his first poetry collection, *El árbol del bien y del mal* (The Tree of Good and Evil); had attended the most prestigious public high school of the time, Vicente Rocafuerte; and was already working as a journalist for the biggest national newspaper in the city, *El Telégrafo*? Contrary to what traditional scholars believe, Silva's fascination with death was probably deeply affected by the racial, sexual, and class expectations that both fueled and constrained him, that were an emblematic contradiction of his ambivalent racialized and spiritual identification with the city's elite families.

Silva was not alone in his obsession with death and race and class dynamics, but he was the only member of a group of writers known as the Generación Decapitada (Beheaded Generation) who came from the coast and was not a member of the elite. This group, representative of the modernist tradition in Ecuador, comprised Arturo Borja (1892–1912), Ernesto Noboa Caamaño (1889–1929), Humberto Fierro (1890–1929), and Silva. It got its name from the fact that all committed suicide. Only Silva represented the class contradictions of the disenfranchised who had been historically excluded from the cultural affairs of the nation. This characteristic also contributed to making his poetry the most immediate in popular terms and probably resulted from his having lived through one of the most dynamic periods of social unrest in Guayaquil's history.

In his writing, both poetry and journalistic pieces (I emphasize the latter in this section), Silva used at least two autobiographical approaches. The first was the use of a French pseudonym, Jean d'Agreve, to sign his literary work. The use of this pen name afforded Silva greater literary license than his social surroundings would have been willing to provide. Key is the leveling power of envy used by Guayaquilean (as a postcolonial) society to undermine his (or anybody's) impressive and ab(ove)-normal talent (see Kincaid 1997). It seems that, in many respects, his compatriots were unwilling to accept him, a poor, sexually ambivalent black men, as their cultural and intellectual equal or, worse, their superior.

Silva was acutely aware of his ambivalent positioning and the crushing power of his social environment when he publicly advised a "young writer" in the following manner (Calderón Chico 1999: 133–134):

The literary profession that you dream of as a road of glory is quite hard, my young friend.
    At the beginning of your literary labor, the elders proven by the sacred anointment of time will call you: {hope of future glories}, but you must resign yourself to being an eternal hope: if they ever

suspect that you might make their imperial thrones tremble, they will stone you . . .

To enjoy the favor of the public you will have to depersonalize yourself, become part of the herd, think in harmony with everybody else: nobody will forgive your irreverence in remaining standing when everybody else is crawling, and the victory, almost always, goes to those who have the least rigid backbones, spines: to obtain it, victory, that is, you must subscribe to the many clubs of mutual adulation where the literary prizes are raffled and awarded.

Silva's pen name allowed him to speak in the first person as Jean d'Agreve without explicitly signifying that it was he who was doing the writing or that he was referring to himself. In a piece entitled "La ciudad nocturna" (The Night City) the writer as Jean d'Agreve is able to dedicate the text (Calderón Chico 1999: 30): "To the hypocrisy of serious people, to the ignorance of the good, to the scruples of the Tartuffe, to the white lies of formal men: to all the false virtues and to all the masked vices, I dedicate this vile piece, sad as Vice and the Night." Jean d'Agreve ambiguously describes himself in the following manner (Calderón Chico 1999: 32): "The hat bent, the hair in disarray, the hands in his pocket 'like a poet out hunting for verses with a trap,' Jean d'Agreve walks his native city, which sleeps at night like a puppet broken by the intensity of the day, under the blinking of the electric lights; with the complicity of the roofs and beyond the hypocrisy of the windows, the fire of debauchery intensifies, its sensual flames egged on by the order of Our Lord the Devil."

Even the use of this pseudonym did not afford him a reprieve from his critics, however, and he soon defended his pen name in an explicit and ironic piece entitled "Malévola interpretación" (Vicious Interpretation) (Calderón Chico 1999: 201): "Those men should know: that Jean d'Agreve is the name of the protagonist of a novel, which goes by the same title of the well-known French writer Vicomte M. de Vogüe, an academic; that who writes these lines has used, for almost two years, this pseudonym; and that I, author of [the article entitled] 'Films,' in spite of my 'egocentrism'—as an improvised critic said—state that these small verses do not augment a little or a lot my literary prestige . . . Do you understand?"[3] It is quite ironic that both Silva and his critics would so explicitly claim "egocentrism" as the author's main problem, since it is his willingness to transgress the hidden cultural scriptures for which Silva is most remembered today, and for which reason he probably had to kill himself.

Another autobiographical approach Silva used was to write about himself, even though he seemed to be writing about somebody else or an isolated cultural phenomenon. This approach is paramount in his literary criticism of two other young Ecuadorian poets, members of the modernist movement, Humberto Fierro and Arturo Borja, both of whom would also commit suicide in their early twenties (see Calderón Chico 1999). As we see in the following lines, the public advice freely given to the young emerging writers could as easily be seen as a more mature (and bitter) Silva reflecting on his own experience and advising himself (Calderón Chico 1999: 134–135): "On such a hard road you will leave bits and pieces of your soul, and when you reach the desired peak—if you ever get there—you will age prematurely with the laurels of your crown pricking your forehead as if they were needles. Meanwhile, if you desist from your objective, be assured, hopeless dreamer, possessed of a sacred frenzy, you will die with your eyes exalted by the light of your unreachable dreams, set upon the ideal peak where that divine dancer called Glory will look upon you with a smile."

Silva uses this particular approach many times to express sexually complicated and socially dangerous feelings that were not afforded poetic license. Another example comes from a piece titled "En la penumbra del cinema: Elogio del claroscuro amor, música y morfina" (In the Shadows of the Movies: Elegy to Somber Love, Music, and Morphine), quite prophetically written a mere month before his probable suicide (Calderón Chico 1999: 50–51):

Indifferent to all, he "butterflies" [*mariposea*] his vague glare as somebody who is about to see a vision.[4]
He has black eyes, they are very black against his pale face: he does not pay attention to the screen, nor does he make love. I am getting quite attached to him. With his convalescent hands and soft touch, with his pose of uncertainty I am attracted to him. Perhaps he suffers from my sickness. He must be sad and also a platonic lover.

Perhaps this is one of those good boys, sick of readings, and perfectly useless; let him kill himself.

We also see this autobiographical element in another piece, entitled "El oso estaba triste: ¿Qué le pasaba al oso?" (The Bear Was Sad: What Was Wrong with the Bear?), in which Silva supposedly refers to a bear named Ursus that had escaped from the private cage of the leading Ecuadorian historian and archaeologist of his time, Don Jacinto Jijón y Caamaño, and "bears" his soul even further. This piece is metaphorically rich because one could wonder if this is not how Silva really felt, encased in the elite's crystal showroom of which Jijón y Caamaño was one of the greatest representatives as governor of the capital and undisputed leader of the Conservative Party. Like the bear, Silva was kept and admired by the city's wealthiest families but only under the implicit assumption of their never acknowledging who he really was: a poor black man with plausible nonnormative sexual mores—in other words, a far superior literary talent born into the wrong class, race, gender, and, most probably, sexual desire. And as in Ursus' saga, you cannot but see Silva's own life drama played out, a life drama that would end with a bullet to his head (Calderón Chico 1999: 41–42; my emphasis):

> Ursus was sad. Ursus got bored. In front of every naked rose-looking arm that sprang from behind the cage, every bronzed villainous body that came to grin its tongue (Have you ever seen such vile behavior: an imbecile mocking the hairy great lord of the Jungle!). Ursus growled, showed his claws, yawned like a Brit in front of this Beaf . . . and nothing happened.
>
> In his cage he had the resignation and philosophical demeanor that are the virtues of his race.
>
> Perhaps—and maybe not—he envies his colleague that jumps, in a public plaza, to the rhythm of the music, in front of a black-eyed and bronze-skinned gypsy.
>
> Good-bye, jungle and honey and sweetness of home—Home Sweet Home!
>
> The unhappy Bear has returned to seclusion and to entertain the grave eyes—expert in finding old Inca jars and reading historical archives—of Don Jacinto Jijón y Caamaño, his good owner.
>
> Ursus resides in the capital of the republic. Condemned to inactivity, *he is destined to die* of sadness or nostalgia.

I propose a Silva who did not live an individual life of sadness and telling nostalgia (see Mitchell 1988; Pratt 1992) but one that foreshadowed a whole generation of Guayaquileans' communal identity; a Silva who escaped the structural historical reading of his time to fully embody its emotional one. In this manner, Silva's work enabled generations of identification with a social life of death due to constricting, normalizing political and social norms that could only be individually experienced and shared (see Duras 1986, 1997). It is this individualized tension between social life and death that I engage in the following chapters.

Overview of Chapters

Chapters 1 and 2 discuss the two major theoretical discourses that structure the book. In Chapter 1, I further develop the analysis of Medardo Ángel Silva's contribution, providing some of the major links between his memorialization and the contemporary production of Guayaquilean identity. Prime in this assessment is the use of the category of *cholo* to define and discriminate (in the violent meaning of the word) the poor and nonwhite majority Guayaquilean population. I also look to problematize the relationship between feelings and a postcolonial experience, thereby highlighting the central role of the mother and motherly love in the constitution of the Guayaquilean subject. The last section of the chapter assesses the role of transgressive love and sin in the ultimate alterity and social alienation of Guayaquileans as constitutive parts of the city's social experience.

Chapter 2 engages the other central metonymic device used by Guayaquileans over the last century, that of the romantic idealization of Guayaquil Antiguo. Particularly important in this chapter is the analysis of Guayaquil Antiguo as pregnant with romantic colonial and nostalgic legacies that have been repressed historically. The second section of the chapter looks to understand how the primarily migrant population has also espoused this romantic imaginary, even though it is continuously denied and erased by its powerful figuration. The last section of the chapter tries to bring together all the elements being elaborated on in both Chapters 1 and 2: sadness, drinking, nostalgic memory, and a problematic sense of belonging in the active production of Guayaquilean identity to this day. This section thus looks to understand the dynamic incorporation of the imaginary past into the daily lives of people in Guayaquil today.

The following three chapters (3, 4, and 5) are specific thematic and case studies of the particular manner in which the romantic notions of Silva's and Guayaquil Antiguo's imaginary have fueled the city's production of popular culture over the last century. Chapter 3 discusses the particular representational power of the musical genre of the *pasillo* in the identity of the city. By assessing the *pasillo's* powerful popular appeal and Julio Jaramillo's role as the city's greatest musical exponent, I review the levels of hegemonic ambiguity, cultural authenticity, and transnational elements that are impregnated in the genre. Another important element I discuss in this chapter is the gender sensibilities that are articulated in the genre's production and the ultimate centrality of gender ascriptions in a Guayaquilean identity.

Chapter 4 moves away from the national fold, in a matter of speaking. By analyzing three migrant life histories, one fictional and two ethnographic, I assess the transnational elements in the city's production of its identity. All three cases deal with the recent historical migration of Guayaquileans to the United States and therefore engage the problematic but dynamic reconfiguration of Guayaquilean identity and modernity through new/old global flows. Although all three case studies are significantly different (chosen deliberately for this reason), they provide new understanding not only of the manner in which Guayaquilean identity is produced but also, and more important, of the constant and central place of this foreign global element in its constitution.

Chapter 5 engages the racial dynamic, specifically, that of the black or Afro-Ecuadorian experience, inherent in the articulation of a Guayaquilean identity. The selections of two Afro-Ecuadorians as Miss Ecuador in the 1990s and the historical figure of a life-sized effigy of a black Christ in the coastal city of Daule problematize Silva's black racial identity. I therefore argue for a much more subtle articulation of blackness as essential in the city's self-defining project. Rather than highlight typical racial discrimination, I use these cases to argue that blackness, or Afro-Ecuadorianness, is subtly articulated to represent Guayaquil in specific and provocative ways, which further serves to support and reproduce the exploitative structure of the city against its black, Indian, mestizo, and *cholo* population.

Finally, the Conclusion reassesses the major themes of the book, providing a discussion of the major theoretical points highlighted by my research. I recap the book's contribution in terms of a more nuanced understanding of the role of sentiment and popular culture in the dynamic hegemonic domination of Latin America's population. By doing this, I look to further our understanding of Gramsci's proposal of hegemony and Raymond Williams' rearticulation of the concept. In many ways, the book is really a concrete ethnographic case study of Williams' cultural hypothesis of structures of feeling.

The success or not of my endeavor is not mine to claim, but I hope it will at least provoke questions about the specific operationalization of hegemony in concrete and local historical ways in daily life. Ultimately, the main concern of the book is to further question how hegemony works, not exclusively, or even mainly, in grand national narratives but, rather, contained within people's cultural reproduction and daily survival, that is, life.

PART 1

SENTIMENT AND HISTORY

CHAPTER 1

Medardo Ángel Silva
Voces Inefables

Dicen que no tienen motivo mis penas,
pues las lloro mías cuando son ajenas . . .
¡Ay! Ese es mi encanto:
llorar por aquellos que no vierten llanto.
—SILVA, "LA FUENTE TRISTE: II"

In this chapter, and throughout the book, I assess the power that Silva's sensibility came to have over his city of origin. I am less interested in providing a systematic hagiography of his life, or even a detailed biography; rather, I want to allow different moments of his life and work to be illuminated by Guayaquil's contemporary citizens and history. Thus, I am not looking to provide ethical or literary judgments of Silva's life and work; instead, I am assessing the problematics he worked on during his short life. At the same time, I believe these problematics were not an obsession for him alone, but are also important for Guayaquileans since his death.

I also am quite aware of the reification that this work will provide as it contributes further to Silva's romantic aura and sentimental status. Thus, I am not excluding myself from the analytical framework. As Foucault elaborates in the first volume of *History of Sexuality* (1990), there is no manner in which one's analysis of social reality does not form part of and contribute to the social reality it looks to study. My analysis is therefore a result of varied realities, including, and above all, my enculturation as an Ecuadorian citizen, but, more specifically, my being Guayaquilean. I have spent countless hours reading Silva's poetry, meditating on his angst-filled existence, and wondering how different our lives really are. However, this nurturing comparison of my life with Silva's was not an isolated act. Even though similar meditations are performed by Guayaquileans as isolated individuals, they are a permanent fixture of our enculturation.

This particular ritual of regional identification is performed by all the Guayaquileans I interviewed, but it is also part of Silva's literary exegesis (see Rodríguez Vicéns 2001). Even former president Jaime Roldós Aguilera (1940–1981), a Guayaquilean, has been described as staying up late at night discussing with friends Silva's life and his complex literary contributions (see Vallejo 1988).

It is this nurturing ritual of idealizing Silva's tragic life, comparing it to one's own, and using his poetic words as a cross-class, soothing inspiration since the early twentieth century in Guayaquil that I discuss in this chapter. What are some of the major sentiments or tropes that enabled Silva's paradigmatic place in the city's understanding of itself and its way of being (*manera de ser*)? What are some of the major effects of sentiments that catapulted themselves again and again into the consciousness of the city's multiple generations? It is many of these same feelings that contribute to Silva's high regard in official textbooks, allowing an initial understanding of how he came to have high status and influence for the generations that have followed him.

This official educational canon, however, is secondary to the larger problematic that Silva represents for Guayaquileans in general. What he symbolizes seems contrary to the traditional mechanisms of official history, which responds, in a pale fashion, to his fellow Guayaquileans' overwhelming understanding and recognition of Silva. The Silva one gets or is able to make out from educational textbooks is quite limited in depth, which gives him implicitly (but erroneously) equal standing with the rest of Ecuador's poets in the popular mind. It is as if, despite Silva's limited official introduction, his effusive sentiments override the constrained official representation of his contribution to Guayaquil's historical life and that this limited knowledge has produced even more evocative hopes for his social recognition.

My sense of Silva's contribution has therefore come not only from those Guayaquileans I have interviewed for this book but also from those with whom I have spoken since the mid-1970s. The city's naming of a small park after him (immediately across from the high school I attended) and his name's prominence on the newly renovated river promenade (the *malecón*) are signs of a depth of feeling that has continuously shaped the city. They are also evidence of Silva's iconic status, which has always reflected the city's ambivalence about its origins and identity. Silva has provided streams of Guayaquilean migrants a mirror that reflects the bitter truth of their unbelonging, the nightmare of colonialism, and the rejection of civilizing manners and norms.

The Wages of Being *Cholo* in Guayaquil

Marcha la luna trágica entre nubes de gasa . . .
Sin que nadie las toque se han cerrado las puertas . . .
El miedo, como un lobo, pasea por la casa . . .
Se pronuncia los nombres de personas ya muertas . . .

El abuelo las lámparas, por vez octava, prende . . .
Se iluminan, de súbito, semblantes aturdidos . . .
Es la hora en que atraviesa las alcobas el duende
que despierta, llorando, a los niños dormidos.
(Silva, "Velada del sábado")[1]

Three significant markers of identification present in Silva's life and poetic imagination are also paradigmatic in the city's social life: (1) what it means to be seen, called, or to understand oneself as *cholo* in the city's social context; (2) the role that one's mother and love for her play in social identification; and (3) the ever-present sense of sin or transgression in the social life of the city, a port. I hold that these social discourses are central elements that, like a "dwarfish devil" (in Silva's imaginary; see note 1), make us cry out about our numbed existence at night, when nobody is looking (see *Pedro Páramo* [Rulfo 2002 (1953)] for similar Latin American ideological specters).

Silva presents an interesting construction when it comes to the ever-present pejorative distinction of being called *cholo* in Guayaquil's contemporary and historical contexts. *Cholo* is an ambiguous racial marker that denotes a class standing lower than that of mestizo, even though both reflect mixed Spanish and Indian ancestry. And even though Silva was black, or had features that suggested African ancestry, his ambivalent racial identification created similarly misplaced feelings of Indian ancestry, which allowed him to find, if not solace, at least common ground for commiseration. In this respect, the racist ambivalence toward the city's population of African ancestry (see Chapter 5) in many ways mirrors or builds on the equally enormous tension surrounding the city's more immediate Indian ancestry.

One can also see this tension in Silva's world, where Indian elements are rarely explicitly mentioned in, much less incorporated into, Silva's and Guayaquil's history. The Indian presence in Guayaquil during and since Silva's time is most vividly a result of highland migrations. Historical migrations saw tens of thousands of Indians flee feudal forms of labor relations and attempt to find a different, and better, life not only for themselves but, most important, for their children. The strong Indian presence traditionally present in marketplaces, construction sites, and the domestic labor market was not invisible to a sensitive man like Silva, thus making his silence about it that much more meaningful and suggestive.

In line with the reality of denial, however, the original Indian presence in Guayaquil was also tempered by silence, as coastal Indians were decimated under Spanish colonial rule and under republican social policies. Coastal Indian populations were the first ones devastated by the Spanish occupation and also the hardest hit by invading epidemics, shifting and oppressive colonial regulations, and outright genocide. As a result of these ethnocidal and genocidal elements, coastal populations went through a rapid transformation, marking the death of most Indian communities and the ethnic transformation of survivors and their descendants. In this manner and reduced to its simplest form, the farther one could get from identification as an Indian, the closer one got to a higher social status and a chance at a better livelihood (Naranjo 1984; Whitten 1984).

Of course, this had complex ramifications (see Benavides 2002 for a discussion of Guayaquil's Indian past), such as the safeguarding of Indian forms of social relationship and labor obligations, particularly the maintenance of an Indian elite that championed colonial policies to secure its own survival. In Guayaquil and vicinity, this meant social practices that, on the one hand, secured a rapid transformation of ethnicities but, on the other, secured some continuity in old/new social traditions. In this context, an Indian ethnicity was maintained through the formation of secular communities and was finally crystallized in *comunas,* the modern form of land claims (see Álvarez 1989).

Meanwhile, two new ethnic groups, *cholos* and *montubios,* also solidified their identity within the multitude of ethnic classifications created by the Spanish crown to answer its angst-filled racial purity riddle and further secure socioeconomic forms of domination. *Cholos* are thus defined traditionally as former Indians who reside on the coast and survive by fishing and small-scale farming, while *montubios* are defined as rural people who occupy the coastal riverbeds and whose inhabitants dedicate themselves more intensely to agriculture and commercial exchange.

It is in this context that both terms have become highly recognizable within Guayaquilean society as markers of a complex history of ethnic identities, colonial legacies, and racism. Both terms, like all ethnic terms, have come to signify much more than they initially meant and have been easily incorporated into the port's vocabulary of racial slurs. After a multifaceted regional historical evolution (see de la Cadena 2000 for evolutionary patterns in Peru), *cholo* and *montubio* have both come to be used less to describe than to question origin, race, and social standing, that is, civilized identity.

Cholo, however, has assumed the worst stigma; *montubio* has become a milder form of a similarly disparaging insult, even though both reflect mixed heritage and Indian ancestry. When used as an insult (and it is rarely used otherwise in daily exchange), *montubio* implies backwardness, ruralism, and even stupidity. But perhaps because it is closer to the city, geographically speaking, it also describes somebody who may have lower-class standards but still has some redeeming qualities. So it is most likely that *montubios* will be transformed into mestizos, white/mestizos, and even full-fledged Guayaquileans and lose their racial classification within their lifetimes in the city's new identity. It is also not uncommon to hear remarks in Guayaquil referring to somebody whose race is categorized as ambivalent (normative) as having been once a *montubio* or as having acted like one when she or he first arrived in the city.

Cholo, or being *cholo,* is a more complicated and devastating status, particularly when used specifically as an insult. To be called a *cholo* signifies a much more essential definition and more distance from what a civilized and, therefore, human being (i.e., a Guayaquilean) should be. Once again, greater geographical distance is hinted at in the term's meaning. Thus, the worst way to be identified in Guayaquilean terms is, along with *maricón* (faggot) or *negro* (black), as a *cholo,* particularly because *cholo* also implies being dumb, backward, or from the countryside and also carries strong racial implications. The main phenotypic features implied are darker skin, shorter height, and Indian features, for men, a lack of body hair, including beards and mustaches, and straight hair (*tener pelo de cholo*). All or a reified combination of these supposedly racial characteristics would mean one would be called *cholo,* and such an epithet would, in a profoundly existential manner, question one's belonging.

It is here that Silva's image has such strong ramifications and bursts into the city's social imagination. Since very few pictures of him have survived, it is difficult to cast him phenotypically into a racial category. His identity as a black is a well-kept secret because of this lack of visual evidence; only those who knew him firsthand or knew of him at the time or have delved into the few published biographies of his life know that he was black. Silva's poetry and journalistic pieces, however, are full of silences and meanings that give life (and the possibility of escape) to a society plagued by colonial specters in the shape of primal racial fears, which include not wanting to be cast as or called *cholo*.

It is quite meaningful that Silva appeared to be oblivious to this racial conundrum; in fact, one would be hard-pressed to find a single reference to it in any of his writings. He seems to have expended an enormous amount of energy in not talking about what everybody was aware of but no one wanted to admit: the complex and racist form of self- and social-identification of Guayaquil's inhabitants. But merely denying this racism as an individual, for Silva, would not have been interesting as a subject for his writing and even less interesting as something with which to identify.

Silva's work, however, as if providing a magical canvas on which the city's socially torn inhabitants can paint their own feelings and ways of being and just like the Guayaquil Antiguo etchings (see Chapter 2), allows for a strong social identification. Thus, Silva's poetry might be devoid of explicitly racial categorizations, but it is not free of the racial context in which he, like the whole city, lived and the puzzles that he and other Guay-aquileans pondered. His poetry is full of racial premises, not necessarily those of his immediate surrounding but, rather, of the larger colonial world that infused his imagination. Poetic references to whiteness, for example, are present in the symbols of water, chastity, the moon, and the body:

A ti la inclinación de las pelucas,
al plegarse los blancos abanicos,
sobre la seda de las blancas nucas;

porque tu nombre sabe a miel y rosas,
y pronunciarlo es evocar los ricos
Trianones de las fiestas suntuosas.[2]

In Silva's poetic economy these symbols are imbued with a magical essence that allows them to be read as belonging to an ethereal world, precisely because, although they are infused by specifically Guayaquilean racial conundrums, they allow for an escape from that same world.

In Silva's deeply rich poetic images, the colors reflecting skin tone are freed from their limited signification and paint a nuanced emotional world that Guayaquileans can relate to more profoundly. The darker, damned, colors, such as black and brown, have less-threatening implications but still fully embody the emotional range that their mere mention conjures up. Silva also works quite forcefully with imagery from the

Arabic tradition and rituals, once again imbuing them with and liberating them from their colonial legacy. It is this complex weaving of colors and meaning which is most readily apparent in the impression-filled words of this excerpt from "A una danzarina":

Tus ojos—perversos magos—
son como dos negros lagos
en cuyo fondo tranquilo,
con musulmana pureza,
duermen en seguro asilo
la crueldad y la tristeza . . .

Tu boca—purpúreo lirio-,
flor de sueño y de delirio,
es una planta de Oriente
en cuyo bermejo seno,
junto a la miel, el paciente
liba también el veneno.[3]

What Silva offers in this complex resignification goes beyond his initial silence about or denial of racist limitations. Contrary to what would on the surface seem to be "escapist" romantic poetry, it is, instead, a much more nuanced reconversion of Guayaquil's intimate and suffocating racial conundrums. Through his writing, Silva offers effusive sentiments that escape officializing scriptures and hegemonic constraints. At the same time and under the guise of individualized sentiments, the poems subtly yet decisively offer, and manage to articulate, the full range of inflexibly denied emotions on a regional canvas, Guayaquil.

It is not insignificant that since his death Silva's poetry has been overlooked by literary critics, social commentators, and intellectuals in general as lacking social content and has been categorized as mere romantic melodrama. Yet it is precisely these ambiguous and far-reaching meanings which have not been lost on Guayaquil's inhabitants. From the moment of his death, city dwellers have championed his poems and sentiments as something that they know to be true, not in spite of but precisely because of strong official policing. Guayaquileans therefore use Silva's lines like soldiers used U.S. baseball team names and players' names as code on the battlefields of World War II.

Silva's words are used as the markers of what it means to be truly Guayaquilean. These sentiments are particularly evident in my interview with Pedro (August 16, 2003). I asked about Silva and his relationship to Guayaquilean identity: "I think it is because his opus was limited but profound, and if I am not mistaken, he was part of a group of poets from the period. I think it is because his work, which, although short, had an enormous impact, and lots of people were able to identify with it." Guayaquileans overidentify with Silva and what he represents, which, in many ways, is that intimately explored anguish of having been excluded from the city's riches and its supposedly unracist existence. In effect, by circumventing the city's constrictive racializing norms, Silva was able to successfully represent them in their full-fledged, symbolic fury. He may not have needed to talk about being a *cholo* explicitly, but each of his poems is full of the anguish implied by being one or by being scared of being defined as such. Through this subterfuge, Silva found a way of expressing the real effects of the racial conundrum experienced by all Guayaquileans and the utterly unbearable anguish of being forced to silence it.

As Miranda (interview, August 15, 2001) states, "These poems, they all carry something in their heart, in their roots, in their life, they have an incredible richness inside." Thus it is that the overburdened signification of Silva's poetry with tragedy, loss, desire, death, grief, and, ultimately, abandonment is not merely melodramatic or over the top. His poetry succinctly captures centuries of defeat and rejection by a colonial past and a postcolonial rereading of that past. This impossible position, most adamantly expressed in but not limited to its racial conundrum, causes the depth of feeling described by Silva's poetry to mean a great deal to a population that lives these social limitations to the ultimate degree.

It is no longer necessary or important that Guayaquileans have read Silva's work very closely; rather, his work has been imbued with tragic meanings which serve to embody the anguish-filled life that Guayaquil represents. In other words, it no longer matters whether Silva uses racial terms specific to Guayaquil's reality to express the Guayaquilean Real (in the Lacanian sense) in the most unbearably concrete ways (see Kundera 1984). It also matters little whether everyone has read his work, or whether Silva or they have consciously aligned themselves with his reworking of the colonial trauma of the Guayaquilean Real. What matters is that the identification with Silva's work is so immediate and so unconscious. The work also imbues with meaning a postcolonial existence systematically crushing and destined to eliminate the Real, which is the Real that Silva cunningly works out in his poetry while writing for himself and his compatriots.

It is not uncommon to be called *cholo* in Guayaquil. People suffer this postcolonial legacy in the same manner that many other racially, socially, sexually, and gender-specific affronts are suffered. I do not want to under-rate the extreme pain and grief that a *cholo* identification brings; no other plausible meaning for the term carries the same weight. It is also because of this pervasive context that no genuine escape is possible. *Cholo* is al-ways the most pernicious racial/racist identification, even if one knows consciously that one is not limited by the physical attributes which serve to define its social role. These attributes still manage to harbor a vast, un-conscious identity formation which marks the frustrating prophecy with both urgent and terror-filled accuracy (see Baldwin 1984; Fanon 1970). Yet the racial identification and unconscious terror that identification as a *cholo* brings is but a symptom of a myriad of other identities implicit in growing up in Guayaquil.

Thus, one slowly begins to paint a picture of extreme sentiments of terror, grief, and tragedy that Guayaquil's postcolonial existence harbors. Any one of these identities—*cholo,* black, or gay, being perfect in colonial terms—can, and for many, including Silva, does lead to despair and death. Of course, nobody is perfect or "normal" in these explicitly inhuman and reified colonial terms, which allow these characteristics to become power-ful normative prescription. Perhaps under these conditions suicide might not be a successful strategy, since it still means death, even though it is a conscious choice. Suicide also provides at least a minimum of control over one's life, and therefore is the most un-*cholo*-like of all characteristics: to live one's life as a free individual and to decide one's own social future.

Since being a *cholo* is also a marker of subservience and servitude, the taking of one's life as if one owns it can also be seen as a form of resis-tance. But it is in the portrait of placid emptiness captured in the black-and-white drawings and pictures of Guayaquil Antiguo that all roads lead to death. It is also in these seemingly peaceful drawings that harrow-ing individual pain, like that expressed by Silva, is the most powerful in representing the Real Guayaquil so actively and forcefully denied in all of its conscious and superficial rituals. At the same time, a more secure form of escape is effected and expressed as love, of which the maternal is the most immediate, although not without its own postcolonial doses of terror.

Postcolonial Legacies and Motherly Love

Mi espíritu es un cofre del que tienes las llaves
—¡oh, incógnita adorada, mi pasión y mi musa!-.

Ya inútilmente espero tus dulces ojos graves
y siento que me acecha en las sombras la Intrusa.

Pero mi alma, jilguero que canta indiferente
a la angustia del tiempo y al dolor de la vida,
te esperará, lo mismo que una virgen prudente,
con la devota lámpara de su amor encendida.[4]
(Silva, "Estancias: XXV")

As Duras elaborates in her autobiographical novel *The Lover* (1997), the figure of the mother and motherly love in postcolonial settings are imbued with complex subsets of limiting and frustrating relationships, intertwined and expressed in the impossibility of love during four centuries of colonial existence. When Duras states (1997: 22), "My beast, my mother, my love," she centralizes the figure of the mother in the ambivalent positioning between the purest expression of love and the harshest colonial nightmares imaginable. The complicated mother figure that Duras elaborates for the personal and political postcolonial legacy of Indochina is also relevant, I believe, to our understanding of the postcolonial production of Guayaquilean motherhood throughout the twentieth century.

This section assesses the complex relationship between Silva and his mother and goes beyond mere biographical information or even psychoanalytical insight. I analyze the effects of motherly love on Guayaquilean identity by emphasizing the work of several French theorists (Duras 1986; Irigaray 1985a, 1985b, 1993a, 1993b; Kristeva 1977, 1982, 1986, 1987, and 1989) and the works of Jamaica Kincaid (1988, 1990, 1996, 1997), who, more than anybody in the Americas, has concretely addressed the Oedipal interplay of colonial relationships as expressed in postcolonial settings. Although Kincaid's literary and memoir analysis deals with the Caribbean, specifically, Antigua, I do not believe Guayaquil, also traditionally claimed as a Caribbean city, is that far removed from this experience.

Guayaquil is perhaps more Caribbean than Andean in many regards, particularly because of its port mentality, its position in the southern extension of the slave trade, and its overall musical and cultural production. I do not intend to argue about whether Guayaquil is Caribbean or not; rather, I believe that the city has systematically used Caribbean imagery to depict what being from Guayaquil is all about. At the same time, the Caribbean imaginary has had decisive consequences for the city in terms of cultural products, including musical genres, fashion, and linguistic variations. Because of this, Kincaid's insights are as readily applicable to Guayaquil as to the Caribbean itself, especially in terms of the complex parent and children relationship within colonialism. That relationship established from the outset the intricate political nature of the family and all interactions within it, traditionally defined as exclusively personal and, to a certain degree, even sacred.

Silva and his mother were incredibly close, their relationship marked very early by the death of his father and Silva's having to take on economic responsibility for the family. His work shows enormous affection toward his mother, who became both a figure to which he owed his life and one that marked the futility of searching for meaning in his existence. This excerpt from "Lo tardío" (That Which Is Too Late), expresses this dual love/frustration in the most succinct manner:

Madre . . .
¿Por qué, cuando soñaba mis sueños infantiles,
en la cuna, a la sombra de las gasas sutiles,
de un ángulo del cuarto no salió una serpiente
que, al ceñir sus anillos a mi cuello inocente,
con la gracia flexible de una mujer querida,
me hubiera liberado del horror de la vida? . . .

Más valiera no ser a este vivir de llanto,
a este amasar con lágrimas el pan de nuestro canto,
al lento laborar del dolor exquisito
del alma ebria de luz y enferma de infinito.[5]

His death made the deep relationship between Silva and his mother quite explicit, and she emphasized their emotional closeness to his main biographer, Abel Romero Castillo. She was one of the first to come running to see Silva's bleeding body as he lay dying in his girlfriend's home. Even fifty years after her son's death, her affection for him led her to write intensely felt sonnets (see Romero Castillo 1970), and, dramatically, she asked that she be buried in his grave (see Figure 5). These expressions of love define the affection between mother and son, affection that could easily be seen as sublimating strong erotic sentiments themselves further complicated by the racial and class elements of a postcolonial context. This type of erotic tension is also present in inherited racial and class identity along with other physical markers and their emotional meanings.

Figure 5. The grave in which Medardo Ángel Silva and his mother are buried. Photograph by Melissa García.

Fanon elaborates these interstices of the Oedipal relationship in the colonial setting in his groundbreaking first book, *Black Skin, White Masks* (1970). For Stuart Hall (1980; see also Julien 1997), Fanon clearly imbues the traditional Freudian understanding of an Oedipal relationship of erotic attachment to one's mother and hatred of one's father with the jealousy and envy produced within a colonial setting. For Hall, Fanon's typical generational structure is particularly problematic when the mother represents the colonial motherland, the native land which has been symbolically (and not so symbolically) raped and ravaged, and when the agency-filled colonial officer who has violated the mother fills himself with the vigorous image of the father figure. In this context, the mother is overburdened to the native land and ethnicity, and the father is seen as the colonizing other, which has brought wreckage and change, that is, the offspring, even when the offspring is the ego at the center of the new, chaotic forms of social relationships (see Hall 1980; Julien 1997).

This newly formulated colonial Oedipal relationship is further complicated by the birth of the postcolonial native, which is only made possible by this rape context; even more important, jealousy and envy are really the other face of love. In other words, jealousy of the occupying colonial figure is also affected because of the enormously ambivalent love of that same colonizing father figure. Because of this ambivalence, it becomes a question of wanting to be like the father in order to replace him, all the while knowing that taking the paternal figure out of the picture leaves the complex and oppressive colonial relationships intact.

To make matters worse, the colonial relationship no longer defines the father figure but ambivalently constitutes the subject of the native off-spring, the ego, as well. It is in this ambivalent love relationship, in tune with inherent mimicry and destruction, where the familial relationship is terribly complicated by the colonial effects of power and the interaction of oppression and repression. At the same time, these familial sentiments are being normatively hegemonized as key expressions of the most authentic and truly genuine and giving kind of love: mother love.

With male children, these sentiments are infused with significations of manhood and masculinity (see Julien 1997), because it is no longer a question of being like the colonizing other but a most intimate taking of one's gender ascription from this problematic father figure. Once again, this is complicated in Silva's case by his father's early death. This personal reality points to yet another of Silva's silences: about his father. I would argue that in such a perceptive young writer his unwillingness to deal with his feelings toward his father reveals an effusively sentimental structure.

At a basic level, Silva's feelings toward his father can be read between the lines, including in his poetic lacunae. If anything, he is narrating the father-son experience in an extremely Guayaquilean way, one that makes sense to most of the city's dwellers. As I found in many of my interviews, masculinity and frustration with one's father are never explicitly addressed, even though they may be the most relevant experience for men (and women) in terms of gender-explicit outlook. Many Guayaquileans expressed this reticence about their fathers when I asked about this relationship.

At another level, Silva and his fellow Guayaquileans' troubled identification with an emasculated native manhood has incredibly powerful sexual implications. One of the foremost of these is compulsive heterosexuality and reigning homophobic behavior, which result in a context in which these mechanisms are elaborated as visible signs of manhood, and in which manhood itself is a contested domain for securing political power (see Rhys 1982; Spivak 1999). In postcolonial settings, the native has been constituted as the inferior other by not being allowed to fully occupy a (masculine or feminine) position as a human being. It is therefore obvious why strong ascriptions to gender rituals are deemed so existentially necessary. It is perhaps because of this that homosexuals, attitudes toward homosexuals, and what is interpreted as loose feminine sexuality in general were repressed throughout the colonies much more than in the colonizers' homelands. In this colonial struggle, it is not an insignificant victory that colonizers had greater freedom (although never total freedom) to define what being a man or a woman was all about.

The flip side of this heterosexist, homophobic behavior is a compulsive heterosexuality that forces men to see themselves as sexual predators and women to let them play the part, even when they know it is only a role. This fracture line is evident in a Latin American literary tradition full of agency-filled women (see Luzuriaga's 1995 film, *La tigra,* for an Ecuadorian narrative of an agency-filled woman; see de la Cuadra 1973, for the short story on which the film is based). Men must be allowed to think themselves superior to women to boost their fragile masculinity. Keeping multiple households and keeping females economically dependent on them does not seem to make men any more masculine, however; if anything, this behavior exposes fragile masculine gender identification (see Andrade 1995, 1997; Guttman 1996, for this phenomenon in Latin America as a whole). It is a dual postcolonial wound: the compulsively heterosexual man is unable to claim his most intimate love and sexual desires; women, especially as mother figures, attempt to heal wounded masculinity by overcompensating their sons and imposing on them their own frustrations and shortcomings as women and mothers.

Anzaldúa beautifully synthesizes this particularly destructive and unending cycle of mothers and sons (1987: 105): "Good son, macho pig." In her exploration of borderlands, she elaborates on how, for centuries in Latin America, women have been shortchanged and repressed not only by their fathers but by their mothers as well. In this postcolonial patriarchal structure, women re-create, through their sons, the only kind of oppressive cultural life they know. Thus, they overprotect their sons because of the wounded past and harsh present they know their children must inhabit in order to survive. A similar phenomenon has been described for African American mothers and their sons in the United States, whose sons, in many ways, are the target of the state's and society's worst discriminatory practices. Mothers, according to Anzaldúa (1987), will also impose on their sons their own erotic frustration, which cannot be resolved within the tortured postcolonial context of silence and sexual repression.

This colonial Oedipal relationship is visibly expressed in Silva and his mother's sharing the same grave. They could not fulfill during their lifetimes the symbolic and unbearable love which was profoundly fulfilled at the level of an operatic Real and which motivated Silva's work. It is in this context of a sublimated erotic and maternal relationship that one could assess Silva's multiple poems about his mother, the absence of a father in his poetic world, and a complex erotic intertwined with sin (see next section).

This scenario would also explain the strong mother figure prevalent in all postcolonial contexts throughout the Caribbean and Latin America; Guayaquil is not an exception. Motherly love holds a pivotal place in Guayaquilean enculturation: the city, like other Latin American cities, has a small but symbolically important park called El Parque de las Madres (The Park of the Mothers); Mother's Day is rivaled only by Christmas and New Year's; and songs that express motherly love are varied, profound, and prevalent (as opposed to the few about fathers) in the *serenatas* (serenades) on Mother's Day and birthdays. A telling example is a popular Peruvian *valsesito* made famous throughout the continent by both Julio Jaramillo and Lucho Barrios, "El rosario de mi madre" (My Mother's Rosary). In this song, a spurned man begs his promiscuous female partner to return to him just two things, "the last kiss I gave you and my mother's rosary, and you can keep all the rest" ("el último beso que te di y el rosario de mi madre, y te puedes quedar con todo lo demás"). These lines capture both the immense vulnerability and the strength of the mother figure in the national and social imaginary of Guayaquilean identity and the pivotal role of sexual and gender markers in that production.

The ideological prevalence of mothers in Guayaquil is overwhelming, which is why there are few, if any, texts that are willing to take on the problematic nature of motherly love, its ambivalent hegemonic positioning, and its overwhelming façade of unquestionable good. This construction and production of mothers as being full of overpowering love and goodness reflects internal contradictions. It is also this ambivalent façade that makes mothers such a powerful hegemonic device and that, like all hegemonic constructions, reflects its own fragile nature (see Sayer 1994). Few crimes in Guayaquil, even murder and rape, are as symbolically reprehensible as not being a dutiful son or daughter. The sentiments associated with motherly love have been normalized, have gone unquestioned and uncontested for a long time, which makes them hegemonically meaningful in Guayaquil.

It is also because of the hegemonic figure of the Guayaquilean mother that Silva's poetry can express his ambivalent feelings toward his parents: his mother is the object of his frustrated wishes for love and life; his father is explicitly absent. This process once again allows for a tradition of single mothers and children with no fathers. It is his ambivalence toward his parents that succeeding generations of Guayaquileans grasp and express as failed fathers and immaculate mothers, neither of which is even half the story.

This same image, which proves so central within the Guayaquilean landscape, is the one carefully elaborated by Kincaid (1990, 1996, 1997) in her ruthlessly honest literary and autobiographical portrayal of her mother. Kincaid (1997) paints a picture of a ruthless woman, hurt by years of rejection and indifference, behind a façade of the ever-giving person and the ever-flowing breast. In this context, her mother, as the hegemonic issue allows, is the best of mothers for her ailing children in a context in which her love exemplifies and expresses hierarchical relationships and control. Thus, as in most toxic mother-child relationships, the worst thing the child can do is grow up, especially emotionally, because that marks the end of the mother's raison d'être and her power or care (see Giddens 1992, for a social reading of toxic parents). It is only in a world of children and childlike behaviors that the mother can assume her rightful place and reign and, therefore, not be robbed of her power and dominion.

Kincaid's work clarifies the obvious colonial connotations of a kin structure which could only be heightened by centuries of political domination and oppressive class, racial, and gender relationships. In this case, the mother replaces the colonial hierarchy as she is normatively installed to rule over all the other subjects in the familial domain. This inversion of gender domination is actually in step and quite logically ingrained in a patriarchal hierarchy—because it enhances women with imaginary and powerful homelands of personal and domestic space—and looks to demean women and perpetually place them on the lower political rungs. However, this greater personal and therefore political role for women, even though they are caught within and replicate oppressive relationships of domination, is made even more possible by the complicated negative images of men and fathers. Men, natives and colonizers alike, are seen either as being unmanly or as outsiders and therefore as unable to fulfill the patriarchal role thrust on them. This ideological construct, coupled with a wounded masculinity that compels heterosexuality and multiple sexual partners, can only contribute further to the denigration of men's reputation and take fathers out of the loving domain of authority within the domestic family (see Benavides 2003; Ferrándiz 2003, 2004).

Yet, it is in this context that the most viable hegemonic device seems to be locked. By weaving women into the patriarchal narrative (see Anzaldúa

1987; Kristeva 1977, 1987), the postcolonial structure secures its own hegemonic ambiguity and ensures that oppressive colonial scripture remains, if not intact, at least very similar in terms of political outreach and social constraints.

It is also in this ambivalent ideological construction of women as more than mothers or mothers as political tools and not simply good that a more realistic postcolonial society comes into focus. The political effects of the Madres de Plaza de Mayo (Mothers of the Plaza de Mayo) in post–civil war Argentina or the reworking of the Malinche myth (see Cypess 1991; Franco 1989, 2002; Mallon 1996) as well as the mothers organizing in Ciudad Juárez, Mexico, to protest their daughters' deaths (Schmidt-Camacho 2004) all serve to complicate a perception of Latin mothers that is complex in reality but whose façade, by not being dismantled and therefore kept intact, has exhausted effusive sentiments for women, men, and children alike (see Santiago and Davidow 2000).

Finally, one can easily imagine why Silva's poetic images of motherhood and his denial of a father figure could only vividly play on the rich Guayaquilean imagery of a pretense-filled existence and the haunting emptiness of a Guayaquil Antiguo (see Chapter 2). It is to these complex and sexually inscribed taboo relationships and their consequent powerful image of sin that I now turn.

The Road of Sin: Transgression and Forbidden Voices

Que lejos aquel tímido y dulce adolescente
de este vicioso pálido, triste de haber pecado! . . .
—Tomó del árbol malo la flor concupiscente
y el corazón se ha envenenado.[6]

In Guayaquil complex colonial and racial legacies are interspersed with the huge sexual effects of power. As the above poem and other pieces of Silva's writing demonstrate, he seems to have achieved a great level of emotional maturity at an extremely early age. In one of his signature poems, "Aniversario" (Birthday), he talks about feeling old and over the hill at twenty. Not coincidentally, he would apparently commit suicide only a couple of days after his twenty-first birthday:

¡Hoy cumpliré veinte años: amargura sin nombre
de dejar de ser niño y empezar a ser hombre,

de razonar con Lógica y proceder según
los Sanchos profesores del Sentido Común!

¡Me son duro mis años—y apenas si son veinte—;
ahora se envejece tan prematuramente,
se vive tan de prisa, pronto se va tan lejos,
Que repentinamente nos encontramos viejos
enfrente de las sombras, de espaldas a la Aurora,
y solos con la Esfinge siempre interrogadora! . . .

¡Hoy no es la adolescente mirada y risa franca,
sino el cansado gesto de precoz amargura,
y está el alma que fuera una paloma blanca
triste de tantos sueños y de tanta lectura![7]

It is impossible to know the personal realities that filled Silva with so much desperation and anxiety that he felt like an old man: "de pronto se va tan lejos" (quickly we go so far). This is a task for future biographers. Here, I explore those conditions that have made it easy for generations of Guayaquileans to identify with and emulate his sentiments. The early maturity of his work found an eager audience that has only grown and that ultimately seems to understand his apparent suicide even when the reasons for it are not clear. His killing himself for love of a fifteen-year-old girl who never felt responsible for his death or traumatized by the event (she married, had children, and lived an uneventful life in Guayaquil) is not taken at face value by any Guayaquilean to whom I spoke. Rather, the problem lies in Silva's apparent turmoil seemingly having been accepted without question, when the excuses and reasons expressed in his poem would be considered unacceptable motives for terminating one's life even today. It is striking how, even though suicide is still socially stigmatized, Silva's apparent suicide is somehow overlooked, even hailed as proof of his superior sensibility, thereby allowing him to become an object of collective sympathy. It is this apparent contradiction between how Silva lived his life (and carried out his death) and how he violently expressed life in his most grief-stricken poems and the normative social façade that Guayaquileans maintain that, I would argue, provides the most insight into the political domain of sentiment in Guayaquil.

I also argue that sexual experience is one of the most important areas in which these troubled feelings are succinctly expressed. It is easy to see in Silva's work a concern with sin, especially as a result of sexual awakening and experience. In contrast to these more sexually explicit poems are a greater number written about the beauty of feminine love as abstractly represented and as devoid of human content (with its set of human follies and inconsistencies). In this sense, these poems seem to hide the ideal of what love should be (what I interpret to have become a useful Guayaquilean image) as opposed to the messy human experience of what it is. A young girl of fifteen chaperoned by her family, barely capable of expressing sexual desire, seems to be an idyllic and wishful recourse for Silva and his society rather than an accurate description of any young woman, then or now.

Contrasted to this fantasy-filled description of love are several poems, albeit fewer in number, expressing a much more troubled existence, one plagued with the burden of knowledge and the contaminating effects of poetry and its intoxicating beauty. One can easily make out the impact of the French damned poets of the nineteenth century and their drug-induced, unconscious exploration of the self. This similarity, among other evidence, has made scholars wonder about whether Silva used drugs and psychotropic substances, which could have contributed to his heightened state of awareness and hopelessness at ever completely fitting in (Patricia Galeano, personal communication):

No alegra la sabiduría,
porque la pena es conocer,
y causa la melancolía
nuestra sola razón de ser.

El prurito de analizar
nos ha perdido,
y el huracán de anhelar
lanzó nuestra nave en el mar
desconocido.[8]

Whether Silva used drugs or not, his unhappy state was enormously popular with his fellow Guayaquileans, even more so after his death. It is also apparent that he owned a burdensome self-knowledge affected by seeing, feeling, or consciously realizing things that were too close to or actively denied by those around him. Silva repeatedly represents this self-knowledge as being a result of having gone too far, transgressed in a particular way beyond the established social norms; his punishment is to be banned forever from a "normal" existence. He returns often to this onerous exile somehow caused by his actions or by subconscious feelings over which he has no control but which ultimately make up who he is:

> Por donde ella pasaba la tragedia surgía,
> tenía la belleza de una predestinada,
> y una noche de otoño febril aparecía
> en sus ojos inmensos y oscuros retratada . . .
>
> Y fue bajo el auspicio del padrino Saturno
> que deshojé a sus plantas mi juventud florida . . .
> Desde entonces padezco de este mal taciturno
> que hace una noche eterna del alba de mi vida.[9]
> (Silva 2000: 97)

At this level we begin to ascertain an enormous and mysterious erotic power that seems to creep up and gain huge control over Silva's life, that thwarts his belonging to "normalized"(civilized) society. What is both interesting and problematic is that Silva is quite clear that this normative civilized and familial behavior is full of hypocrisy and lies; he refers to it with disdain and sad epithets:

> La enfermedad que yo tengo
> mi corazón sólo sabe:
> como él nunca la dirá,
> nunca ha de saberla nadie.[10]

Once again, Silva is caught within an apparent contradiction: being banished from civilized society, but being hurt despite understanding the emptiness of normative practices of domestic bliss and accepted social convention (or, as he describes them, as being as empty as shallow graves and maggot-infested corpses [see Silva N.d.]).

Yet, there is a recurring theme here of the normative precepts of good manners and the pull of the Real, with its volatile surge of desire and its unwillingness to simply be silenced and to comply. There is no doubt that Silva's contradictory behavior would prove to be enormously attractive to Guayaquileans and, more important, would hold a paralyzing interest for Guayaquileans until the present (see Calderón Chico 1999). It is also toward this contradictory nexus and transgressive behavior that his narratives, particularly his journalistic pieces, seem to turn to dark spaces such as the night and the interior of movie houses, all pointing to the transgressive and forbidden nature of his desire.

It is perhaps to Silva's credit that he left the nature of his transgressive desires vague. In doing so, he was able to channel more unrealized—and perhaps even unspeakable in the civilized quarters where these desires were most rampant—cravings. Thus, Guayaquil has from its inception exhibited repressed sentiments that have charged any feeling that does not fit into the normative pantheon with alienation and destructive guilt. Along with low-class, Indian, and black racial features, homosexuality and independent female sexuality have become the most threatening sexual expressions to be subversively represented. It is these two sexual images—of homosexuals and whores—that have been hailed in the Ecuadorian literary canon by Javier Vásconez (1986), Pablo Palacio (1986), and Jorge Enrique Adoum (1983, 1995), among others.

I want to state explicitly that I do not assume Silva to have been a homosexual or to have had homosexual feelings, although I maintain that a thorough biographical exegesis might easily lead to this conclusion.[11] Rather, I assume that Silva was aware of the explosive content of sexual desire and personally crossed the line to understand the debilitating effects of its real, infused sentiments of guilt and exile. Only firsthand knowledge of transgressive sexual experience could have been strong enough to provoke feelings of sinfulness, guilt, death, and unrelenting physical desire, as he continually expresses in his poems:

¡En la actitud del que ya nada espera
nos embriagamos de teorías vagas,
soñando hacer brotar la primavera
de la infección de nuestras propias llagas! . . .

¡Señor, contra tu ley pecado habemos
y, en vez del alma dulce que nos diste,
en el día final te ofrecemos
un corazón leproso, viejo y triste![12]

What these desires were specifically, and how they ultimately contributed to his death are of less importance, at least in this historical and ethnographic enterprise, even though it is his personal dimension or, rather, his expertise at intimately expressing a social situation plagued by postcolonial undertones that has made Silva the iconic figure he is. The national identification allowed by Silva's work expresses the generations' understanding that here stood a man alone in his sin, unrelenting in his knowledge of the hypocrisy of normative social relations, and able to understand the sharp pain afforded by the pull of sexual desire versus supposedly normative behavior. He was unwilling to negotiate a truce or find a safe harbor; instead, he confronted life and death in their most vivid honesty. What else could provide the fantasy-filled image to which so many Guayaquileans continually return to reflect their oppressed existence, to, as Silva ambiguously puts it, express and hide their personal suffering at the hands of ambiguously hegemonic sexual norms?

> ¡Oh, vida inútil, vida triste
> que no sabemos en que emplear!
> ¡Nos cansa todo lo que existe
> por conocido y por vulgar!
>
> ¡Frívolos labios de mujeres
> nos brindan su hechizo fatal!
> ¡Infeliz del que oyó en Citeres
> la voz del pecado mortal!
>
> Y con aquella calma fría
> del que en un principio no ve,
> iré a buscar mi paz sombría,
> no importa adónde . . . ¡Pero iré![13]

CHAPTER 2

Guayaquil Antiguo
Sentiment, History, and Nostalgia

Se encuentra mi ciudad circundada de cerros
y, si sobre los cerros la corva luna brilla,
en los patios ululan tristemente los perros,
al vagabundo espectro de la diosa amarilla.

Tienen sus calles reminiscencias provincianas,
infantil alegría sus casas de madera,
dulzura familiar sus sencillas mañanas,
y es siempre una mentira su fugaz primavera.

¡Oh, ciudad de Santiago, ciudad pequeña y mía,
que abrigas mi alegría y mi melancolía
y el universo lírico que dentro del pecho llevo!

Imagen de mi alma tantas veces vencida,
que resurges más bella, cada vez más erguida,
con un ritmo más puro y con un ideal nuevo.

—SILVA, "MI CIUDAD"

Like most cities, Guayaquil has its share of beauty and enchantments.
Few Guayaquileans, however, will recommend that tourists visit the city.
Residents have learned to love the city as a result of living in it rather
than because of the city's physical or natural beauty, or even its social
comforts. In many ways, it is the city's characteristics as a port—seafar-
ing flux, urban chaos—and a romantic colonial vision of rural harmony
that has fed Guayaquil's evolution as Ecuador's economic capital. That
the cemetery (*el cementerio*) has traditionally been one of the city's most
awe-inspiring sites says a lot about the nostalgic representation of Guayaquil (see Figure 6). This is the same cemetery across from which Medardo

Figure 6. The General Cemetery, Guayaquil. Photograph by Melissa García.

Ángel Silva lived while reflecting on life in his poetry as he saw one funeral procession after another bring the dead to their final resting place. It is also the cemetery where he is buried in the same grave with his mother (see Figure 5, Chapter 1).

In this chapter I discuss the historical structures of feelings that fueled Guayaquil throughout the twentieth century and enabled the city to maintain its dominant regional and national position. Again, how Guayaquileans identify themselves is highly political and prone to the precise power effects, because the historical process is supposedly devoid of explicit political characteristics. Guayaquil's emergence as Ecuador's socioeconomic capital and its nostalgia-laden identity are not natural or logical outcomes other than its continuous drive to hide the complex racial, sexual, and class constraints that sustained the city's hegemonic representation of itself. The metonymic device par excellence in this political representation has been the production of a nostalgic discourse referred to as Guayaquil Antiguo, initiated in the late 1800s, to which the city and its inhabitants have obsessively referred since. This atemporal version of Guayaquil is present in Pedro's comments (interview, August 16, 2003), "I believe that time in that manner is relative. He [Silva] did it [committed suicide] because of his own decision, quite independent of the period in which he was living. If he did it during that period, he would do it today as well, in modern Guayaquil. I think it would have been the same."

The late 1880s marked the emergence of a long period of unrest for Guayaquil that would last almost for half a century, until the 1930s. It is during this period, which saw one social upheaval after another and continual cultural and artistic rearticulation, that many of the traits recognized today as authentically or traditionally Guayaquilean emerged or were invented (see Hobsbawm and Ranger 1983). Guayaquileans symbolically return to this time on July 25 to celebrate the city's founding with *verbenas* (social gatherings where people wear traditional colonial dress from the 1880s), visits to the ship *Buque Escuela Guayas* (the country's only traditional wooden naval ship), the Daule-Guayas swim meet, and official exhibitions of the black-and-white representations of the port's seemingly pristine existence.

Prime among Guayaquil's invention of traditions is the discourse of Guayaquil Antiguo, which never existed but is provocatively Real in providing Guayaquileans a vibrant form of identification and historical agency. In the midst of political conflict and exploitative social relationships, the discursive device of Guayaquil Antiguo allows for a more utopian vision of what many Guayaquileans, particularly but not exclusively the elite, believe their city to be. Thus it is important to analyze the power effects of this hegemonic device and to explore the inherent social processes that have fueled rather than limited Guayaquil Antiguo's hegemonic ambiguity and popular appeal.

The most blatant contradiction is the one between the pristine images of the city in photographs, etchings, and sketches (produced roughly between 1890 and 1920 [see Figures 1–4 in the introduction and Figures 7 and 8 here]) and the violent history of the city during the same period. While historical accounts, academic analyses, intellectual histories, and even some literary production describe a city caught in the midst of intense political conflicts between Liberals and Conservatives, these same conflicts are completely absent from the visual representations of Guayaquil Antiguo, even though, or perhaps because, many of these conflicts encapsulated much larger class-based and colonial racial distinctions that have never been acknowledged.

The description of Guayaquil Antiguo always implies the hegemonic ambivalence of a master trope as described by many Guayaquileans I interviewed: "I think it is a very welcoming city, it is a nice city. It has its history, its colonial past. And from that a whole set of attractions, which

CASA DE LAS 100 VENTANAS   GUAYAQUIL ANTIGUO

Figure 7. House of the 100 Windows, Guayaquil Antiguo. From Roura Uxandaberro (N.d.).

if I told them all, you wouldn't have any tape left" (Juanito, interview, October 11, 2002). For Guayaquileans, this master trope always brings with it specters of authenticity and a traditional manner of being. All master tropes—including the sentiment-infused trope of Guayaquil Antiguo —precisely because of their successful hegemonic ambiguity, are really difficult to define.

The most empirical element in the production of this historical discourse is the visual images left to us mainly from the first two decades after the turn of the twentieth century and the continuous reproduction of these images since their creation.

These representations have been so hegemonically successful that owning original pictures or sketches from the period, or even early reproductions, confers social status and historical legitimation. A person or household with images of Guayaquil Antiguo projects a sense of privileged class, historical knowledge, and civic pride, which reflects social character. In other words, knowing about or being able to afford these archival representations of the city implies a level of national feeling that reflects power on the owners of the reproductions. The Archivo Histórico del Guayas (Historical Archive of Guayas) has felt the need to obtain as many of these representations as possible to maintain an officializing record for the city (Archivo Histórico del Guayas N.d.).

There is little more than these images to support the account of a pristine utopian period in Guayaquil's social life, a period devoid of the conflicts and extreme poverty in which most of the city's population found itself immersed (Macías 1983, 1986). This does not mean there are no conflict-filled images from the period, such as of poor port workers; rather, these are conveniently excluded from public display. Also absent from this visual economy are the angst-filled images of Indian faces and Andean desolation typical of highland representations from the period.

The visual economy of Guayaquil Antiguo is keen on depicting large wooden buildings and romanticized *caña gadúa* (bamboo) houses, quaint streets and alleyways, large avenues, and, above all, the romantic image

JOYA COLONIAL   GUAYAQUIL ANTIGUO

Figure 8. Colonial jewel, Guayaquil Antiguo. From Roura Uxandaberro (N.d.).

of the Río Guayas, either as backdrop or frontispiece for the nostalgic representation. Rarely are there people caught in this visual frame, and when there are, they appear from such a distance that individual faces are lost and, perhaps most important, any racial distinction (phenotypic or sartorial) is blurred. Surprisingly, class distinctions are visible, including men wearing suits and crop hats and women with long flowing dresses, emblems of higher status, particularly in long shots. These contrast with the few poorer individuals or Indians in the photos. As Laura Wexler (2000) powerfully argues, these images, in their silences and privileged icons, express the larger subset of relations of domination and racial formation that frames them.

The images have continuously reinforced a particular vision of Guayaquil at the turn of the century that has slowly but surely come to represent the period, beating out alternative historical versions. Other types of popular narrative have appeared that convey traditional legends with the romantic overtones of rural customs (*costumbrismo*), convent life, ghostly appearances and hauntings, and iconic figures which reinforce the images caught in these particular visual discourses (see Pino Roca 1973). I explored these visual and narrative economies and the particular investment they embodied to assess how these discourses were reworked to formulate Guayaquil Antiguo as a powerful hegemonic device, both an expression of Guayaquil's limited historical longing and Silva's reworking of an essential emergence of new structures of feeling.

The question here is one of relationship and not of supposed exclusion, of how revolutions, social conflicts, and exploitative relations were all normalized to infuse differing levels of Guayaquilean reality as expressed and coalesced around particular structures of feeling and a fantasy-filled hegemonic device like Guayaquil Antiguo. I would argue that the representational violence is as present in descriptions of Guayaquil Antiguo as they are in Silva's life and poetry; otherwise, neither could serve as contrasting hegemonic vehicles of Guayaquilean self-identification.

It is precisely because both Silva and the discourse of Guayaquil Antiguo ambiguously embody not only Guayaquilean reality (in its multiple contradictions) but also the wishful longing for something that Guayaquileans know they do not have that both elements serve as hegemonic strongholds of Guayaquilean identity. Just as Silva's work represents great social tension but has been represented as merely personalistic, as imbued exclusively with romantic concerns, the recourse to a reified past in Guayaquil Antiguo captures conflicts and violence hidden beneath the veneer of the city's historical longing to be seen as a utopian, tropical, urban paradise (see Shank 2000; Wexler 2000).

Silva and Guayaquil Antiguo are the two most potent devices of structures of feeling, which, informed by the Liberal and Socialist revolutions, enabled Guayaquil to assume a conscious identity vital to the economic productivity of the city, for both those born in the city and those who found their way to it. It is also due to the primal discursive place of Silva and Guayaquil Antiguo that hundreds of thousands of migrants have claimed Guayaquil as their own, contributing even further to making the city the vital economic heart of the country. It is the centrality of these discourses that makes them essential to an analysis of the emerging "structures of feeling" at the turn of the twentieth century.

My analysis of Guayaquil Antiguo therefore relates more to its investment and power effects than to an argument for or against historical truthfulness, always a problematic endeavor (see Benavides 2004a). The version of this discourse put forward by its visual images and by many of the city's popular mythical narratives, unlike other academically legitimized historical accounts, speaks to the investment in a pristine past as demonstrated by these particular images. It is precisely because the structures of feeling are caught within this melodramatic narrative and active memorialization of the city's past that they are activated and dynamically reworked by Silva and continually reproduced by generations of Guayaquileans in cultural gatherings, academic literary traditions, musical reconversions, and, above all, cultural self-identification. It is also thanks to colonial legacies inherent in this visual economy that nurturing a Guayaquilean sensibility slowly became normalized into the experience of modernity to which I now turn.

Guayaquil Antiguo: Colonial and Nostalgic Legacies

(Barrio de San Alejo)
Rueda, como una lágrima, en la atmósfera fina,
la voz del campanario antiquísimo: la una . . .
Y su eco pasa, leve como un ave marina,
sobre los techos blancos de escarcha de la luna.

Finge un lanzón la antigua torre de San Alejo,
a cuyo extremo brilla, temblando, una estrellita . . .

Húmedos callejones . . . *Casas de tiempo viejo,*
con ventanas que el viento, como un ladrón, agita . . .

Una copla canalla tiembla en el aire puro . . .
Guiña un farol: su guiño se refleja en el muro
y hace mayor el duelo de los sucios portales . . .

El paso de la ronda se pierde en la calleja
y el rumor de las armas, en la penumbra, deja
épicas remembranzas de días coloniales.[1]

One of the most obvious silences in the metonymic device of Guayaquil Antiguo is the absence of any mention of a colonial ethos, even when the device itself is profoundly steeped in a vision of the past complete with nostalgic and romantic colonial forms. This is clearly evident in the yearly celebrations of the city's founding by the Spaniards (the date settled on is July 25, but it is still contested; see Gómez Iturralde N.d., and Muse 1991, for romantic problematization), when *verbenas* are organized in El Parque Seminario and middle- and upper-class Guayaquileans wear traditional dress to commemorate the city's founding. The traditional dress worn mimics that worn by upper-class men and women of the late 1880s and early 1900s, as evident in the very few pictures of people (more often men than women) from the period.

This highlights the complete rejection of any Guayaquilean "traditions" before that time, including the two centuries of colonial control and over fifty years of Ecuadorian independence. It also speaks to the complete denial of centuries of indigenous occupation, of the continuous Indian presence during colonial and republican times, and of the constant migratory streams of other coastal, highland, and foreign groups.

The definition of Guayaquilean tradition in the form of dress and social rituals from the turn of the century does not merely preclude alternative expressions but really sets the tone for the incorporation of other time periods and groups into the contemporary reinvention of Guayaquil's past and sense of self. The city's colonial past is embedded in the particular reformulations of the city's imaginary or, rather, of the agent-filled image that Guayaquileans project of themselves and their city. This particular colonial ethos is imbued—as most colonial legacies are (see Stoler 1996, 2002)—with a singular nostalgic investment of what the population wishes the city to have been. They have convinced themselves, in an operatively obsessive manner, that this was what Guayaquil was really like.

Similarly, it is this vision, and not any other historical account, that is used to delineate the city's contemporary social order. What this obsessive attachment (see Butler 1997a) provides is a rejection of the city's problematic articulation of racial oppression, patriarchal structures, homophobic and heterosexist behavior, and exploitative class conditions. All of these social maladies, therefore, are seen, and can be understood as mere anomalies, sociohistorical accidents not in keeping with the rich pageantry of tradition reified in the expression of Guayaquil Antiguo.

Of course, this particular imaginary provides for a complete denial of oneself, principally one's social self, and of alternative historical formations. This self-denial is in itself one of the most pervasive colonial legacies imbedded and reworked within myriads of contemporary postcolonial existence (see Kureishi 1998; Rushdie 1994, 2000; Said 1978, 1999, 2000). It is an innate and continuous rejection of oneself based on foreign standards of class, race, status, gender expectations, and religious beliefs which were introduced and relate to the moment of Europe's conquest of the Americas. The postcolonial moment is defined when these mechanisms of control, which are now locked into place as identity markers, no longer are external forms of oppression but have become internalized by the colonized populations at large (see Butler 1997b; McClintock, Mufti, and Shohat 1997).

In other words, the postcolonial conundrum is that the colonizing officers are no longer needed and that the colonized populations are able to do to themselves, even more successfully, what the colonizing process started centuries ago. In this manner, the struggle to be less Indian and black and more white, to see oneself as of higher status and with economic privilege, as well as to define one's worth based on the control and exploitation of others are all indebted to the colonial legacy. Guayaquil has developed its own postcolonial existence to deny a gruesome past that, more than ever, is an essential part of who Guayaquileans are and what the city is all about: "Well, I think that back then there must have been more romanticism and, without trying to exaggerate, that is, in a manner of speaking, they brought down the stars and put them on earth. But really, if you put the period back then in which they were writing on a balance with the period today, I prefer theirs. Because now everybody [writes] such superfluous stuff, very superficial, and back then, you know, then there was much more feeling; one really lived them" (Juanito, interview, October 11, 2002).

This characteristic postcolonial condition has left Guayaquileans ambivalent about their history, since they are aware of an Indian past and use it as much as possible to their advantage, for example by reclaiming an ethos of courageous resistance and strength. Ancestral claims to a Huan-cavilca heritage are constantly reified by politicians and official rhetoric. Yet Guayaquileans also look to distance themselves from their Indian past, since it literally darkens their desire for what is Spanish and white. The latter is no longer represented by a Spanish ideal but by the neocolonial image of the United States (see Benavides 2002). In this postcolonial reworking of the city's past, Guayaquileans in general, and the reification of Guayaquil Antiguo in particular, gloss over the obvious historical continuity between the Spanish colonial occupation (which meant the demise of the indigenous population) and the Spaniards' reeducation of that population within colonial parameters and a neocolonial class, racial, and sexual ordering of the city that closely resembles the initial colonial structures and hierarchies (see Allende 2003; Dorfman 1998).

The unwillingness and, at some point, the inability to see this historical continuity make the Guayaquil Antiguo device devoid of social maladies not merely a sign of schizophrenic desire (and a symptom of self-hatred) but a necessity (Žižek 1996). Thus, Guayaquil Antiguo is a logical result of a scenario of social oppression and distinctive disordering and, as such, is a more profound description of the Real (see Žižek 2002) than any academic or intellectual historical account could ever be. Therefore, a nostalgic account of the city's past is to be taken very seriously and looked at for its reified content as well as its greater productive context, from which it emanates and is sustained, instead of simply arguing for its demise or historical inaccuracy. This is especially true when all historical interpretation is merely that: interpretations with enormous effects of power and based on always questionable empirical exigencies and evidential constraints (see Foucault 1993, 1998).

Therefore, the imaginary of Guayaquil Antiguo is a direct result of a colonial existence and, as such, of a postcolonial legacy that looks to separate itself from its origin. It is this particular romantic colonial ethos, and its resulting problematic nostalgia, that is evident in the two poems I have quoted in this chapter. Both of them contain explicit references to a more provincial and colonial existence, which is readily infused with a nostalgic romance. Silva uses of these colonial images and infuses them with problematic nostalgic memories of a struggling city constantly revisited by death, sadness, lies, tears, theft, and unsanitary conditions symbolic of larger implications.

At one level, it is clear that Silva's poems are a representational reworking of these stark historical and existential realities into operative structures of feeling for the new century (see García-Canclini 1968; see 1992 for what he refers to as a process of reconversion). At another level, it is also Silva's honesty (or emotional truth) in singing about and beautifying the city of Guayaquil simply because it is his city, without eliminating the harsh and denigrating reality that marks his success in capturing the pulse of the City, thereby allowing generations of Guayaquileans to find the expression of their feelings in his words. That success, I believe, is also evidenced in Silva's poetry's being reformulated to occupy the ambivalent hegemonic status of representing the city's national sentiment along with the metonymic device of Guayaquil Antiguo. One could thus say that Silva's century-old poetry is used alongside an image of a Guayaquil in which he never lived and yet knew quite well emotionally. This reality is grasped by one of my interviewees: "But from the *pasillo*'s point of view, the lyrics are very heartfelt. Up to a point, they are lyrics full of experiences that the writers who wrote these songs had, where they narrate the past, their past, right? Their life experiences, their things" (Juanito, interview, October 11, 2002).

In her work on Antigua, Kincaid expresses the void to which a postcolonial desire drives people, who wish into existence a blank past that everyone knows not to be true: "I only now understand why it is that people lie about their past, why they say they are one thing other than the thing they really are, why they invent a self that bears no resemblance to who they really are, why anyone would want to feel as if he or she belongs to nothing, comes from no one, just fell out of the sky, whole" (Kincaid 1997: 12–13). In this sense, Guayaquil Antiguo fills the longing for a past that all Guayaquileans know never existed. In profound ways, they refuse to accept this, and thus are unable or unwilling to acknowledge what they know to be true: "It is the denial of oneself. The topic of race is quite present but nobody talks about it. Nobody talks about it, nobody wants to touch those topics" (Ana, interview, August 15, 2001). The vivid expression of that void or the nature of the Real in postcolonial Guayaquil permits such realistic imaginaries as Guayaquil Antiguo not only to be created but also, more important, to maintain its hold on the population. This obsessive attachment to Guayaquil, as expressed in homage to a past that did not exist, is also indicative of this cultural production's erotic emotions and love: "Because as a good Ecuadorian I like those tragic sentiments. I love the romantic poets . . . But that means to talk with a simple language that makes you understand things. Not only to understand here [points to her head] but also what is over here [points to her heart]. To identify oneself, perhaps" (Ana, interview, August 15, 2001).

A basic understanding of love makes it easy to understand why one would paint a favorable picture of the object of erotic desire, even if that object is a city, particularly when one knows that the love object (Guayaquil is a prime example) is not the chaste and honest subject one wishes to have fallen in love with. This ambiguous love also might be reflected in the hundreds of *pasillos* describing the pure love of men for women unworthy of it. Once again, the gender implications of this uneven structure speak volumes about the modern ordering of the city. The initial traumatic experience of loving a city that is not what one would like it to be may be more an expression of an inherent inability to love oneself as a postcolonial subject, after almost four centuries of social processes that have made one unworthy of loving recognition. This process of symbolic misidentification is also a clue, I believe, to why love-torn *pasillos* are one of the best ways through which to grieve for a postcolonial identity (see Chapter 3).

It is also perhaps this central paradox that is contained in Demetrio Aguilera Malta's suggestively rich racial narrative: "El cholo que se enamoró de Guayaquil" (The *Cholo* Who Fell in Love with Guayaquil), published in the paradigmatic collection of short stories *Los que se van* (Gallegos Lara, Gil Gilbert, and Aguilera Malta 1973).[2] Once again, the richness of the story might explain its success, as Malta describes the inherent failure of the main character, *el cholo,* to live in Guayaquil because he has fallen in love with the city. Unable to have sex with and make love to the city, and unable to live within its erotic grasp, he must accept his defeat and loss and departs the city forever.

Perhaps this story and its paradigmatic success can help us understand the device of Guayaquil Antiguo as a marker of failure or as the denial of failure. In other words, those who subscribe so vehemently to a Guayaquil Antiguo are those who, unlike the *cholo* in Malta's story, refuse to leave the city and use this metonymic recourse to hide their racially and sexually ambivalent desire from their violent past and exploitative present. Because of the impossibility of admitting one's failure in love, the image of Guayaquil Antiguo becomes an obsessive attachment that upholds the status quo and contemporary social existence. Questioning the past would only bring down the current social order and, with it, the only identity Guayaquileans have known and inhabited up to now.

Because of this, I argue, nobody consciously believes Guayaquil Antiguo existed, yet the lie/hegemony is secure, since one would have to be crazy to dislodge this discourse (or to tell the emperor he is naked). This also would explain why the harsh and violent enculturation of Guayaquilean children begins early—to spare them a physical death which only secures their emotional one. And there is Silva, whose death is officially reenacted in schools and tributes. Contradictorily enough, Silva's memory also secures some degree of life, at least in the intimacy of his poetry or in the sharing of feelings. It is this degree of life which is shared by Guayaquileans with the help of music (*pasillos*) and drinks when night has fallen and the emperor is fast asleep, as they cry over what, intimately, they know to be true. It is no surprise that Silva's love and his poetry speak at such a basic level to a population caught in the grip of a postcolonial obsessive attachment that produced Guayaquil Antiguo to nurture its troubled and troubling soul.

Migrants to the City and the Past: A Historical Hagiography

Cae de los aleros, sobre la estrecha vía,
una larga sombra húmeda en el aire pesado,
una pena opresora, una melancolía
contra la que no puede nada el sol enclaustrado.

Y es un dolor mayor, al áureo mediodía,
mirar el cielo azul y la calle fangosa,
y ver, como a través de angosta celosía,
un palmo de la inmensa bóveda luminosa.

¡Ah, pero en las celestes noches aurinevadas
de luna, *qué lirismos en la oscura calleja*
y en las casas que fingen ancianas inclinadas!

¡Qué leyendas se evocan si de un portal oscuro,
a la luz de un farol, se proyecta en el muro
la sombra de un transeúnte que se aleja![3]

"Of course I feel Guayaquilean. Perhaps I was not born here but I feel Guayaquilean, this is where I live, where my daughters were born" (Miranda, interview, August 15, 2001). Like many Guayaquileans, Miranda was not born in Guayaquil, but as we gather from the above quotation, this does not preclude her from identifying as Guayaquilean and, most important, from securing a Guayaquilean identity for her children, who now can claim the identity as a birthright.

These particular forms of identification belie complex mechanisms of historical and social appropriation, not the least of which are the ambivalent heritages that combine with new and hegemonic Guayaquilean identity in migrants and their families. On the one hand, they claim to belong to and be part of Guayaquil; on the other, there is the consistent pull of the migrant's roots, in other coastal or highland cities and towns. Contradictorily enough, foreigners find it easier to feel like they belong in Guayaquil, as they are less problematically incorporated into the postcolonial ideal of what being Guayaquilean is all about (see Chapter 4).

How most migrants in Guayaquil identify themselves is problematic within Guayaquil Antiguo, which is so readily enshrined within the myth of Guayaquilean authenticity and turn-of-the century tradition. What would seem to be problematic development between migrant origins and Guayaquilean heritage is far from the case, however. Even Silva was the grandson of Spanish migrants. To an enormous degree, this combination of national, ethnic, and racial ambivalence only served to fuel his ambiguous self-identification as Guayaquilean.

The migrant experience of moving to Guayaquil, attracted by the greater social and economic freedoms that Ecuador's largest port city provides, is an essential element of Guayaquil's identity. As such, this element is not too far behind the discourse of Guayaquil Antiguo, although the necessary (and reinforced) initial reading might make one think the opposite. Like all port cities, Guayaquil has been a magnet for internal migration since its founding in the seventeenth century. The archaeological evidence for pre-Hispanic populations is not scarce, but its interpretation is unclear at best (see Muse 1991). This points to large mercantile polities up and down the coast. To a large extent, migrant histories have also been readily developed by Guayaquileans themselves, beginning in the 1960s, when they migrated in large numbers out of the country to the city's U.S. counterpart, New York City, and later to Venezuela and Spain. In many ways, New York City has come to represent for Guayaquil what Guayaquil represented for the rest of Ecuador's cities at the turn of the twentieth century (see Chapter 4).

Migration has been a constant theme throughout the city's existence. A brief genealogy of traditional Guayaquilean names connects many of them to other highland and coastal cities, including the capital of Peru, Lima. However, it was really in the early 1900s when migration became intense. The social upheaval of the Liberal Revolution of the 1900s and Eloy Alfaro's ascent to power in 1905 created social relationships that allowed new racial hierarchies to be reinscribed, particularly in the coastal provinces of Guayas, Manabí, El Oro, and Esmeraldas. Esmeraldas became the stronghold of the Liberal ideal being imposed on Quito and the rest of the highlands.

In terms of race, this meant the reworking of oppressive hacienda-like relations of production for the nation's Indian populations and the political emancipation of black (Afro-) Ecuadorians, who, since the end of slavery in the 1880s, had withered in similarly oppressive socioeconomic conditions. Even though this modern reworking of the relations of production would bring the workers closer to a proletarian existence within the new modern global order of world capitalism, it still meant a significant break from the colonial forms of latifundismo that sustained the economic agricultural order of the nation (Ayala Mora 1983). The reworking of the relations of production on the coast was decisive, and the coast's transformation to an exporting agro-industrial economy did not prove less appealing to the mass of Indian laborers migrating from the highlands. These populations, along with other coastal laborers, initiated an exodus which continues to this day, marking an essential identification of what the City of Guayaquil and its inhabitants represent for the rest of Ecuador.

It is this same migrant drive that was highlighted in the Socialist-inspired revolts in Guayaquil during the 1920s and the 1930s, leading to massacres of large numbers of workers, the founding of Socialist-inspired political parties, and a new social consciousness in the national literature, which would begin to focus on society's political problems (Gallegos Lara, Gil Gilbert, and Aguilera Malta 1973). Luis A. Martinez' novel *A la costa* (To the Coast) is titled for the battle cry of a whole generation of laborers wishing to escape four centuries of exploitation and domination. The country's literature saw similar narratives by Demetrio Aguilera Malta (1970, 1977, 1980), Joaquín Gallegos Lara (1980), Enrique Gil Gilbert (1983), Nelsón Estupiñan Bass (1983), and Adalberto Ortiz (1982, 1983). Aguilera Malta returned to this period to try to understand the conditions that would shape not only Guayaquil but the whole sociopolitical structure of the country in the twentieth century. All of these authors seem, in one way or another, to return to this period as if constantly reminded (and believing) that this is when it all began, where Guayaquileans' current social identities first manifested themselves. Afro-Ecuadorian writers like Adalberto Ortiz and Nelsón Estupiñan Bass have proved essential in recounting this period of upheaval and violence, and, in many ways, their intellectual experiences speak to a reworking of a black racial identity. It is this same Afro-Ecuadorian identity that allowed them to claim a black pride that was closed off to Silva and that marked one of his most personal race-related frustrations and obsessions (see Chapter 5).

It is important to elucidate how a migrant reality essential to all Guayaquileans and continually reinserted into the regional and national literature is silently and evasively inscribed within the imagery of Guayaquil Antiguo. In other words, the migrant histories of many Guayaquileans are necessarily part of the discourse formation of Guayaquil Antiguo, even when that discourse denies their roots and existence. This disremembering is not only exhausting (see Coronil and Skurski 1991; Davis 1998; Morrison 1993) but also essential in the complex structures of feeling put in place at the turn of the century.

This migrant reality also saw its most empirical realization in the construction (made possible by a loan from the British government that took a century to repay) of a national railroad that connected the highlands with the coast and, more specifically, the economic capital, Guayaquil, with the political capital, Quito. In a profound sense, the railroad, along with legalized divorce, is often proclaimed as one of the greatest contributions of the Liberal Revolution and administration of Eloy Alfaro (see Ayala Mora 1995). The railroad serves as a metaphor of the greater regional integration that this period saw, the possibilities opened up by greater freedom and more rapid movement from one region to another. Until this happened, transregional movement was extremely dangerous, marked by landslides and muddy roads during the rainy season and criminal attacks all year around. The danger also made travel mostly a male affair, so the greater freedom afforded women with the building of the railroad is obvious, even though it is rarely mentioned in the literature (see Yáñez Cosíos 2000, for an exception).

Freedom of movement was expanded with the opening of highways and increased car transportation throughout the Andes in the 1930s, leaving the railroad to decompose slowly. It would, however, continue to serve as a metaphor for regional integration, a reworking of labor conditions and racial identifications, and, perhaps most important in Guayaquil's case, it marked reoccupation of the city by a wider array and diversity of national populations. It is not a coincidence that as the city grew throughout the twentieth century from an influx of indigenous and highland peoples, it became more important to maintain a homogeneous Guayaquilean identity. Most national identities are vital precisely because they are less apparent in reality.

Thus, nostalgia grew for a city that not only never existed but that also claimed a homogeneous origin, which, now more than ever, is clearly not an accurate portrayal. Slowly the city began to present itself as populated by migrant populations that had come to work and live in this new urban center. The reality belies the question of belonging, identity, and roots, which, unlike economic gain, is not easily answered. Thus, it was the migrant populations—elites and non-elites alike—that needed and used a standardized device to produce a cohesive identity like Guayaquil Antiguo would provide. It did not matter that this metonymic device would exclude them and their ancestors from the city's historical picture, since, after all, this was what they were looking for: a sense of belonging that would allow them to feel at home in the new city of their choosing, Guayaquil, and would erase as completely as possible their having been born and lived somewhere else.

Guayaquil Antiguo therefore provided migrants with the same feelings they were bringing to the city: a way of making a fresh start, even if it meant leaving behind their places of origin in a physical and an emotional sense. Only a metonymic device as powerful as Guayaquil Antiguo would allow migrants to feel Guayaquilean during their lifetimes and allow them to claim first-generation Guayaquileanness as authentically as possible. The process can easily be followed in the following remarks: "I am Guayaquilean with all my heart. I consider that my roots are from Zapotal, and that I will never forget. But here is where I am developing, where my kids were born, and I am just another Guayaquilean" (Giovanni, interview, August 8, 2003). However, this process of belonging would also trigger a different, if not necessarily greater, regionalism (*regionalismo*) from that tackled by the railroad system.

The fragile need for a Guayaquilean identity coupled with the powerful representation of a homogeneous historical past for the port slowly has transformed itself into a divisive form of regionalism that ridicules highlanders (*serranos*). Guayaquileans see the former as backward and stupid (not least because of the highlands' closer Indian genealogy) while they represent themselves as smart and sassy. It is this uneven regional identification that makes an insult of being called *serrano* (which is already imbued with the pejorative meanings described above) but not *costeño* (meaning from the coast). In Guayaquil the effort to not be called *serrano* is surpassed only by the effort to not be called *cholo* (as discussed in Chapter 1). This unequal signification also marks the anxious emotional distance needed by new and first-generation migrants (since they have a greater investment than other Guayaquileans) wishing to feel that they belong and marking their difference from their problematic historical roots.

In the process, the elitist and xenophobic rendering of Guayaquil's past as Guayaquil Antiguo has proven productive for the burgeoning industrial and landed elite of the coast. It has also proved paradigmatic for all Guayaquileans, migrants and poor alike. It is also not lost on anyone who can claim "Guayaquileanness" that they are immediately seen as superior in status because of their greater economic potential and relationship to the outside world (afforded by now belonging to a port city); a similar process is undergone by Guayaquileans living abroad, mainly but not exclusively in New York City, who return with higher status to their homeland (see Chapter 4).

In this manner, the new global migrants are doing to Guayaquil what earlier migrants did to their homelands, although how Guayaquil incorporates this process is different from and in tune with its investment in the identification of self-denial and the postcolonial legacy of legitimation from abroad. Ultimately, Guayaquil Antiguo turns out to be the perfect marker for migrant populations eager to belong to the country's number one port city, not only in spite of its denying but precisely because it does deny their place of origin. It is also this new national identification that produces an emotional scenario of rejection in which alcohol consumption and lovelorn *pasillos* are the best antidote for this new kind of being and living in emotional exile.

The Past as Ambiguous Signifier: Sadness, Alcohol, and Belonging

Entre tanto individuo que charla, bebe y fuma,
el poeta se siente extraño. La neblina
del tabaco rubrica en el aire, y se esfuma
con cierta voluptuosa levedad femenina.

La fatigada frente a los sueños se inclina
y se añora el encanto de esa mujer de bruma
leve, como en la copa de Sèvres cristalina
la fugaz explosión de la pálida espuma.

¿Soñar, soñar . . . ? Qué valen alegría y tristeza,
semejante a una copa de espuma de cerveza,
que dura lo que duran las huellas en el mar . . .

Vale más la mentira, ilusión que perdura,
del ensueño imposible la eternidad segura
y la estrella remota que no hemos de alcanzar.[4]

Rather than seeing the production of a homogeneous past (which has little evidential support in academic or other intellectual historical accounts) as merely historically inaccurate, wrong, or in need of revision, it would seem more worthwhile to investigate the powerful effects that the imagery of Guayaquil Antiguo supports. Why is it so successful in maintaining its hegemonic ambivalence in the face of such strong evidence to the contrary, and how does it ultimately fit into the greater picture of what I am calling a Guayaquilean modernity? Looked at from this perspective, the constant reproduction of Guayaquil Antiguo, *verbenas, chivas* (party buses; see "Las chivas" 2003), and narratives of Old Guayaquil produce a cohesive whole that fits into the picture of the modern metropolis of Guayaquil that has been created since the turn of the twentieth century.

It also is this nostalgic longing for a past that never existed, as well as for the reversal or denial of a present that one wishes to escape, that complements Silva and his poetry, particularly since Silva addressed the same kind of feeling that would contribute to the growing musical movement of the *pasillo* (see Chapter 3). It is these same structures of feelings of rejection, longing, and unattainable goals (as expressed in Silva's poetry and inherent in the postcolonial legacy) that fuel the different cultural productions that gave way and came to symbolize Guayaquil's modernity.

Silva's reworking of these themes (see Chapter 1); the passion-driven inspiration of Julio Jaramillo and the *pasillo* (see Chapter 3); the fleeting, ecstatic quest of global migrants to the United States (see Chapter 4) are all intimately tied to a regional cultural production similar to that of Guayaquil Antiguo. All of them share sentiments and a cohesive normative ordering that not only makes all these forms of cultural production mutually intelligible but also reinforces them against each other. Thus, it is artificial (albeit necessary when analyzing social reality) to talk about them individually, since they form a coherent whole in expressing these vital, according to Raymond Williams (1977), hegemonic structures of feeling in the ultimate assessment of how hegemonic national domination is normalized day to day.

What the representation of Guayaquil Antiguo therefore allows is the crucial incorporation of the past into the hegemonic and historical process of Guayaquil's modernization process. It is also clear that, to an enormous degree the nature of this representation allows the incredible feat of believing oneself to be what one may not be but would really want to be. It is, after all, the effusive effects of power, not history, which ultimately convinces one of who one is (see Baldwin 1990: 480). Thus, the representation of Guayaquil's modernity complete with a seamless ethnic past is as essential as other more concrete forms of modernity in helping Guayaquileans achieve modernity and give themselves permission to see themselves as modern. The past, therefore, is an essential part of Guayaquilean modernity, as it is of all contemporary political projects. Precisely because of the past's essential place, this inherent hermeneutic process of historical reconstruction must be erased.

The need to reinvent the past in tune with the modern invention of the city is not lost on a population that safeguards reputation and *buenas costumbres* (good manners) as sacred elements of character, both personal and national. This reality once again immediately brings into the picture gender and sexual prescription as the most highly charged in terms of social reputation claimed as a result of class origin, national/ regional roots, and education. There is an intricate exchange between the denial of a present mired in exploitative class, racial, and gender/sexualized relationships and the production of a Guayaquilean modernity devoid of such social prescriptions. The longing for a past imbued with the fantasy of a future, neither of which actually exist, speaks to a complex, yet fragile, hegemonic production. It is this same hegemonic production that is being balanced on the (pillarlike) structures of feeling and the complex reinsertion of the repressed (or what Žižek [2002] refers to as the return of the Real in the Lacanian sense). In other words, this is why an unvisited history always returns, refuses to go away forever.

The past, like the present, finds a way of inserting its Medusa-like head back into the picture, and, just as with other mythical figures, the more you cut down and try to deny them, the more they grow, both in visual imagery and power. Therefore, it is not surprising that the decade of the 1990s saw the construction of Malecón 2000 on the traditional river promenade, the rebuilding of El Cerro del Carmen, and the construction of a new historical park (Parque Histórico Guayaquil; see Figure 9), all obsessively historical ways of holding onto an identity that never really existed and whose reality is, more than ever, beyond one's grasp. What better way is there than (re)constructing monuments to a period that only metonymically exists in the heads and emotions of Guayaquileans?

This metaphor has doubly interesting implications for my analysis of Guayaquil's modern ideal. On the one hand, as I have mentioned, one cannot simply disregard the imagery of Guayaquil Antiguo because, in denying its historical accuracy, one secures its place even more solidly. Guayaquil Antiguo and its hegemonic force do not stem from historical evidence but from an outright, almost explicit, denial of the historical palimpsest

Figure 9. Historic house in the Parque Histórico Guayaquil
(http://www.parquehistorico.com).

(see Foucault 1993) of what Guayaquil was or wants to be. Therefore, proving Guayaquil Antiguo's historical inaccuracy only strengthens its allure and leaves its power intact.

Similarly, Guayaquil Antiguo is a concrete denial of an interpretation of the city's past. As such, it also looks to erase historical elements, accurate or not, that would seem to distract from the political project of modernity, in terms of a hierarchical status afforded to the city, and which it invested on soon after its republican independence in the mid-1800s. The constant representation of Guayaquil Antiguo also brings threads that disrupt and, at the same time, fuel the modernization project put in place by this representation and the myriad other forms of popular cultural production. It is as if the representation of Guayaquil Antiguo is at its most fragile when not tampered with, precisely because discussion of it always produces effusive sentiment that, even as a simple reaction, makes its image purer and more adaptive to the social norms.

Either approach, however—dismissing Guayaquil Antiguo as merely historically inaccurate and failing to understand its hegemonic potential, or continuously presenting images of Guayaquil Antiguo which constantly reinscribe its historical and emotional shortcomings—seems to be a setup for disaster, or at least for constant emotional upheaval. Neither the use of Guayaquil Antiguo nor its dismissal provides a safe harbor; rather, each seems to push for an elusively final ideal that is the most seductive precisely because it is out of reach.

Yet the seduction created by this construction is most successful both because it is out of reach and is alluring, always while managing to present itself as not being either. This ambiguity is what marks Guayaquil Antiguo's success and its intimate relationship with the *pasillo* and drowning one's sorrow. It is also this ambiguity, so essential and yet so impossible to describe, that songs about lost love, sublimated sexual desire, and a bar full of smoke and beer foam (as in Silva's poem) can represent so succinctly that which one can never have: a cohesive and homogeneous Guayaquilean identity. It is also because of this problematic of the Real within Guayaquil's postcolonial legacy that all of Silva's poetry about the city is so damagingly precise, perhaps none more so than the last stanza of "En el bar":

Vale más la mentira, ilusión que perdura,
del ensueño imposible la eternidad segura
y la estrella remota que no hemos de alcanzar.

PART 2

MUSIC, MIGRATION, AND RACE

CHAPTER 3

Musical Reconversion
The Pasillo's *National Legacy*

Si yo muero primero es tu promesa,
sobre de mi cadáver dejar caer,
todo el llanto que brote de tu
tristeza y que todos se enteren de
tu querer.
—JULIO JARAMILLO, "NUESTRO JURAMENTO"

The *pasillo* is Ecuador's national musical genre, described by all as the country's *música nacional* (national music). *Pasillos* are not unique to Ecuador but are also present in neighboring Colombia as well as Costa Rica. *Pasillo* musicians have a long history of singing about frustrated love, although the genre initially developed, surprisingly, in town bands (*bandas de pueblo*) and even *retretas* (military orchestras). The *pasillo* evolved during the late 1800s in close association with an emerging national elite, and the radio and recording industries made it the national musical form par excellence. In 1911, of the 272 pieces recorded in the country, 67 were *pasillos,* and by 1930, *pasillo* composers and musicians, such as Nicasio Safadi and Enrique Ibáñez Mora, were touring New York City as official representatives of the nation (Wong 1999).

Guayaquil and Guayaquileans intimately relate to *pasillos,* although coastal *pasillos* are differentiated from those from the highlands by being rhythmically brighter and more upbeat; the lyrics of both coastal and highland variations are sad, grief-stricken, and tragic. As many Guayaquileans told me, the city's *pasillos* are systematically unhappy and express despondency caused by a lost or betrayed love: "*Pasillos* are the country's national music . . . , it is a sad music, a music that refers a lot to stories about relationships, unrequited love, not reciprocated" (Kathy, interview, July 3, 2002).

The nature of the *pasillo's* melancholic aspect tends to be ambiguous; however, the tragic discourse of this national rhythm, similar to that elaborated in Medardo Ángel Silva's poetry, makes the genre interesting in terms of popular cultural production and hegemonic positioning. As a result of the intimate relationship between the *pasillo* and the national melancholy, it is not surprising that what many consider Silva's suicide note, "El alma en los labios," has been transformed into one of the most evocative Guayaquilean *pasillos* and immortalized by Julio Jaramillo himself.

I am particularly interested in the interstices of cultural production as an ambiguous, and therefore successful, hegemonic symbol of power. In this chapter, I look at the *pasillo* as a regional Guayaquilean representation, as many other authors have done with other musical genres throughout the American continent (see Austerlitz 1992; Davis 1998; Otero Garabís 2000; Quintero Rivera 1989). This kind of analysis points up subtle articulations of national sensibility, cultural production, and hegemonic domination. A historically informed ethnographic analysis of the *pasillo* allows us to explore the structures of feeling that have imbued Guayaquileans with the capacity to represent and identify with their city, because *pasillos* in the city mark an interesting intersection of several of the variables essential to understanding the relationship between power and sensibility in the production of a national Guayaquilean identity. The creation of Guayaquil's cultural identity (or its lack of one) is particularly salient in the mythical Guayaquil Antiguo discourse, Julio Jaramillo's position as the city's musical icon, and a tragic national identity, which was, contradictorily, essential to the city's development as the economic capital of the country throughout the twentieth century. All of these variables are an inherent part of the same structures of feeling Silva reworked.

One must wonder why a genre whose apolitical lyrics overwhelmingly tell of unfaithful women and tragic love affairs would be the most symbolic for a population that espouses patriarchal identification, gender/sexual discrimination, and popular political participation (as the proliferation of social movements and political parties attests). Many Guayaquileans I interviewed saw through the cultural contradiction, with its elements that supposedly were not part of their daily reality (Ana, interview, August 15, 2001): "It is due to the fact that the country's life is tragic. Everything you see, the social system, the economy, it is all a tragedy; it makes you want to cry. I believe the music reflects the soul, the feelings of a people. And I don't believe it can reflect much happiness, because people really suffer a lot. In one way or another, the people suffer and they have different ways of expressing it, and one way is through music."

The *pasillo* also holds a central place in the tragedy-filled inspiration for the migrant history of Guayaquil's identity. Guayaquileans with whom I spoke elaborated on the power of *pasillo* lyrics in sustaining their identity when they left the city: "[When I listen to *pasillos*] I remember a lot about that period, right? The period in which I was there [Guayaquil], that is what comes to mind. I identify it with the country of my parents, the place in which I lived a long time, and I identify it with Ecuador, with a national identity" (Pedro, interview, August 16, 2003). Beatriz, another informant, began to find *pasillos* more meaningful while living in Chile (interview, July 7, 2002):

When I traveled, when I went to live in Chile, I learned to really enjoy *pasillos* [laughs]. That is, Julio Jaramillo became my idol! Without a doubt! I liked him before, it's not like I didn't like him, I liked his songs, I even liked the typical "Nuestro juramento." But when I got there [Chile] and that feeling of belonging that appears when you are away from your country, and anything may make you start crying ["chorreando el moco"]. It is really sad that you have to leave your country to really start appreciating it, right? Because I used to like them, but it really was when I was living over there that I learned to appreciate it, because I took a tape, and when I was there, with some wine and with my friends, I memorized all the lyrics that I didn't know before; I just knew a couple of them. And, for example, when we got together with friends, with guitars, we began to sing *pasillos,* the songs from Ecuador, you understand? And then one begins to feel nostalgic. One should not have to leave the country to feel that, but at least in my case and in my experience, you realize the importance of the things you have . . . Don't get me wrong, I adore Santiago [Chile], let me tell you, I love the city. I was very happy there, but every time something reminded me of Ecuador or Guayaquil it was unbearable ["como que te daba"] . . . and it was the music, it is a very important part, it sort of transforms you, with the songs.

The pain-filled migrant reality Beatriz expresses is equally present in the large Guayaquilean population living in New York City today (see Chapter 4).

In the complex articulation of the *pasillo* as the hegemonic cultural device that it is, however, it is the apparent contradiction between the lyrics and the lived-in reality of the over two million Guayaquileans that is most intellectually productive. It is in this largely unconscious process between what Guayaquileans feel, on the one hand, and what they know, on the other, that allows them to not only identify but also express their lives through this musical genre. It is also through their national identification with the *pasillo* that the cultural ambivalence of doing what is normative in a postcolonial context of domination and good manners (*buenas costumbres,* or its Guayaquilean racial counterpart, *no ser cholo*) obtains powerful hegemonic dimensions. It is this same contradiction between what is personally and intimately felt and what is socially allowed (inherent in Silva's life and oeuvre; see the Introduction and Chapter 1) that is apparent in the *pasillo*'s hegemonic articulation. Guayaquileans have many social reasons for tragedy and despair, from extreme poverty and political corruption to concrete racial exploitation and gender discrimination. But to criticize all these social maladies, which everyone knows to be true, would mean the demise of Guayaquil's social structure and of any personal Guayaquilean identity. As Sayer (1994) notes, telling the emperor he is naked (or exposing hegemony for the fakery that it is) is not a sound idea unless one is a fool or willing to die. And interestingly enough, *pasillos* proclaim death (which Silva so eloquently immortalized) to be the most logical solution to an emotional or a physical life devoid of meaning and dignity.

Therefore, it would seem that *pasillos* allow Guayaquileans to express intimate frustration and grief in a personal manner, in spite of the innumerable social constraints that are never articulated. Gender and sexual constraints have been even harder to critique and analyze (with very recent exceptions; see Andrade 1995, 1997; Andrade and Herrera 2001; Cifuentes 1999) than Guayaquilean political realities, which are treated in a more detached and academic manner. The *pasillo,* I argue, embodies and responds to a historical tradition similar to structures of feeling, which emerged at the turn of the twentieth century. This tradition has ambiguously resolved social limitations by being expressed as supposedly depoliticized intimate feelings, feelings that, through cultural and musical transformation, are shared with less threatening force but with even more powerful sentimental—and therefore intimate—political meanings.

It is because of this particular structure of feelings that Guayaquilean singer Julio Jaramillo's death in 1978 was publicly mourned by over 200,000 people, who went to see him lying in state and accompanied his funeral procession. There has not been any similar demonstration of grief since the mid-twentieth century for any public figure other than Pres. Jaime Roldós Aguilera in 1981.

It is this same emotional and political ambivalence, inherent in the structures of feeling reworked in postcolonial Guayaquil, that allows

Silva's poetry to express the pain of Guayaquil's reality. It would be erroneous to think that this identification could have occurred while Silva and Julio Jaramillo were alive, since tragedy, grief, and death are the emotional building blocks that inhabit Guayaquileans' daily lives, however subconsciously. In this sense, grief and pain, as expressed in Silva's poetry or in Jaramillo's evocative *pasillos,* are but crystalline metaphors for Guayaquil's emotional life and both social existence and national identification.

National Misidentifications

> Si tu mueres primero yo te prometo
> escribiré la historia de nuestro amor
> con todo el alma llena de sentimiento
> la escribiré con sangre, con tinta
> sangre del corazón.[1]
> (Jaramillo, "Nuestro juramento")

The *pasillo* has surpassed its initial Andean boundaries of Ecuador and Colombia; it is now sung and appreciated by Latin Americans throughout the continent. But it is important to note that national fault lines are essential in this continental endeavor. The *pasillo* has not remained unchanged in its continental voyage; rather, it has adapted to each national interpreter and audience. The *pasillo* is a lens through which identification speaks loudly to the genre's ambiguous national representation and does not deny the transnational or ambivalent hegemonic reach of the music. It is precisely because the *pasillo* may disregard (or displace) questions of authenticity that it is a good vehicle for national and postcolonial representation. The *pasillo* is invested with strong national readings, and it is because of these readings, not in spite of them, that the genre has made its way through the continent, is so popular, and has so many meanings.

Ecuadorians and Colombians living beyond the borders of South America continue to invest the *pasillo* with national, albeit different, sentiments and meanings. As my interviewees told me, for many it was only when they left Ecuador that they fully invested the *pasillo* with the sentiments that made them see themselves as participants in that imagined national community that they thought they had left behind. Since nostalgia rather than civic pride takes center stage, for those Guayaquileans living abroad, the *pasillo* is reinvested with national markers that make listening to these songs more nostalgic than when they heard them in Ecuador.

The *pasillo*'s particular grammar and rhythm contribute to the creation of a transnational identity that blurs the geographical boundaries of Guayaquilean and Ecuadorian citizenship. But the genre creates this identity by reemphasizing national markers, although different ones, from the *pasillo*'s original signification. It is this phenomenon, of which the *pasillo* in migration is a prime example, that allows a generation of people born in New York City, for example, and who have never even visited Guayaquil or Ecuador to consider themselves authentic Ecuadorians. There are interesting postcolonial implications in this, since the center and periphery model seems to be overturned as people identify with the neocolonial possessions, not with the colonizing entity, even when they have never been to the former colonies. In short, the transnational drama exemplified by Guayaquileans and *pasillos* points to the complex interaction of national markers and the superfluous desire to maintain a strict center and periphery, or West and non-West. At the same time, these processes point to the need to reassess the nation-state's underpinning of cultural phenomena, such as the *pasillo,* to understand the complex articulation of identification across the unsteady yet resilient fault line of national identity, as well as the role played by race, class, and generational markers.

It is useful, albeit somewhat problematic, to use Anderson's (1991) "imagined communities" to assess the modern production of socially meaningful gatherings of peoples and physical bodies. His imagined communities present a viable metaphor for expressing the fragility and vulnerability of the national ideal while representing it in its solid configuration, one which has been responsible for so many violent uprisings and invasions, so much ethnic strife, so many national liberation movements and refugee scenarios, and so much genocide (Malkki 1995; B. Williams 1991). However, Anderson's proposal also has quite visible limitations, which do not necessarily hinder the concept's utility but express the need to reassess it in terms of greater historical, geographical, and cultural specificity.

Anderson's work presents specific problems within the Latin American context, primarily because of the Eurocentric nature of his initial formulations. I am not speaking about the usual West versus non-West dichotomy (which it is so important to demystify) but about the profound colonial divide that separates the national ventures of European and Latin American nation-states. Unlike their European counterparts, Latin American nations did not undergo a communal movement for modern forms of sovereignty and an escape from feudal and monarchical regimes; rather, they had to overcome colonial regimes. Many of the new national ventures in Europe not only did not lose their colonial strongholds but they expanded their control over their overseas colonies as they (the colonizers) transformed themselves into modern nations. The Latin American nation-states were the colonial possessions that, under the new configuration of national identity, looked to provide a political situation different from that during colonial times. It is also interesting that national-liberation movements in Latin America, Africa, and the Middle East would use this same cultural model again in the 1940s, the 1950s, and the 1960s.

This distinction is essential, I believe, in assessing the political and social context in which different national embodiments took shape. This postcolonial model is central because it also marks the forms in which the different national traditions, or those customs that would be brandished as traditional (Hobsbawm and Ranger 1983), would evolve. It is in this particular context that dance and musical traditions such as the Andean *pasillo* developed, not as a neutral cultural trait but as a rich social product invested with profound historical, cultural, and political implications and hegemonic ambiguity. It is also instructive to understand the "national community" from this particular postcolonial vantage point and to realize the subtle and not-so-subtle articulations that make national identity and tradition complex forms of ritual exchange rather than the homogeneous production they are normally thought to be.

Anzaldúa's (1987) work, along with that of others (Mignolo 2000; Minh-ha 1997; Spivak 1999), points to the disjunctured nature of the national ideal and the constant reconversion of cultural traditions and practices (García-Canclini 1992). Anzaldúa's work has perhaps been more critical of Latin American audiences because of her particular engagement with the ideology of *mestizaje,* which occupies a central place in the continent's national production of identity. The discourse of the ideology of *mestizaje* is a prime example of the cultural ambiguity expressed in musical genres such as the *pasillo.*

As I have previously noted (see Benavides 2002, 2004a, for a similar but lengthier discussion of *mestizaje*), the idea of a mestizo race superior to its black, Indian, and even white European constitutive components was initially put forward in the late 1800s in Mexico (Smith 1996). Vasconcelos (1997) and other ideologues proposed a "cosmic race" that served to legitimize the aspirations of the local elite in the face of European and North American intruders and to distance that elite from nonwhite national citizens. Soon afterward, this mestizo ideal swept through the southern part of the continent, and by the beginning of the twentieth century was an essential part of Latin American ideology (Quintero 1997; Quintero and Silva 1991).

Thus, the *mestizaje* process serves not only as a pillar in the construction of a national identity but also as a viable ideological tool for the maintenance of the status quo and oppression of the majority of the continent's population (Stutzman 1981; see also Hale 1996). However, Mallon (1996) and Anzaldúa (1987), as well as several other scholars (the majority of whom are women) (e.g., Cypess 1991; Morraga 1986, 1994), strive to emphasize the liberating or counterhegemonic elements of this traditionally exploitative state ideology. They do this by appreciating the contradictory nature of a mestizo ideology that both creates inequality (Smith 1996: 149) and liberates us from absolute identities (Anzaldúa 1987). It is this essentially contradictory nature of *mestizaje* that becomes a source of contention and that allows for a thorough critique of many of the traditionally accepted social categories through the vantage point of a "strategic marginality" (Mallon 1996: 173; see below).

Thus, it seems more useful to, along with Anzaldúa (1987) and other scholars of color (Fusco 1994, 1995; Gómez-Peña 1991, 1994, 1996), take the national community in Latin America as a "fault line" rather than a homogeneous entity. The *pasillo* and other national traditions are good markers of this hegemonic ambiguity. On the one hand, they represent an official national identity; on the other, they represent an emblem with different socially meaningful significations. The *pasillo* is very much a vibrant (and hot) national item, and its national characteristics are central to understanding its migratory and ambiguous hegemonic potential.

The migratory status of *pasillos* is best exemplified by the different versions of Guayaquil's paradigmatic popular testament, "Nuestro juramento," whose lyrics tell of the promise of two lovers to love and cherish each other after death. This song, written by Puerto Rican Benito de Jesús and initially sung as a bolero by Rosalino, catapulted Julio Jaramillo to stardom and earned him the nickname of "Mr. Juramento." Therefore, Julio Jaramillo's version of "Nuestro juramento" (1997), although not the first, is considered the most authentic and original (originally issued in the 1950s); a third version is offered by the Cuban/Puerto Rican icon Daniel Santos (1995) in his distinctively slow Spanish Caribbean drawl (originally issued in the 1960s); a fourth belongs to the "Nuyorican" José Feliciano (1991) and mixes the *pasillo* cadence with R&B and soulful melodies that speak to the Latino experience in New York City (originally issued in the 1970s). The most contemporary pop version by Colombian Charlie Zaá has reintroduced the *pasillo* rhythm to a whole new generation of listeners (1990s). Charlie Zaá's remake, like Astor Piazzolla's remake of traditional tangos, created an enormous amount of controversy over the *pasillo*'s authenticity being polluted by modern pop forms and Zaá's version's absence or melodramatization of real sentiments. But it is this productive revision of "Nuestro juramento" which speaks most easily to the migratory nature of the *pasillo* and its capacity to adapt to differing geographical and racialized spaces and to produce ambiguous transnational and emotional social meanings.

The *Pasillo,* Popular Culture, and Hegemonic Ambiguity

And even then [Julio] had to wait for the love we saw at his funeral to understand the impact and influence of his life and music. (Estaentodo.com)

Julio Jaramillo (or JJ, as he is referred to popularly) is by far the most renowned exponent of the *pasillo*. He was born into extreme poverty on October 1, 1935, in the heart of one of Guayaquil's traditional neighborhoods (*el centro,* the same neighborhood where Silva had met his death sixteen years earlier), in a small apartment at the corner of Gómez Rendón and Villavicencio. His existence is easily portrayed as larger than life. He was left fatherless at age six, lived a bohemian lifestyle until his death, had numerous female lovers, was father to twenty-seven children, and had a musical career that popularized him throughout the American continent. His life has been depicted in both fictional and nonfictional accounts, although his popular allure and the legacy and social implications of his ambiguous emotional productivity are far from having been exhausted.

JJ contributed in innumerable ways to the increasingly ambiguous identity of a hegemonic Guayaquilean way of being and feeling. He literally gave voice to contradictory elements essential to the city beginning at the turn of the twentieth century, when Silva lived. Like Silva, JJ inherited a chaotic city reeling from the Liberal and Socialist upheavals and slowly adapting to the new capitalist world order as a regional center of cacao production, which would fuel the new agro-exporting model of the city's elite (Macías 1983, 1986). JJ's emotionally infused songs slowly came to symbolize the struggling modernist contradiction inherent in a

Guayaquilean identity of intimate emotional frustration caught in the postcolonial struggle of the emerging Latin American metropolis.

The *pasillo*'s tragically formulated lyrics, more than any other artistic expression, sorrowfully symbolize the life of the city and the nation that were to be hegemonically erased from official imagery. Who other than JJ could have successfully represented, through his songs, the lives of hundreds of thousands of Guayaquileans with less commercial success than he enjoyed? The population could easily identify with a man who had to leave Guayaquil to find renown in other American countries; who, like them, came from extremely humble beginnings and refused to depart from "popular" forms of being (or forms constructed as such) like womanizer, having dubious sexual practices, and, most important, a *cholo* identity, with its ultimately discriminatory social consequences. All of these characteristics allowed him, not surprisingly, to be given both a hero's burial and to be nicknamed the "ruiseñor de las Américas" (nightingale of the Americas). Therefore, JJ lived in many parts of the American continent, including Mexico, Colombia, and Chile, places where he produced over four thousand recordings and starred in several hit film musicals.

The *pasillo*'s history is very much a product of the early part of the twentieth century (see Wong 1999). JJ did by far the most to popularize this musical tradition, but he is not its only exponent; Carlota Jaramillo (no relation), Nicolás Safadi, and Carlos Rubira Infante are but a few of its other cherished national composers and exponents. Although the *pasillo* is indigenous to the northern equatorial Andes, it has become renowned throughout the continent since the 1970s. Its continentwide expression was initially made possible by its dissemination by singers like JJ and Olimpo Cárdenas. Cárdenas lived most of the later part of his life in Colombia, where he died at age sixty-five while on stage.

Although there are few significant scholarly analyses or assessments of the genre (see Wong 1999 for a synthesis and discussion), it seems to be a result of localized Andean adaptations of European (Spanish) rhythms. Paramount in its production is the central place (and, in many instances, exclusive use) of guitars. In many respects, it is similar to other American genres such as the tango and the *valsesito* in its mixed European and American imagery and, perhaps even more important, in its emphasis on the tragic nature of love, desire, life, and lust. All of these genres are particularly interesting postcolonial vehicles of identification that allow for subtle cultural markers to be expressed and reprocessed for immediate and intimate social naming. Thus, it is not surprising that there are significant regional differences between coastal and highland (*serrano*) *pasillos*.

Ecuador's two broad regions mark the genre in distinct ways. While the coastal version is typically described as lighter, happier, and faster (just as is the coastal population in general), the highland version is considered much slower, more melancholy, and nostalgic (as the highland population is normally portrayed). Not surprisingly, the *pasillo* falls into a rabid and violent category of regional representation and discrimination (*regionalismo*), with enormous effects of power (see Benavides 2002).

This identity marker facilitated by the *pasillo* is but one of the many ways that the genre enables the productive ambiguity of popular cultural origination. The *pasillo,* in this regard, plays a role in both the hegemonic maintenance of the exploitative class and the social relations of the nation, as it does in the subversion of these same oppressive social relations in unique and intimate ways. Following Angela Davis' analysis of the role of the blues in the United States (1998), I am not arguing that the *pasillo* is exclusively a form of political manipulation or of cultural resistance. Rather, I maintain that, as part of a dynamic popular cultural production, the *pasillo* is strategically in a position to do both things at the same time: dominate and resist as opposite sides of the same coin, and not as either/or options. As many would argue (e.g., Foucault 1980; McClintock 1995; 1997; Sayer 1994), each position seems to enable the other, since exclusive resistance or domination not only disempowers the other position but also, and perhaps more realistically, is an impossibility in social life. As García-Canclini has elaborated (1992), popular culture is infused with a reconversion process that allows the reworking of traditional cultural markers with a social meaning significantly different from the original. It is García-Canclini's particularly vibrant analysis of Latin(o) American culture that allows us to understand the ambiguous political and social roles played by soap operas (*telenovelas*), cartoon characters (such as Superbarrio), and music (e.g., groups such as Fabulosos Cadillacs and Café Tacuba, which mix ska, punk, salsa, bolero, and rock) in contemporary cultural production. This same analysis of reconversion is essential to both the maintenance and the subversion of a national ethos beyond territorial borders.

As I have already stated, the *pasillo* is without equal as a representative of national musical in Ecuador. Since the early twentieth century, generations of Ecuadorians have grown up listening to *pasillos*. It is the music most supported by the state, including the endorsement, not surprisingly, of weekly official television shows that highlight national *pasillo* singers. This official sanction, as well as the support of earlier generations, produces a particular dislike or distrust among the younger generation, which sees the *pasillo* as belonging to the older, more conservative folks. This generational divide, which is (or has been) cyclically resolved, since the *pasillo* would otherwise lose its national status, is quite unlike the homogeneous interclass identification engendered by the genre.

Although Ecuador, like all Latin American nation-states, comprises primarily an impoverished population, the *pasillo* is one of the cultural markers that serve to override socioeconomic differences. It does not matter what side of the economic divide one comes from, being Ecuadorian allows for a complete and intimate identification with the *pasillo* as a national way of life. This projected classless identification, however, does not preclude the *pasillo*'s being represented as a "popular" form (like other Latin American musical genres) and one that supposedly allows the masses a cheap and intimate form of entertainment. As an example of this representational reality, thousands of people stood outside of the hospital during JJ's last days, and his funeral was held at the largest sports coliseum in Guayaquil and broadcast over the most popular local radio station (Radio Cristal), as befitting a national icon.

The *pasillo*, as does soccer (see Galeano 2002), allows a national form of identification that transcends class distinction while maintaining a strong sense of "popularness" and rootedness. Thus, it is not hard to begin questioning a musical tradition that, at one and the same time, can provide an illusion of equality (or at least make it seem as if money does not matter) while maintaining and reproducing strong class definitions of what is popular (*lo popular*) and belonging to the people (*del pueblo*).

It is also important to consider that, although economic differences seem to be almost explicitly targeted by the *pasillo*'s popular appeal, generational differences are not. On the contrary, the generational divide between younger people reacting against the *pasillo* and the older ones embracing it seems to be, if not encouraged, at least actively produced within the cultural dynamics of the official representation. As one informant in her mid-twenties explained (Kathy, interview, July 3, 2002), "Well, I listen to it a lot. Because that is the way I am, I listen to it a lot, but I believe young people do not. Young people do not like that music very much. Maybe, perhaps, at 2:00 AM, after many beers, everybody is dancing, but nobody is going to go out and buy the record." It is as if the generational difference allows older Ecuadorians, legitimated by the backing of the state's political apparatus, to express their discontent with the younger generation, thereby enabling an enculturation mechanism that allows the younger generation to be formed within the reactive field of force of the national ethos. In other words, the generation gap is much more productive than a homogeneous entity would be, since it allows for the political control of younger Ecuadorians under the guise of culture, by training them how to be Guayaquilean and Ecuadorian and how to accept what is true national music, and therefore true national culture. According to Miranda (interview, August 15, 2001), "it would be a sin for them not to like it, to not like something from their own country."

Miranda's statement highlights the political underpinnings of culture, since the national drama of the *pasillo* has matured these reactive youngsters (among whom I count myself and many other colleagues) into becoming staunch enthusiasts of the *pasillo,* even to the point of reconversing it in unique rock rhythms or making it the object of scholarly research and articles (Kathy, interview, July 3, 2002): "Well, there is also a new period of this national music, a lot of talented Ecuadorian groups have reinvested in the genre, with lots of talent and persistence . . . They have fought and invested a lot of their time and money, with better instruments, composers, and they have succeeded." And as Kathy told me later in the same interview, "For example, take Charlie Zaá, who sings the same songs that Julio Jaramillo made famous. Well, imagine that, an artist from another country gives credit to our own music. A lot of our own groups play our music. They change the rhythm a bit, make arrangements. But they do it."

One of the most important elements in accounting for these class and generational dynamics is the lyrical content of the *pasillo* and the abundant consumption of alcohol that accompanies active listening. The *pasillo* is usually a vehicle through which to express sad or melancholic feelings. Most *pasillos* deal with love gone bad or, even more poignantly, with an unfaithful lover. Unlike what one might predict from Ecuador's *machista* ideology and patriarchal tradition, few of the songs encourage physical violence; on the contrary, they express an emotional outburst of male loss and tenderness, which at its most extreme leads to personal paralysis, heavy alcohol consumption, and/or suicide. This contradictory gender dynamics is ambiguously represented by the *pasillo* and its popular appeal.

Gender and Wounded Identities

Hemos jurado amarnos hasta la muerte
y si los muertos aman,
después de muerto amarnos mas.[2]
(Jaramillo, "Nuestro juramento")

It is easy to argue for the postcolonial origin of much of the *pasillo*'s lyrical content. These expressions of unrequited love are intimately related to a postcolonial reality of repressed desire. Identity is based on not having what one wants or needs; what makes us who we are (Ecuadorians, in this case) is that we do not have what the other (in this case, Europeans or gringos) has (Kathy, interview, July 3, 2002): "I believe that it is because we are still in that period of society where we still want to pretend ["aparentar"], we are in a place where we do not want to do certain things, or we prefer others, better ones. In other words, we have not gone beyond that frontier, at least I think so, of discriminating so much. There are still tons of people here who care only about how you look, where you can go or be, and where you are in terms of status."

It is not about material comforts so much as having the socioeconomic agency to obtain these emotional comforts and control those of others, according to Guayaquileans with whom I have spoken. Love more than any other feeling—anger, shame, or pride—is the emotion expressed in *pasillos* through which to play out forbidden desire, power, and transgressive identity formation (Beatriz, interview, July 7, 2002): "It's like that's the way we are, we are more tragic ["corta venas," literally, wrist slashers], cry more, women cry, men suffer, I do not know why. But maybe when it is sad it gets to us easier, like, I don't know, like it reaches us better." As Pedro (interview, August 16, 2003) told me, this tragic love is essential to a gendered way of being, as a man or a woman:

> Unfortunately, in Ecuador people tend to identify with what is tragic, and because something is tragic that is what people remember the most, and people, people do not tend to see the good that is going on but, rather, they identify with what is tragic, the negative, with some kind of tragedy. And also unfortunately, when you love, when they love, unfortunately, we pick the negative side of love, that is when we feel the passion. No, what happens; well, I consider myself like that; I am also like that. Many times we feel too much passion and sometimes we do not see the sublime part of love but, instead, we feel too much passion, and when we feel passion we do not think, we do crazy things, things that are not rational. And this is what happens to most of us, and I also include myself in this, we love too much so that we no longer think, we go against certain things . . . Because I think our people love to suffer, at least at times. I believe people enjoy suffering. It is like the national pastime. The love to suffer. For example, see the newspaper [*El Extra*], that is what people love, to buy *El Extra,* and it breaks records ["bate sintonía"]. If you

see something that causes a stir, it is a tragedy; no matter how small, people make it gigantic. But why do our people love to suffer? I think it is because people have been badly hurt, and they have suffered tragedy after tragedy after tragedy so that it becomes normal for people. And if something more tragic comes along, they will say, this tragedy that is happening to me is not as bad as the one over there; perhaps my tragedy is not so bad, as that one is, and it is a way of surviving.

The representation in *pasillos* of pained suffering, rejection, but fulfilling love is not devoid of a transnational, albeit a colonial, nature. One can see in this loving image a painful reification, developed through years of colonial rejection, of the native or local population. There is in this process an anguished desire to be recognized and loved, only to be rejected and spurned; at the same time, those who are rejected count on rejection to be constituted as human. It is as if the only thing remaining of the colonized self is the possibility of rejection—as a testament to existence, to being alive, and as a last sign of humanity. As Oscar Wilde, another colonized and sexually oppressed writer, notes (1964: 71), "Suffering—curious as it may sound to you—is the means by which we exist, because it is the only means by which we become conscious of existing; and the remembrance of suffering in the past is necessary to us as the warrant, the evidence of our continued identity."

Undoubtedly, there are interesting implications, and I do not mean pathological ones as much as realistic ones, when rejection is essential to the constitution of the self, personal, national, and historical. One of the interesting implications in this regard is gender articulation. As I have stated, *pasillos* ambiguously reinforce oppressive social relations in spite of or, most probably, because they find ways of subverting them. An initial assessment of the social dynamics involved in drinking while listening to *pasillos* might envision a patriarchal world with misogynistic tendencies and the social exclusion of women; however, this is far from the case. Although going to bars and publicly consuming alcohol is definitely more recognized as a male "sport," as Pedro ironically notes, women are by no means excluded from consuming alcohol. In keeping with Andean tradition, alcohol is an essential element or social lubricant in the ritual practice of communal gatherings, and women are also expected to participate (Allen 1988). Women express their agency, if not their social equality, by participating in the intensity of the emotions being expressed in the *pasillo*, and they keep up with the men in their own way and in their own social settings.

The setting for drinking while listening to *pasillos* is yet another space of active hegemonic contestation, however. Since the 1970s, women have been more willing to publicly express their pleasure and to challenge men's control of the traditional bar setting. More *peñas* (see Wong 1999) and women's nights out have also constructed a different form of gender interaction linked with appreciation of the *pasillo*, and in doing so have transformed traditional gender relationships.

Perhaps even more telling in the gender configurations of the *pasillo*, however, is that, although singers tend to be more or less equally male or female, the subjects of the songs are not. Most *pasillos* paint females as the wrongdoers in love and the cause of heartbreak, even the reason for the loss of a man's life. And even though one could take this as a misogynistic tendency in a patriarchal society that looks to speak to or prove women's inferiority, there are disquieting and quite essential subversive elements in the lyrics. The *pasillo*'s speaking to women's emotional and sexual infidelity belies a very different construction of women's identity from that espoused by the traditional national hegemonic norms. Far from being the chaste, content, subservient female that the national *machista* ideology encourages in all social settings, women in *pasillos* are full of a dangerous and disrupting sexual agency.

As Mallon (1996) and others have pointed out with regard to other popular cultural practices, *pasillos* seem to exemplify the hazardous effects of women's moving out of their nationally defined gendered and sexual scriptures. The female narrative that makes up the lyrical content of the *pasillo* relates to other social narratives, such as the ambivalent history of La Malinche (Cortez's Indian lover and partner), who is seen as a traitor, from an authentic Indian perspective, or as a liberator, from the vantage point of a mestizo nation (see Cypess 1991), and even Rigoberta Menchú's (1985, 1998) uncharacteristic narratives as an overtly recognized political leader.

All of this points to the centrality of feminine sexual discourse in the maintenance of the national status quo. Sexuality, specifically female sexuality, becomes a major locus of contention and domination as well as the site of the policing of boundaries, which is essential for the maintenance of the character of both the nation and the state (Mallon 1996). The ambivalent relationship between gender, sexuality, and hegemonic domination is thoroughly expressed in these popular songs; a relevant example is the third stanza from the song "Un disco más":

Si recuerdas esta melodía
recordarás también que fuiste mía

cuando me besabas locamente
jurando eternamente quererme a mí.[3]

These gender-specific lyrics, and countless others, express fulfillment from that which we no longer have but which constitutes, more than ever, our existence. The central place of the absent gendered object in the constitution of the contemporary subject reflects a wounded masculinity (see Ferrándiz 2003, 2004) that is activated only through a transgressive, and equally wounded, female figure, one in which the Oedipal mother figure is not left too far behind (see Kristeva 1989).

Once again, these gendered utterances bring us back to the central concern of unattainable desire: hegemonic articulation and postcoloniality. Today, even a man can publicly weep for his love, for his lost youth, or, ultimately, for all that this is translated into: an identity based on self-rejection. In essence, the *pasillo*'s structures of feeling are composed of the anguish and pain that come from not fitting in. Therefore, it is this identity of rejection that makes Guayaquileans identify with the *pasillo* and that, at the same time, allows us, by analyzing the *pasillo*, to begin to understand these socially constitutive sentiments more fully. In this colonial-identity mode of rejection, translated into a postcolonial setting, one is no longer exclusively, or even mostly, sustained by empirical official constraints, because they have been triumphantly internalized. At this juncture, the *pasillo*'s ambivalent articulation of structures of feeling expresses how essentializing sentiments are formulated and classified into normative behavior.

Ultimately, the critical study of popular culture, such as *pasillos*, contributes to the hegemonic understanding of the relationship between the development of popular icons/semantic figures such as JJ and Medardo Ángel Silva, the officialization of memory in the discourse of Guayaquil Antiguo, and the daily construction of people's livelihood in a postcolonial setting. I hope it helps us understand how, when we hear these musical notes, Guayaquileans are intimately moved, and cultural hegemony is seductively and consecutively locked into place.

The *Pasillo*, Transnationalism, and Cultural Authenticity

Fatalidad sino cruel
que en mi rodar se llevó el
más valioso joyel
que tu querer me brindó

el calor permanente de un cariño
que ávido como un niño de ti tanto
esperé
¿Por qué te fuiste mujer?[4]
(Jaramillo, "Fatalidad")

Pasillos display a particular rhythmic language, individual gestures, social drama, and grammar of movement that are productively meaningful. The movement produced by dancing (rarely done today) or actively listening to *pasillos* delineates subtle articulations in terms of both racial/geographical and class dynamics. In this section I want to pay particular attention to how the different *pasillo* forms both align themselves with and contest an imagery imbued with national implications constrained within ethnic, racial, gender, sexual, and class parameters in their voyage.

One of the main effects of the *pasillo* is that it allows Guayaquilean migrants to reidentify with the city of their origin. In this manner, even migrants who no longer necessarily identify as Guayaquilean still see in the *pasillo,* specifically, in JJ's music, a source of solace and comfort. For example, Ana (interview, August 15, 2001) told me how she turns to JJ's music when she feels defeated and downtrodden as a way to overcome these harsh emotional realities. As we have seen, listening to his music is always accompanied by alcohol and linked to a manner of living more vicariously the feelings that seem shut down in day-to-day existence. Pedro (interview, August 16, 2003), also a Guayaquilean migrant in New York City, found it quite interesting that he came to appreciate *pasillos* much more acutely when he was no longer in Guayaquil (for an extended analysis of Ana's and Pedro's life histories, see Chapter 4). This particular relationship was experienced by all Guayaquileans with whom I spoke. All found themselves relating to the *pasillo,* significantly, to JJ's renditions of them in a different and much more intense manner abroad. *Pasillos* were no longer just a way to express personal feelings of love and rejection, efface class differences, normalize hierarchical age relationships, or even homogenize national identity; rather, they became a new and profound way to redefine themselves as Guayaquilean. It is particularly interesting that *pasillos* take on this transnationalizing element and redefine national origins precisely when Guayaquileans find themselves physically removed from their homeland.

Rather than seeing this phenomenon as merely a traditional recourse to one's roots, heightened by exile and socioeconomic migration, there seems to be a profound tie to a globalized existence and a modern constitution heightened by cultural mechanisms such as the *pasillo*. It is not that Guay-aquileans do not stop being Guayaquilean when they leave but, rather, that they are ambivalently constituted as even more Guayaquilean by leav-ing. As a port city, Guayaquil sees itself as actively mimicking anything that comes from the outside, giving credence to Guayaquileans' nickname as *monos* (monkeys). Evolving foreign and nontraditional cultural traits in dress, customs, status, language, and so on are all envied and soon enough incorporated as authentic Guayaquilean forms of behavior.

Thus, Guayaquileans living abroad, particularly in the *yoni* (slang for the United States), are seen as authentic Guayaquileans who reinfuse the city with new (and more genuine) ways of being or aspiring to be (see Chapter 4). This ambiguous reality of a "foreign authenticity" has been actively portrayed in artistic ventures such as plays (put on by the El Jug-lar theater), literature (Ulloa 1992), nostalgic *pasillos* (i.e., "El romance de mi destino" [My Destiny's Romance]), and even popular television commercials for the lottery, such as one about a returning migrant who protests when strangers refer to him as cousin (*primo*) to gain access to his money. This kind of authentic foreignness would seem to be inti-mately connected to a postcolonial existence and subject that are revital-ized by the absence of the naturalized object of love (see Butler 1997a; Žižek 1996).

From the inception of a mythical Spanish founding (ambiguously play-ing on the enormously controversial date and place of the city's found-ing), the city has been constituted of a way of being that suffers from not being what the Spanish masters told the native inhabitants they should be racially, in gender ascriptions, status markers, civilizing normative be-haviors, and religion. The list is open-ended precisely because the city has never been able to express itself except in negative terms: "But when you are far away you feel that sadness, although it is a love-hate kind of feel-ing, that rejection, but that is why it is something that is yours, it is your world of contradictions, it is yours, it is who you really are in some pro-found way" (Ana, interview, August 15, 2002). Thus, longing becomes a parameter within which a subject is constituted, but also has dangerous hegemonic implications, beautifully crystallized in the nostalgic rhythm and lyrics of "Fatalidad":

Nocturno de celaje deslumbrante
tu encanto rememoro cada instante
romance de un momento que viviera
con el alma ilusionada en tu mirada

un amor que nadie tuvo para mi
aunque aciego el destino, dividió nuestro camino
y angustiado para siempre, te perdí.[5]
(Jaramillo, "Fatalidad")

Thus, the migration of Guayaquileans to the United States that began in the late 1960s is really a neocolonial continuation of a colonial legacy and a postcolonial identity. Guayaquileans might be foreigners in the United States (and even that warrants some discussion), but they are not foreign to longing and negative identification. At this juncture, it seems as though *pasillos* fulfill a role in terms of continuing a postcolonial identification that started over four centuries ago for Guayaquileans, from the moment they are born. The *pasillo* already embodies a sense of nostalgic longing and impossible constitution expressed in futile love attachments that are continually relived, only now in exile, or in "in-xile" within Guayaquil, as the case might be. Migration itself constitutes a particular way of achieving Guayaquileanness that might be out of reach for most Guayaquileans, since their migration ideals are never fulfilled, but are actively integrated into their imaginary homeland in exile as felt and sung in *pasillos*.

Seen from this vantage point, it is not uncommon for Guayaquileans to continue to migrate to Spain or Venezuela, and for new Guayaquileans to be born in the United States or to become U.S. citizens. The *pasillo* maintains an "apparent" aura of authenticity and tradition, apparent since what makes it both authentic and traditional is not that the genre is the same, homogeneous, or even static (as we have seen in its multiple reconversions) but, rather, that it continues to embody a form of being lacking in self-constitution. Thus, the *pasillo*'s authenticity is most afforded by its lack of it. And it is this national positioning, always looking outside of oneself, which is essentially expressed in the new migrants' wish for a utopian homeland that they have never experienced or have had to leave in order to miss it the way the *pasillos* say they do (or allow them to fool themselves into thinking they do).

Two other elements are interwoven into this fact. First is the ever-changing nature of Guayaquilean identity, which the migrant experience has proven by reinfusing Guayaquileanness over the last four decades of migration to the United States. Therefore, it is not surprising to see Guayaquilean identity stronger than and as vital as ever, even when such a large percentage of the city's population now lives or wants to live abroad. So in truthfully identifying with this nostalgic discourse about essential exiles, *pasillos* are far from static, authentic, or traditional in any way.

Rather, it is the *pasillo*'s ambiguous identification that allows Guaya-quileans to use it as a vehicle of social cohesiveness, even though it only ever sings about lost love, social frustrations, and personal prohibitions. There is nothing more intimately constitutive of Guayaquilean iden-tity than those personal feelings that dare not speak their name in the ever-changing, prohibitive postcolonial context. It is also this far-from-immobile meaning that allows Guayaquileans to find in JJ and his voice the same saga of national, racial, and gender misidentifications that al-lowed him to achieve full national recognition only when he could no lon-ger enjoy it: at the moment of his death. One could also argue that living in exile afforded him a closer approximation to death, central throughout his life, that, unlike physical death, everybody can feel but not see.

Thus, there is nothing (or everything) authentic or traditional about the *pasillo* other than its historical investment in expressing a postcolo-nial identification of longing, nostalgia, and grief for not being socially who one must be, and of being destined to live out this destiny in a per-sonal and pain-filled manner. It is also these postcolonial misidentifica-tions that are implicated in the life histories of migrants and the regional recourse of an unlived past epitomized in Guayaquil Antiguo, a past that never existed but has always defined the city's imaginary and identified itself with Silva's poetry. Thus it constitutes itself as the most Real of Guayaquilean realities (see Lacan 1977). Modern rock and pop groups like Tradiciones (appropriately named), Cacería de Lagartos, and Tran-zas, to name a few, have reinfused the *pasillo* with modern rhythms and new/old reconversions (see García-Canclini 1992; Hall 1997a, 1997b). Finally, it is to this new/old phenomenon that Kathy refers when she says (interview, July 3, 2002), "Let me tell you, there are a lot of people who will react negatively when you say, 'Play that song,' and they will say, 'Oh no! How low class' ["que cholada"] . . . but wait until it is two or three in the morning, they will know the lyrics even better than you do!"

CHAPTER 4

The Migration of Guayaquilean Modernity
Problemas Personales
and Guayacos *in Hollywood*

Yes, there is a little bit of everything, good, bad, nice, ugly. I have
written a few things, nothing to be published, comparing my birthplace
with where I live now, sort of the same question you are asking.
I always end up comparing New York City with Guayaquil. We have
the Hudson River here in New York, and in Guayaquil we have the
Guayas River; in New York we have New Jersey across from us, and in
Guayaquil we have Durán. That is, there is a certain relationship, I am
not sure if I am making it up or even if I am confusing you . . . That
is, as soon as I arrived, I had this nostalgia, I remembered Guayaquil;
New York City actually reminded me of Guayaquil.

—JUANITO, INTERVIEW, OCTOBER 11, 2002

This chapter is an ethnographic exploration of the major ideological conundrums of Guayaquilean migration to the United States, specifically, to
New York City. My main concern is how migration relates, although not
exclusively, to issues of postcolonial identity formation, globalization,
masculinity and gender definitions, and regional ethnic identification,
both in Guayaquil and abroad. Thus, the chapter is part of my larger
research question concerning the translocation of politics, particularly
Guayaquilean modernity, through Silva's work and the regional recourse
of the representation of Guayaquil's past (Guayaquil Antiguo).

This chapter also calls on my personal immigrant experience and life
history. As a son of immigrant Guayaquileans, I have spent half of my life
as a "legal alien in NYC" (to borrow from a Sting song), the other half as
an "estrangeiro em Guayaquil" (to borrow from a Caetano Veloso song).
As a result, this chapter, as does my whole research endeavor, involves
both my immigrant identity and my participation in the Guayaquilean
modernity that I am studying.

When I was about a year old, my parents brought me to live in what was, from the late 1960s throughout the 1990s, the third-largest Ecuadorian city in the world—New York. As millions of other New Yorkers have done, and thousands of other Ecuadorians, I learned to claim as my own a city in which I was not born. Early on, I developed a sense of nostalgia for and a romantic memory of a nationality that I had lost almost as soon as I had obtained it. I thereby made an ambivalent commitment to an identity as a Guayaquilean (and through it, as an Ecuadorian) which was kept alive by my family's daily endorsement. The early nostalgic stance afforded by my hybrid migrant experience directly influenced my constant need to bridge two worlds. As it has been more poetically described, I had the "bilingual blues" (see Pérez-Firmat 1997).

This form of uprootedness has received attention in literary circles (see Anzaldúa 1987; Dorfman 1998; Kincaid 1997; R. Martínez 1992, 1998). These scholars have investigated the Latin way of "unbelonging," which makes one a stranger in the world (see Allende 2003). I now realize how my immigrant experience contributed to my career choice of the study of anthropology, to how I have defined my life. Only a discipline caught between ever-moving mainland (Eric Wolf, personal communication), in constant battle with its colonial origins, and adapting to the changing effects of global culture could provide a safe haven for somebody exposed very early to the changing nature of social identification. Therefore, this research is very much a result of "mis problemas personales" (my personal problems).

I use the notion of *problemas personales* as proposed by Rivera and Sarmiento's documentary on Ecuadorian migration to Spain since the 1990s. The film uses powerful and moving vignettes of their life to follow three Ecuadorian migrants to Barcelona. It is clear that none of them undertook this gigantic and often tragic move with a sophisticated understanding of globalization and its transformative politics. For them, migrating to Spain resulted from a dilemma which they had to address personally, despite the frustrating circumstances. This does not imply that these migrants were devoid of agency or unaware of the national ramifications and international tensions of their decisions.

Any and all global considerations, however, are overshadowed by individual choices reflecting these migrants' aching nostalgia for what they thought was a secure homeland in Ecuador. This melancholy reality comes through quite readily as one of them sits at midnight in a park in Barcelona, wondering if he should ask his wife to come and share his hardships. As he ponders this question, he covers his eyes and states, "Es triste la vida, es triste" (Life is sad, it's sad; see Lancaster 1986, for a similar analysis of postrevolutionary Nicaraguan migration). It is this personal dimension, precisely because it is not merely personal (see below), that I believe is useful in assessing Ecuadorian migration.

The other motif of this chapter's title, "*Guayacos* in Hollywood," comes from a couple of Guayaquilean theatrical and literary representations. In the mid-1980s, the regional Guayaquilean theater, El Juglar, produced "Un guayaco en Hollywood," which deals with the diasporic character of Ecuadorians living in the United States. The play highlights the lives of migrants who have maintained their Guayaquilean identity, even becoming more Guayaquilean while they are living in New York, as well as the conflicts they face on their return to Guayaquil. This diasporic character is also a popular motif succinctly captured by Edwin Ulloa's (1992) narrative, "Johnnie the Man," from his collection of short stories *Sobre una tumba, una rumba* (A Rumba Atop the Grave). Ulloa represents this diasporic identity as a mixed blessing, since it possesses everything Ecuadorians want in terms of global commodification but also, precisely because of this characteristic, is envied and despised for being a Guayaquilean (or *guayaco*) in Hollywood.

These two concepts have fueled my research into the Guayaquilean diaspora in New York. These images, I maintain, offer an entry point for assessing Guayaquilean migrants' transformation of politics and identity. I shall discuss the situations, one literary and two ethnographic, of three migrant subjects who share many of the experiences of their compatriots. I am not, however, looking for typical scenarios in these three subjects. Rather, I have chosen them precisely because they are not representative in terms of birthplace, national affiliation, or life choices. Instead of seeking homogeneity, I have looked for disparities and the heterogeneity essential in producing hegemonic national identities and unique forms of historicity and citizenship (see Hall 1997a, 1997b).

I have tried to distance myself from traditional social science approaches to migration, which are more invested in seeking fixed answers and eschew the insights of other disciplines, particularly the humanities. As Foucault states (1996: 225), I would much rather envision a scholar as the "destroyer of evidence and universalities, the one who, in the inertias and constraints of the present, locates and marks the weak points, the openings, the lines of power, who incessantly displaces himself, doesn't know exactly where he is heading nor what he'll think tomorrow because he is too attentive to the present." I therefore envision this work, and my general research endeavor, as contributing to a "history of the vanishing present" (from Spivak's suggestive subtitle [1999]).

Bacán and Sabroso: Migration, Popular Culture, and Being Guayaquilean

Aquí soy alguien, afirmas allá no era nadie, agregas y mientes: Johnnie the Man.[1]
(Ulloa, "Johnnie the Man")

Guayaquil, as do many other port cities, enjoys a vibrant popular culture which defines the city and its ad hoc regional and national citizenship (see Genet 1974). As the magnet for the country's internal migration throughout the twentieth century, Guayaquil is the largest urban center in Ecuador (it has almost twice the population of the capital, Quito). Due both to its being a port and its attraction of internal migrants, Guayaquilean identity is never a result simply of birthplace. As several of my interviewees pointed out, not being born in Guayaquil was an accident that did not negate their claims to being fully Guayaquilean. This reality is easily understandable in a city where a third of the population was born elsewhere. The similarity between the patterns of national and regional citizenship of Guayaquileans and New Yorkers provides the backdrop for the logical translocal flow of Guayaquileans to the Big Apple.

Complex cultural features, principally, language, manner of being (*manera de ser*), and gender definitions, are essential elements in Guayaquilean identity. These features tend to be much more closely examined when defining a person's regional and cultural identification as Guayaquilean than is birthplace. These categorizations are reflected in Guayaquilean slang, popularly referred to as *coba*. *Coba*, with its own grammar, vocabulary, and cadence (see La Zona del Trago N.d., for an on-line glossary of Guayaquilean slang), has dynamically developed over the last century. Traditionally viewed as a low form of speech and discriminated against, as most popular culture variations of Spanish tend to be (see del Valle and Gabriel-Steethman 2002), *coba* has a distinct rhythm that substantially reflects the city's characteristic violence and high crime rate. For example, in Ulloa's use of it, one can see both the rhythmic and the transgressive beauty of the dialect: "Méteme solamente la cabeza te pedían y respondías libidinosamente: cual cabeza si la paloma no tiene hombros"(1992: 46).[2]

One of its origin myths states that *coba* developed as a code language for thieves and lowlifes, which would partly explain its seductive allure for the younger generation. However, as became immediately apparent to me while living in Guayaquil, *coba* is quite a rich and vibrant dialect and is constantly reenergized by new situations, including migration to the United States, for example, the words for *man* and *woman* in *coba*, *el man* and *la man*. Perhaps even more poignant is the phrase used to describe an urgent moment or activity: "de uan" (pronounced "one").

Edwin Ulloa (1992) uses this particular linguistic trope to represent the central place of popular culture in the production of Guayaquilean identity. In "Johnnie the Man," Ulloa develops the story of a returned migrant from Los Angeles who unsuccessfully tries to reestablish himself in Guayaquil. After several frustrating flashbacks, including remembering his short stint as a porn star in the United States, Johnnie returns to Los Angeles. Although unable to claim the status he enjoyed in Guayaquil as a result of his gringo experience, he ultimately settles for the decent living he can make in Los Angeles, which eluded him in Guayaquil. The tragic dimensions of Johnnie's life are intimately tied to a transgressive erotic reality, which is what forced him to migrate to Los Angeles: "Estabas perdido . . . comerse un maricón no solamente trae mala suerte sino que es un estigma"(Ulloa 1992: 42).[3]

This narrative successfully expresses the multiple layers in the Guaya-quilean immigrant experience. Ulloa's narrative ingeniously incorporates elements of popular culture as central to the form of his narrative. In do-ing so, he captures the *coba* elements of *sabroso* (sly) and *bacán* (cool), essential in the maintenance of popular Guayaquilean identity and inher-ent in other locally produced narratives (see Andrade 1995, 1997, for a discussion of the popular icon Pancho Jaime and his cultural-political implications). The degree to which Ulloa is successful in assessing the power of the popular in Guayaquilean identity is also the degree to which he is able to express language as a vital marker of the production of pop-ular culture. At the same time, Ulloa argues for the need to recognize the significant place of popular culture in the lives of most Guayaquileans, particularly those most economically deprived. In this regard, it is telling that the main character thinks of initially settling forever in Guayaquil (Ulloa 1992: 47): "Estoy perdido, sentencias gravemente, porque sabes que dentro de poco tiempo volverás a ser Juanito el Burro, con una se-ñora honorable por esposa y un negocio lucrativo como repuesta a la vida de perro que llevaste."[4] Thus, it is not surprising that two of the most successful Latino authors in New York today, Emanuel Xavier (N.d.) and Ernesto Quiñónez (personal communication), although born in the

United States of Ecuadorian parents, have made small forays into their Ecuadorian homeland. It is therefore not out of character for Ulloa's main protagonist to be accepted immediately into the Guayaquilean fold.

Guayaquilean identity in the narrative, as well as in many of my interviewees' lives, is afforded more by a manner of being and belonging than by any external feature. For the main character, identity is expressed by his use of *coba* and by the distinctive attitudes and experiences that he opens himself to. One of the things that makes Johnnie most Guayaquilean is his incredibly vibrant individuality, which enables him to go against, and beyond, the normative conventions of most of the other city dwellers. Even though he goes to Guayaquil to improve his social behavior, he soon enough finds himself carrying on and behaving worse than he would have been able to in Los Angeles. It is this pattern of regeneration (as in the case of Emanuel Xavier, see above), successful or not, that characterizes the return of many migrants—particularly males—to Guayaquil as full-fledged citizens. The returned migrant, however, in many ways is also considered in local terms as representing a more progressive, or much more evolved, example of what it means to be Guayaquilean: "Ahora tienes el ceño fruncido y desgastado por la decisión de regresar para nunca más volver, en mucho tiempo, corriges, ante una de las preguntas que te formulan los tuyos, incansables y admirados por las camisas y el corte de pelo; eres un sueño Johnnie" (Ulloa 1992: 42).[5]

This particular process, experienced by me and many other return migrants, is not the easiest to grasp, which makes Ulloa's narrative that much more perceptive. It is perhaps in its most problematic disruption of a hegemonic Guayaquilean identity, and even in the close throes of death faced by the return migrant, either emotional or physical (see Baldwin 1984) that the return-migrant experience proves most productive. Initially, the foreignness of having been born or having lived outside of Guayaquil resignifies the return migrant with an enormous amount of power and status not independent of the global dynamics which, ultimately, play out in very intimate and personal dramas. Thus, Johnnie is recognized as a Guayaquilean, but a better one, a more evolved one, improved by his superior livelihood in the *joni* (U.S.).

This resignification of status has serious implications in terms of power. On the one hand, Johnnie, as any return migrant would be, is confused by being represented as a superior being and placed on a pedestal, a very seductive position for someone insecure about his national identity. At the same time, there is an invisibility in this global seduction—global because Johnnie was brought up in the shadow of the U.S. empire, since nothing inherent in his being affords him superior status. However, it is this global seduction that denies his individuality, which is supposedly being celebrated. As the narrative points out, pretty soon, Johnnie finds himself having to fulfill his character's socially projected role rather than having any chance to discover who he really is. One can therefore almost sense the tragic foreshadowing in Ulloa's narrative of the unraveling of the main character: if at the outset he accepts the "superior" caricature projected onto him, however grandiose it might be, he is still left longing for his "real" self. This caricature is only an "unreal" portrayal of him, grown out of his (and other Guayaquileans') global needs and wish to be what they think they should be. It is because of this displacement that tragedy ensues, since the Real Johnnie is ever-changing but not allowed to find fulfillment, except in the caricature of himself (see Lacan 1977; Žižek 2002).

This scenario is heightened and made more understandable when one realizes that Guayaquilean identity embraces this global seduction by displacement as one of its most active essential features. This setting expresses the nostalgic nature of popular cultural production, which not only allows but also actively instigates tragedy as a sine qua non of personal and social identification. My research therefore assesses a postcolonial Guayaquilean identity that nourishes itself with nonbeing, that is, with the rejection of oneself as the most active and cherished form of self.

The self-inflicted wound of seeing oneself as not being good enough, as being less than, as always desiring and being seduced by the desire of the commodified global other, is an active element in the postcolonial construction of Guayaquilean identity. This is why drinking (and crying over one's personal problems) in a group mainly, but not exclusively, limited to men is recognized as a legitimate form of social activity. This is also why the *pasillo* is hailed as the local form of national musical expression. These tragic sentiments, I argue, are the sign of the modern in Guayaquil today. These exact sentiments are highlighted in Medardo Ángel Silva's poetry. The sign of the modern, therefore, is closely linked to a sign of the tragic related to a general form of postcolonial legacy which Quijano (1995) refers to as colonialities of power.

It is this inherently disrupted self as the sign of the modern, of course, a tragic modern, that I have assessed in my interviews of migrants, and that Ulloa seductively elaborates in his work. Ulloa's narrative evaluates this process of the modern in what I believe is a powerfully insightful fashion, as we will see in the two life histories I discuss below. In Ulloa's narrative, we are privy to a sinuous sign of the modern that continuously resignifies itself in similarly different ways (Hall 1997b) and utilizes migration as yet another modifier, a global one, of Guayaquilean modernity.

To spell it out further: Johnnie, as a return migrant, is immediately invested with tragic elements because he returns to represent that which the local population does not have but so desperately wants. It is this return of the repressed (see Žižek 2002) that continues to haunt the sign of the modern, calling it progress, civilization, modernization, or any other new/old global configuration (see Hall 1997b). The return migrant, therefore, is both hailed as someone whom everybody adores and wishes to be like, and, precisely because of this, is also despised and resented, for having what everybody else wants but does not have (see Kincaid 1997; Rhys 1982; Spivak 1999). It is in this game of non-self-identification that envy raises its incredibly destructive head and claims its central place in the production of postcolonial identities (Ulloa 1992: 45–46): "No lo han olvidado, este mundo ha dejado de ser tuyo, no te pertenece y, aún cuando han pasado tantos años, sigues siendo un delincuente juvenil, cachero de maricones." [6]

So in Ulloa's narrative it is the return migrant who fulfills the tragic role, with utmost economy and consummate acting. The character tragically accepts from the outset that identity which he knows not to be his. And it is this acceptance of the sign of the modern as a signifier for the city's repressed identity that clinches the tragic resolution of his life. It is at the moment of signification that Johnnie loses (and productively gains) his authenticity as a person of superior status, which would seem to be the only thing he has going for him. Yet he chooses, interestingly enough, to return to invisibility in Los Angeles. So it is in that playing of roles and identification, in accepting that which he is not and striving to be the other's projection of himself, that he becomes the most authentic, precisely because Guayaquilean identity is imbued with tragic self-identification and a permanent desire to be what one is not (Ulloa 1992: 46): "Te ríes, eres un hijueputa Johnnie y lo admites mientras preparas los papeles para regresar nuevamente a Los Angeles en busca de tu identidad y núcleo." [7]

It is no coincidence that the most common nickname for Guayaquile-ans is *monos* (monkeys), because Guayaquileans have a long tradition of aping everybody they meet, including themselves (or who they think they should be). This characteristic is tragically replayed in infinite foreign arrangements and silk trappings (as noted in a popular expression,

"Aunque el mono se vista de seda, mono queda" [even dressed in silk, a monkey remains a monkey]). Implied in this popular saying is the powerful social leveler that fuels both Guayaquileans' envy and their desire. Yet this is not the only Guayaquilean migration experience or sign of modernity. In the following scenarios I discuss two ethnographic subjects who continue to live in New York and who have made different life choices, have different identities, and have reacted differently to the seductive effects of the modern.

Born in the USA: "Guayaquileño por Excelencia"

Pedro was born in the United States and has been a U.S. citizen for over thirty years. At the time of our interview, he lived in Long Island. When I asked him whether he felt Guayaquilean, Pedro (interview, August 16, 2003) answered that during adolescence he "began to feel Guayaquilean, to feel the traditions, the manner of thinking. I became interested in the things that were happening in Ecuador, politics, economic development. I became really interested in the history of Ecuador, and therefore of all Latin America." Pedro's adamant response is clearly a result of personal (and therefore global) life choices. At the same time, this national identification also reflects the secondary place that place of birth holds in terms of claiming to be Guayaquilean.

Pedro was born in the United States but returned to Guayaquil while still in grade school. His initial years in Ecuador were quite traumatic, paralleling my experience of not fitting in in a hostile environment. Not surprisingly, Pedro's response to suffering hostility while being accorded superior status projected onto him was to suppress his American (U.S.) identity. This was the only way he could live in Guayaquil as a Guayaquilean, even when this repression also meant denying who he really was. The only way he could escape his false identity as a superior—foreign—being was to assume another false identity, one that silenced his having been born abroad or having had a significant life outside of the local fold.

Pedro, with his newly silenced identification, finished grade school and enrolled in a traditional Guayaquilean high school–level naval academy, the Liceo Naval. This experience only further inscribed the masculine role he had played in grade school by instructing him in military ideology, pushing him to suppress his emotions, and instilling a strong drive to succeed. All of these values were deemed natural, possessed by all male Guayaquileans, even though their imposition would seem enough to belie their "naturalness."

After high school he made the expected middle- and upper-class transition to college, working toward a degree in economics at the city's elite Catholic University, Universidad Católica de la Ciudad Santiago de Guayaquil. At this point, his American (U.S.) past resurfaced. During this period (the early 1980s), continuing migration to the United States, particularly to New York City, intensified because of worsening socioeconomic conditions in Guayaquil and throughout the country. The decade of the 1980s was marked by a fragile transition to democracy after the newly elected president, Jaime Roldós Aguilera, died in a suspicious plane crash on a national holiday, May 24, 1981. The transition to democracy also encountered challenging economic conditions as the nation faced enormous debt repayments for loans accrued during the previous decade of military rule. In this troubled global economic context, Pedro returned to New York, using his U.S. citizenship to regain entry into the country.

Pedro's adolescent years were critical in marking his Guayaquilean identity. According to him, *la música nacional* marked a central place in his development of ethnic sentiments toward Guayaquil. He stated that he started liking *pasillos* in early adolescence, especially after seeing his father use these songs to serenade Pedro's mother. In his words, his own emotional-erotic awakenings were tied to *pasillos,* and he easily recognized the importance of this music in seducing (*enamorando*) members of the opposite sex: "At the beginning I did not like them [*pasillos*], when I was young, but then as I got older I started to like them, at around sixteen or seventeen years old. That is when I started to pay attention to the lyrics, to the music, and I began falling in love, and I liked it. I thought, it would be great to take these songs ["dar serenatas"] to a girl, when I get married I want to do this to, this is what I used to say, so I started liking it more. At around sixteen or seventeen I began to like them" (interview, August 16, 2003).

In Pedro's life, as I found with several other interviewees, national and sexual awakenings seem to have gone hand in hand. Most of the interviewees also described their early dislike of *pasillos* and stated that it was only during adolescence that attraction to this kind of tragedy-driven music became central in their lives. Pedro, however, commented that his burgeoning ethnic identification was further complicated by his ambivalent origins. On the one hand, he had to hide not where he was born but his having had any profound contact with the United States; on the other hand, he struggled to catch up to the national sentiments that all his friends already seemed to espouse. In this sense, it was less an issue of naturally effusive national identification than of a conscious process of ethnic resignification, of which, because of Pedro's national duality, he seemed to be highly aware.

The process by which one becomes Guayaquilean starts with an early and unconscious figuration of cultural forms that are later officialized through parental and school media. Traditional national music, *pasillos,* plays a central role in this process, as Pedro and others pointed out to me, by contributing to the national hegemonic ideal and then effacing the music's contribution. With the aid of *pasillos,* presented simply as neutral music, a series of national values and standards are continually paraded in front of young people. Guayaquilean youths are then forced to accept this music and its set of national values or to feel guilty for rejecting it, and thereby the nation of their parents. This guilt comes not only for supposedly rejecting one's own music but also for rejecting one's own way of being. Not liking *pasillos,* tellingly enough, is raised to a form of self-hatred, or at least self-denial, with multiple cultural and political implications.

The nature and discussion of the *pasillo* as a national musical form introduce the discussion of larger national representations because the *pasillo* reinforces the sentiments that make up Guayaquilean ethnic identification as a discrete form of Ecuadorianness. Of course, being Guayaquilean is represented nationally as being a superior Ecuadorian, a racist element highlighted in the city's ongoing regional construct (*regionalismo*) against its highland compatriots. It is not surprising that this regional difference is also reflected in a coastal form of the *pasillo,* with its happier rhythmic arrangement. This essential contradiction, inherent in coastal *pasillos,* of a tragic form contained within a happy exterior also reflects the contradictions of a Guayaquilean identity.

This particular form of official representation in the *pasillo,* in Medardo Ángel Silva's life, and in the representation of the city's past functions as a central axis in Guayaquil's self-representation. Gone from the city's self-identification, and understandably so, are any negative readings that might complicate one's smooth self-identification as Guayaquilean. Thus, one begins to accept the national style of sentimentalizing (see Anderson 1991), as Pedro did during his adolescence—love, loyalty, self-effacement, heritage, and strength as an individual—and not social characteristics. These cultural values, therefore, take on the appearance of individual emotions and qualities which seem to deny their national and social hegemonizing role. Therefore, it would not be surprising for one to begin to feel national pride and attachment to Guayaquil's regional musical tradition at the same moment that love and other forms of obsessive attachment began to burgeon (see Butler 1997a).

There is a high price for feeling this way without wondering out loud if anybody else feels the same way. Guayaquilean identity is shared, as all identities must be, but only as long as these feelings are not acknowledged as social. It is this particular form of postcolonial ethnic construct that, understandably, makes listening to *pasillos,* drinking oneself into oblivion, and crying one's heart out the national pastime in Guayaquil. What else could provoke as much pain as an identity that does not allow itself to be expressed other than in tragic and self-denying forms? Even more problematic is its inability to be acknowledged as other than a unique form that demands constant concealment and national reification. That is, you can cry in public as long as you admit that what is making you cry is yours and yours alone. Now that is what being a man (or a woman) is really all about.

It is in this context, I argue, that one can understand Pedro's constant reaffirmation of his Guayaquilean identity, even though he was not born there and lived most of his life away from the city (interview, August 16, 2003): "Yes, I think about the love I have for my country, that it gave me so many opportunities, a land where I learned a lot, and I think of the love I have of the region. I see it as another opportunity, where I learned to value things . . . I owe a lot to Guayaquil, absolutely, the education, the friends, everything, a lot of things, and that is what has enabled me to live in a better way here [New York City]." And yet one also begins to understand his reticence to listen to *pasillos,* especially since they, at a very personal level, problematize his ambivalent regional and national identification, as they do for all Guayaquileans: "No, I do not listen to *pasillos* here. I pay more attention to them when I am over there [Ecuador], but I am not sure why I have not paid more attention to them here, unfortunately, I do not know . . . The period in which I was over there, that is what comes to mind. I identify *pasillos* with the country of my parents, the country where I lived for a long time, and I identify them with Ecuador, with a national identity."

She's Got a Ticket to Ride:
Guayaquil as Entry to Latin America

It is precisely that feeling of being and not, to be and to not want, to deny one's being in some way. You are also identified by your way of feeling, as part of a people, as a woman, as a human being. It is precisely that. To be there in front of your own image and to not want to accept it, all of a sudden to trip over your own image and to say, "That is not me," to deny. That image is many times a racial one, about rebellion, racial in the sense that there is always this idea that I want to be one thing and not what I really am. (Ana, interview, August 15, 2001)

Although she is young—twenty-six at the time of our first interview—life experiences have made Ana an intelligent and provocatively insightful woman. She was born in Guayaquil but lived most of her life in the Province of Azogues. She and other family members moved to Guayaquil when she was an adolescent. Her stay in the city was not long enough for her to develop a close identification with it, however, since, at eighteen she moved again, this time to New York City. She had lived there for about eight years when we spoke and considers the city her home. Although she has been back to Guayaquil only one time, she describes her visit not only as emotionally unsatisfying but also as frustrating because she was not able to spend as much time as she wanted (and needed) to.

Ana's perception of her responses—primarily her being struck by how insular she now finds Guayaquil—is interesting to her because, when she first moved to Guayaquil from the highlands, she thought the city incredibly cosmopolitan and open. But in comparison to New York, she finds the racial and sexual restrictions in Guayaquil limiting and extremely problematic. According to Ana, the racism, against both blacks and people of Indian descent, and the sexual repression experienced by both women and gay people, makes returning to Guayaquil very difficult.

My research assistant and I interviewed Ana on two occasions, the first before she became a single mother, and the second after she had her baby. The second interview took place at Ana's job at a City University of New York media center and was marked by its vibrant multicultural setting: a young Italian American woman (married to an Egyptian man) and a young Asian American man were arguing over world music so forcefully that, at times, we were forced to referee.

The multicultural setting of our second interview highlights what many Guayaquileans living in New York talk about in terms of their exposure to enormous cultural, racial, and sexual difference. For several of them, this exposure was problematic and even frightening at first. Ana, however, and others (myself included) not only have found themselves growing more tolerant of these ambiguities but also have found themselves exploring many ambiguous racial and sexual identities, which were initially taboo. This same racial and sexual ambiguity then gets projected onto return migrants as the embodiment of greater social freedom.

Several informants pointed out that, even when visiting Guayaquil, as Ana has, they found that they no longer felt at home with normative racist jokes and the limited sexual expression given to women and gay people. They quickly found their own recently acquired sexual and racial ambivalence to be more and more of a burden. They were torn between their memory of having actively contributed to these racist and sexist attitudes in the past and a new way of being that made them the center of attraction (and attacks) from something for which they had previously had little public tolerance. There is no doubt that in this instance envy is mediating between the seductive allure and social resentment of what the returned migrant represents.

For Ana, this and many other considerations make her feel little need or desire to identify herself as Guayaquilean or even Ecuadorian. Rather, she says that as the years have passed she has grown to see herself more and more as Latin American and understanding her Guayaquilean identity simply as an entry point for a Latin American one (interview, August 15, 2001): "You know, now my idea of being Ecuadorian, Guayaquileña, is really much broader, right? I feel more Latin American. It is more than Ecuadorian, Guayaquilean, my intuition is a Latin American one. Because this is my own small world, or rather, my world is New York. Where having a Guayaquilean identity or being a highlander [serrana] is only useful in some Ecuadorian social circles, but you live in a world where you meet people from different parts, you become more Latin American." For Ana, interestingly, Guayaquil is equated with Ecuador, since she seems to have little concern for localized identity representations. In a way, this regional denial is an essential first step in the denial of herself as Ecuadorian, which makes a Latin American identity and, significantly, not a Latino one, even possible. Ana's understanding of her identity is even more striking when you take into account that all my other interviewees, including those discussed above, make national claims only through the specificity of a regional one, in this case, Guayaquilean.

It is easy to understand the normative process by which a regional locale, like Guayaquil, is essential in producing a national Ecuadorian representation. This normative process brings into focus the nature of social identification and the fact that, although they are abstract generalizations, identities must always be empirically and locally (or regionally) grounded (Duras 1986, 1997). What is more problematic is how a regional identity maintained outside of Guayaquil is still a path to national identification, even though it attempts to differentiate itself in a hierarchical fashion from other Ecuadorian regional identities. But in Ana's case, the question is how her national identification allows both greater supranational identification as a Latin American and a denial of an exclusively national identity.

Perhaps it is the ambivalence of possessing an identity but consciously moving it to one side that provides the most insight. It would seem that Ana's negative self-identification—I am (Guayaquilean/Ecuadorian) but refuse to be (Guayaquilean/Ecuadorian), or I am (Guayaquilean/Ecuadorian) but wish to be (Latin American)—is yet another, albeit more sophisticated, form of a reworking of the sign of the modern. Ana's reworking of her identity is similarly different (Hall 1997b) from Pedro's assumption of a more explicitly normative Guayaquilean identity.

Furthermore, in Ana's analysis one still sees both primary elements: the pervasive denial of who one is, as well as the productive desire to be something that escapes national boundaries or local definitions. Her analysis, however, also makes us ponder the central nature of this double-stranded form of identity production. Precisely because Ana's response would initially seem to be so different from the others', it is more striking to assess how a similar structure of tragic desire informs her vision of herself and her identity. Ana is quite aware of this possibility, as she expresses how the life of the country is so tragic, and music is a particular way of expressing that suffering.

It also is not surprising that Ana is fully aware of the multivocality of music, particularly the *pasillo,* in the effective production of sentiment and social identification, what Foucault (1980) refers to as the power of effects in the realm of sentiment production (see Davis 1998). Perhaps precisely because of this, unlike Pedro, Ana refuses to stop listening to *pasillos* but, rather, with the majority of her compatriots, returns to them in moments of supreme personal sadness and anguish (interview, August 15, 2001; my emphasis): "I do it when I am depressed. When I want to drink a couple [hits her neck with her fingers to signify alcohol] . . . of you know what. Yes, when I am depressed, especially. Well, because this music speaks to your heart. Where I come from, I grew up in a region where it is pure feelings, pure heart, to slice your wrists and all, you see? And yes, when you feel like that *you obviously are going to look for something that is going to make you feel even more pain, to feel that loss."* Thus, it is significant that Ana, who refuses an explicit personal identification as Guayaquilean, returns to Ecuadorian forms of cultural identification through music and the tragic dimensions of personal emotion.

This apparent contradiction speaks to two phenomena relevant to the larger research question. The first one refers to the nature of hegemonic constraints, principally in terms of the maintenance of a nationally hegemonic ideology and history. In this case, all social identifications react to similar historical constraints, which allow individuals to play the field in varying ways but never allow the hegemonic (game) identification to be broken. At best, the varying differences create new rules for the game, as in Ana's reworking of a productive Guayaquilean identification, but, ultimately, the hegemonic structure remains the same (see Wylie 1992, 1995).

The second element, also related to the malleability of hegemony, is the completely internalized yet ambivalent notion of the signifier (Barthes 1972, 1982, 1992; Bataille 1986, 1988; Hall 1997a, 1997b). It would be problematic, therefore, and, to an enormous degree, erroneous to interpret not only Guayaquilean identity but also one of its main cultural forms, the tragic *pasillo,* as meaning the same thing to everyone. Rather, what is striking is how this cultural form allows varied meanings and applications while producing similar effects of social identification. It does not matter if one listens to *pasillos* or not, or even if they mean the same to everyone; rather, what is important is that all variations respond to similar constraints of hegemonic structural identification. It is this structural identification which I am calling the sign of the modern, which in Guayaquilean identity means the tragedy of knowing that one cannot be who one wants to be. This modern identification is activated either by representing it as a "personal problem" or by being pushed to seek that which is beyond one's personal (and national) borders.

This analysis makes sense for a port city such as Guayaquil, which has been historically shaped always to look outside and beyond the national scriptures of the nation (Maiguashca 1994). This looking out, however, as expressed by Guayaquil's high number of internal and international migrations, is never devoid of a central structure constantly being reworked in similarly different ways (Hall 1997) to the benefit of the nation. Therefore, both kinds of migration are intimately linked to the city's ruling modernity and a normative means of expressing one's Guayaquilean identity. Ana's case provokes a powerful requestioning of Guayaquil's future social identification in the following sense: migration does not signal the end of Guayaquilean identity but, rather, its continuous transformation into a new global, translocal form.

Ana, significantly, contributes to the dynamic reworking of Guayaquilean identity and modernity not only in her own life but also in her
unrestrained pride in being a single mother. She reflects, perhaps with
her child's identification in mind, "Ecuador is like the umbilical cord to
Latin America, the womb, to say it in some way, but it is also Latin
America. I cannot say that I identify with Ecuador as I did two or three
years ago. Now it is more like Latin America, and Ecuador also shares
that part of Latin America, that is the way it is, right?" (interview,
August 15, 2001).

Guayaquil, Migration, and the Sign of the Modern

The three representations I have discussed, one literary and two ethnographic, reflect the interplay between migration and identity and what
I have referred to as the sign of Guayaquilean modernity. My interest
has been to understand the underlying implications of Guayaquilean
migration, particularly in terms of the continent's current global flows.
Although I have taken an ethnographic approach, I am less interested in
discerning general migration patterns than in assessing the multiple constraints, both structural and global, that define the movement of people
between Guayaquil and New York.

There are three basic cultural transformations of interest in terms of
migration effects: regional identities; racial/sexual definitions; and globalization. A regional identity—like that of being Guayaquilean—was
present in all the subjects I interviewed. This regional identification has
not been lost but, instead, seems to have intensified with distance from
the Guayaquilean homeland. My three examples therefore reflect the
powerful regional identification through which the subjects have gained
either a national (Ecuadorian) or a supranational (Latin American) identity. Perhaps Ana's example best demonstrates how the pervasive nature
of Guayaquilean identity, even in its less-explicit form, maintains its
quality of tragic representation and ambivalent self-identification.

This pervasive regional way of feeling, I maintain, heightens a particular form of Guayaquilean modernity, one inherited from previous generations (Guayaquil Antiguo), and their structures of feeling (see R. Williams
1977) point to a way of rethinking the global as a local global (see Hall
1997b). Thus, a tragic sensibility primary to Guayaquilean modernity
is necessarily represented as local, even though it moves with incredible
assurance through global flows. There is no doubt that Guayaquilean

identity has always benefited from global flows, as a result of the city's both being a port and having a history of immense migrations. The reworking of a regional Guayaquilean identity in different parts of the United States, Venezuela, and now Spain is a continuation of this global tradition.

Guayaquilean identity is therefore a good example of a specific form of a local global that has resulted from migration and that utilizes particular notions of racial and sexual mores to maintain its dynamic articulation. Guayaquil continues to maintain ambivalent racial and sexual identifications. It is not that the city's identity expresses total racial and sexual liberation; rather, it has traditionally maintained a significant form of greater sexual and racial freedom than the rest of the country, particularly the highlands. The ambivalence in this openness is apparent, however, as experientially captured by Ana when compared with the even greater, not just different, sexual and racial tolerance present in a metropolis like New York City.

In this framework, Guayaquilean identity is represented as providing more sexual freedom and racial equality than the rest of Ecuador but less than the desired (but morally reprehensible) hedonistic North. This ambivalence is present in all three examples but is perhaps more creatively expressed by Ulloa's Johnnie, whose belonging is both constrained and enabled by the greater sexual freedom and fewer racial constraints with which he grew up. The degree of sexual liberation and racial equality is not what is at stake, however; rather, it is the delicate balance between going farther than expected (or than the rest of the country) but not too far (as they do in the United States and New York City), ultimately, an impossible position to maintain. In Guayaquil's more restrictive sexual and racial mores one can see both the ambivalent hegemonic constraints of the city's modernity and its inevitable structural limitation: a form of the modern that gives way to its tragic representation in the most vivid Guayaquilean terms.

All three examples dutifully express the interrelated phenomenon of global flows and local representations. These cases argue for the impossibility of talking about the global and the local as separate entities; instead, they are unique productions of a greater level of plausible social relationships. It is glaringly clear that Guayaquilean identity has never been local, devoid of global parameters, from its colonial past to its postcolonial present, and from its port characteristics to its being the historical center of enormous social upheaval and revolution. It is even more poignant that migration, internal and international, has never stopped being an essential part of Guayaquilean identity formation.

As my interviews with migrants to New York City exemplify, Guayaquilean identity has afforded itself a particular place in global, translocal flows. It is this heavy global burden of translocality which, in its own way, has continually contributed a tragic sign of the modern to Guayaquilean identity. It is not insignificant that Guayaquileans have impregnated their national musical form, the *pasillo*, with beauty and that this musical tradition legitimizes identification as never being fully who one is and sings about it with unsurpassable passion. The fact that this tragically unfulfilled desire must be sung about in personal terms only makes the pain sharper and opens Guayaquileans to the powerful political dimensions of these *problemas personales*.

Finally, this same sign of the modern expressed in pain-filled *pasillos* is further burdened by translocal, global flows experienced by Guayaquilean migrants in New York and Guayaquileans at home. They are never able to be who they really are: globally liberated persons. Even more problematic is the representation that, when approaching this ideal of a globally liberated self, they are publicly represented as steering away from their primal connections to a Guayaquilean identity. It is here, however, that the hegemonic constraints (Sayer 1994) and the field of force (Roseberry 1994) prove even more deadly, because it is in the pain afforded by the loss of a Guayaquilean identity that a Real (see Žižek 2002) Guayaquilean identity is secured and reiterated as the tragic sign of the modern.

CHAPTER 5

Instances of Blackness in Ecuador
The Nation as the Racialized
Sexual Global Other/Order

It really enrages to be black and to live in a country of whites. Not to be able to escape. To have to stand the discrimination, the ridicule, the mistreatment, the exploitation. And to not be able to escape.

—DEMETRIO AGUILERA MALTA, CANAL ZONE

Ecuador's participation in a long-standing tradition (inherited from the conquest) of racial oppression against its nonwhite populations is not surprising (see Cervone and Rivera 1999; de la Torre 2002; Muteba Rahier 1999; Phelan 1967; Rueda Novoa 2001), and less so to me as an Ecuadorian native. My invariable categorization as a *cholo,* at best, or, at worst, as having strong indigenous features has never sat well in the racial reasoning of most, if not all, Ecuadorians. The Western ideal which elevates whites to the highest level of civilization (and therefore makes them representatives of urban culture) and characterizes blacks and Indians as savages (one step removed from the jungle and present in rural, backward settings) is not new (or news) and no longer demands much complex social analysis (see Gregory and Sanjek 1994; Haraway 1989; Wade 1993, 1994). Rather, these racial junctures of white, black, and Indian identity strike me as the most visible and fragile interstice of the Ecuadorian nation's nationalizing discourse of *mestizaje.* The century-long rhetoric of "we are all mestizos here," espoused by presidents, national leaders, and historians (e.g., Cevallos García 1960; see also Whitten 1984), has done little but expose an inherent need (i.e., neurosis) to hail whiteness as the preferred form of identification and strengthen color-blinding to any other form of racial demarcation (E. Silva 1995). As many scholars (e.g., Hale 1996; Mallon 1996; Stutzman 1981) have pointed out for Latin America, the discourse of *mestizaje* is an ideological recourse that has worn out its schizophrenic need to incorporate its mixture of Indian and black heritage while striving to hold onto European standards of social and physical body politics (see Anzaldúa 1987 for the most enlightened revaluation of *mestizaje* since the 1980s).

I have spent several years assessing the racial ordering of Ecuador's hierarchical structure, incorporating my personal experiences into the anthropological knowledge I have gained while researching the nation's past and culture. I strongly believe in the advantages afforded me by my Ecuadorian identity and by my having lived in Ecuador for over ten years as a full-fledged "native" before choosing anthropology as a method for understanding the cultural incongruence that pervaded my life and social surroundings. My research and lived experiences, as well as the time and distance to reconsider them in comparative perspective, have enabled me to carry out my exploration of the national racial/sexual ordering (Benavides 2001).

Instead of accusing the Ecuadorian nation-state and its related construction of a national identity of inherent racism and sexism (an undeniable reality), I am more interested in exploring the complex manner in which these racial/sexual structures are productively intertwined. In this chapter, I hope to assess the transnational othering/ordering of black racialized bodies that, although indebted to Western global ideals of postcolonialism, is articulated in singularly localized ways in Ecuador. At the same time, by problematizing a much more local embodiment of racial meaning (for an understanding of the local as a product of the global, see Hall 1997a, 1997b), I also hope to acknowledge the interrelatedness of the racial and sexual othering/ordering central to the production of a postcolonial national identity. One of the main elements that I study is the myriad of racial (and inherently racist) categorizations that are produced by contesting forces, which results in the ever-ambivalent and fragile construction of an Ecuadorian national identity.

As my research in Ecuadorian national history(ies) and national identity(ies) evidences (Benavides 2004a), neither of these cultural processes is singular, although both are highly invested in presenting themselves as such. National histories and identities are hegemonic and contain forms of domination not because they are static or monolithic; rather, national discourses are successful precisely because they are able to articulate counterhegemonic discourses and incorporate them into the changing face (and body) of the nation. Contemporary Ecuadorian national identity is clearly very different from the one espoused by the leaders of the late 1800s or even the early 1900s. In this regard, the remarkable feature of the country's national identity is not that it has remained the same over the centuries but that its people believe it has. The national identity process is supposed to have an inherent continuity, but everybody knows that it does not, even though they are unwilling to acknowledge that fact for reasons of emotional (the chaotic loss of identity) and physical (the military force of the state) survival.

A number of scholars (Alonso 1988; Baldwin 1984; Duras 1986; Taussig 1992; B. Williams 1991) discuss the fragile nature of the nation and the state, but perhaps the most succinct are Phillip Abrams and Derek Sayer. Like Sayer's (1994) understanding of hegemony, Abrams' (1988) elaboration of it in an article published posthumously assesses our "fictive" understanding of the state. The state, according to Abrams, is not a monolithic entity with clear political dictates but an ever-changing political project constantly in the making, only reified by our own fears and social necessities. It is this approach that I would like to use to look at the racial reconfiguration of the social other/order in Ecuador. In the process, I will use three examples to argue the complexity of racial ordering as a means to "other" a black population as a way of grounding the Ecuadorian nation-state's cultural difference. Racial ordering is clearly visible in places like the United States, where an enslaved population was essential in defining what the Constitution meant by being free (as succinctly expressed in Toni Morrison's [1993] essay on U.S whiteness and literary production). But in postcolonial settings, like those of Latin America, this particular distancing is even more essential, since so many qualities of the other(s), in this case, Indians and blacks, are dispersed throughout the population (see Lancaster 1986). Thus, it is not only that the other is needed exclusively as an essential distancing mechanism but that it is also needed to constitute oneself, in this case, the nation. As Minh-ha (1997) argues, it is not only a case of "not like you" (to distinguish oneself) but, more problematically, a case of being more and more "like you" (and not being able to distinguish oneself or deny the similarity completely).

I shall elaborate on this complex, dynamic racial articulation of othering, and therefore of hierarchical ordering, by looking at three examples of national production or engagement with blackness (or Afro-Ecuadorianness). I first discuss Medardo Ángel Silva, who is hailed as the most representative icon of Guayaquil in spite of (or, ambivalently, because of) his Afro-Ecuadorian identity. The second example involves two recent selections of a Miss Ecuador to represent the country in the Miss Universe Pageant. In two pageants, in November 1995 and November 1997, the women selected by the judges as Miss Ecuador were black, setting off a national debate on the racial representation of the nation. The third example is Daule's powerful Señor de los Milagros (Lord of the Miracles), a colonial representation of a black, life-sized, crucified Jesus that, to this day, is venerated by the predominantly Catholic coastal population.

I will discuss each of these cases separately and return to them at the conclusion to problematize the localized production of blackness as inherently linked to global Guayaquilean interactions. It is not my objective to argue that the racist underpinnings of postcolonial nation-states should not be highlighted; rather, I believe that they should be problematized more fully before we attempt to rescue those communities involved and perhaps replicate Western intervention yet again. I would also argue that the difficulty in denouncing the racist underpinnings of postcolonial societies lies precisely in the ambivalent role played by racial discourses and their usefulness in implementing not only "not-you" distinctions but also "like-you" ones as well (see Minh-ha 1997). Finally, I also sustain that the following examples explain how racial othering/ordering is inextricably linked with not only global "national" projects but sexual ones as well. Racial othering/ordering is strongly linked to sexual and engendered bodies that are as ambivalently sexualized as they are racialized (Morrison 1993; Omi and Winant 1994; Stoler 1996, 2002).

Medardo Ángel Silva: A National Representation of the Ostracized Other

"I don't think he killed himself because he was black. If that would be true how come there are so many black people that don't kill themselves" (Miranda, interview, in Benavides and García 2001). This response to a question about why an interviewee thought Silva had killed himself brings to the forefront the painful characteristics of the poet's life and his ambivalent representation as Guayaquil's most cherished poet. Miranda's comment also brings out her own anxiety, and that of many other Guayaquileans I interviewed, about the racist ethos that is secured within a viable Guayaquilean identity. Guayaquil is particularly important to the production of Ecuador's national identity because it is the country's largest city and its economic capital. As is logical, Quito and Guayaquil stand out as the largest metropolitan centers and where the most extensive national refurbishing is produced, if not exclusively, at least most meaningfully articulated regionally (see Maiguashca 1994).

Guayaquil's role in the national reimagining of what it means to be

Guayaquilean, and thus Ecuadorian, becomes especially meaningful in the memorialization of Silva's life. That Guayaquil would celebrate one of its Afro-Ecuadorian citizens as its most venerated national icon is particularly intriguing, especially as demonstrated in public monuments and ritual events ("Medardo A. Silva" 1999; "El arte se junta con la medicina" 2001). This memorialization of Silva is meaningful for at least two reasons. First, his name is invoked to explain what it is to be Guayaquilean and is used in official events to define a particular way of being Ecuadorian. Second, Silva has enormous popular appeal and is thus translated into a meaningful symbol of national identification.

Silva's inscription into the national canon of Guayaquilean and Ecuadorian identity would seem insignificant if one were quickly to gloss over his self-acknowledged troubled racial identity. The manner in which Silva's blackness is represented elides mechanisms that demonstrate the contradictory balancing act inherent in the national identity's configuration of a black racial identity. An initial reading, and a quite superficial one, could see a democratic incorporation of nonwhite racial identities into the national fold. After all, Silva is not only Guayaquil's most cherished poet but also the only one that most Guayaquileans have heard of or read. My interviewees repeatedly came up blank when I asked them about other favorite Ecuadorian poets (see Benavides and García 2001), and this despite the "problematic" reality of his black racial traits.

The fact is, most textbooks which actively endorse Silva's literary value to the nation are quick to ignore his blackness (see Romero Castillo 1970). As a result of this racial amnesia, most high school students never learn that Silva was Afro-Ecuadorian. The official willingness to hide his identity as a black man makes a democratic understanding of his iconization difficult to sustain; even the idea that at least one black icon has been adopted as a way of making the masses happy seems difficult to support empirically. Even if one takes into account the racist underpinnings of Ecuador's national identity, there would seem to be little room for a black icon, least of all a black poet, to be heralded as the nation's intellectual heir of Guayaquil's heritage.

This racial conundrum also elaborates a much more complex reading of the racial content of the country's identity. The puzzle is not a simplistic, prejudiced discrimination against nonwhite racial identities; instead, it selectively incorporates these racial identities to sustain a much larger hegemonic entity, which, by necessity, must be nonmonolithic and vary over time and space. Thus, it would seem that Silva is raised to the level of icon not only in spite of his blackness but also precisely because of it. It is therefore possible to see in Silva's (and his mother's, friends', and other Ecuadorians') problematic dealings with his own racial difference a more ambiguous relationship with a nationalized black racial identity.

To a large degree, I am reassessing Flores' (1992) interpretation of the changing nature of Puerto Rico's racial definition. Even though Flores never makes a direct association with national identity, very similar postcolonial structural constraints mark the definition of Puerto Rican culture, on the one hand, and Ecuadorian national identity, on the other. In this regard, Flores utilizes a small (and, from a surface reading, quite insignificant) incident in which the name of a popular black Puerto Rican musician (Cortijo) was proposed by a desperate candidate for governor as the name of the island's foremost cultural arts center. This immediately stirred protests from conservative elites and support from progressive circles. The discussion disappeared as fast as it erupted and seems to have had no concrete impact.

Flores argues quite insightfully, however, that the simple fact of the incident, however small, exemplifies a differing and ever-changing context in which a national culture is being reassessed. Far from blackness being a mere epiphenomenon in the central debate over identity, it represents a much more complex relationship in the discussion of identity. Blackness, as a racial identity consistently denied and hidden, is also enormously subversive; otherwise, why so much investment in denying it? It is the ambivalent nature of all denied and oppressed racial identities (a position held by black identity since its initial devalorization through Western global-capitalist relationships on the eve of Europe's mercantile expansion [Gregory and Sanjek 1994]) which is important to explore within the national debate over an Ecuadorian identity.

The Puerto Rican (Cortijo) and the Ecuadorian (Silva) cases present interesting contrasts. Even though a larger percentage of Puerto Rico's population is African/black, Cortijo seems reduced in representative status (see Flores 1992). Silva is regarded as a larger-than-life national figure, even though only around 10 percent of Ecuador's population identifies as Afro-Ecuadorian (see Santacruz 1995). Thus, one could argue that Silva's iconization as a national figure is in some ways a regional realization of the difficulty of using Cortijo's memory as a national representation.

In Silva's case, without a doubt, there has been an attempt to "whiten" him and his memory. This is evident in the scant attention his blackness is given in the official popularization of his memory. As another interviewee told me (Juanito, in Benavides and García 2001): "I had no recollection that he was black." This "problematic" relationship is not only an official (mis)representation of Silva but also a (mis)representation (although one must wonder about the signifying value of calling something a misrepresentation) that Silva himself quite actively argued for (Silva in Romero Castillo 1970: 323): "I despair in poverty and I am offended by blackness. It is curious: I am a man of pure white race. My grandfather was Spanish. It is useless to explain a freak phenomenon of nature. But you must know that in me is harbored a pure Iberian heritage. However, I look like a black Moor."

Silva's and his mother's difficulty in dealing with his blackness is far from contradictory (see Romero Castillo 1970); in fact, within Ecuador's social reality, it is to be expected. How sad his mother felt because of his racial plight (without her, or anybody else for that matter, acknowledging her contribution to it) signals how much both of them were caught up in national racial prescriptions. But neither of them was merely a pawn of national appropriation; rather, they were active agents of their own appropriation, and therefore were also regulators of new forms of dominative agency (see Butler 1997a, 1997b). Silva's dual nature (as oppressed and oppressor) is essential in the popularization of his memory as well as in its officialization by the regulatory powers of the state. It is precisely because so many Guayaquileans can relate to Silva's ambivalent position as both oppressor and oppressed that his work takes on such intimately meaningful social significance. His poetry could have been possible only because he was black; only a person operating within so much racial oppression and exclusion could have written poems of such desolation, and thereby allowed future generation of Ecuadorians to relate to his national experience. Even though the majority of Ecuadorians are not black, they equate themselves symbolically with a productive blackness as they try to understand the exclusion that being Guayaquilean/Ecuadorian means. Therefore, the legacy of *mestizaje,* and the ongoing transformation of Indian identity into one of pain and suffering, is expressed in productively complicated ways.

There is also a sexual element in the national discourse of Silva's representation that has been necessarily and significantly silenced. There are several passages like the following that hint of a much more "problematic" sexuality, which neither official nor popular venues are ready to tolerate. As in the following example, prophetically written a mere month before his probable suicide, Silva uses this distancing sexual-narrative approach to express sexually dangerous feelings of homosexual attraction that had not been afforded poetic license (Silva, in Calderón Chico 1999: 51): "It is almost a quarter of an hour since that cute and pale boy has caught my fancy, with an air of elegant fatigue and with a beelike body."

But, once again, the silencing of Silva's sexuality is not as meaningful as how productive this silence has been in reifying his national importance. The denial of its existence or the refusal to discuss it is, once again, a secret reference point from which to discuss and portray his national reality (see White 2001). As Žižek (1996) elaborates, this central void or silence is essential because it allows us to hold onto the repressed norms essential for our self-representation, and thus our cultural survival.

I do not intend to minimize Silva's ambivalent sexuality; rather, I choose to give it a central position, along with his ambiguous racial identity. It would seem that both identities allowed him to constitute himself as "the self" and "the other" at one and the same time. This contradiction—expressible only in a muffled poetic voice—is ever present in his work, life, and death. This is how the postcolonial identities of oppressed (and agent-filled) Ecuadorians continue to cry, in their individual pain, by singing along with intensity of Silva's social pain. When his "El alma en los labios" is sung with enormous feeling (see Benavides and García 2001), all know that more than an individual weight is being carried. But as all Ecuadorians also know, if one questions the emperor's (hegemony's) new clothes, death—emotional or physical—is sure to follow.

Miss Ecuador: The Racial/Sexual Wages of National Representation

As I noted earlier, Ecuador espouses a very explicit *mestizaje* discourse (Stutzman 1981), which, among other things, is a clear ideological recourse for propagating an implicit whitening of national society as it looks to both erase and efface the threatening identities of Indian and black populations. Both Indians and blacks are constructed as dangerous productions that threaten the seams of civilized and orderly norms (E. Silva 1995). That national Ecuadorian markers are produced as a homogeneous identity, thereby creating a dichotomy between civilizing, urban white images and savage, rural Indian and black imagery is not surprising. In many respects, this trend is very much in line with a Western global perspective that is responsible for Ecuador as a modern nation-state. After all, Ecuador had five centuries of brutal awakening to reach its contemporary state of Westernness. It is this same racist ideology that privileges the whiteness that traditionally pervades the Miss Ecuador Pageant ("María Luisa Barrios" 2004).

It is more difficult to understand the ambiguous underpinnings of a national identity that not only denies but also connects with an ostracized identity, particularly a black identity. This social reality was highlighted when, on two occasions, Miss Ecuador was an Afro-Ecuadorian: Mónica Chalá in 1995, and Soraya Hogonaga in 1997. (It is interesting to note that the first black Miss Colombia was not chosen until 2001; see *Cromos* 2001a, 2001b). In both instances, the audience and the population at large reacted strongly to the judges' choice to represent feminine beauty and the nation. In 1995, the choice of Mónica Chalá caused a stupor among the general population, symbolized by an embarrassing moment of silence in the theater after her name was announced before a round of polite applause; the announcement in 1997 of another black Miss Ecuador was no less problematic (see Barnes 2001, for discussion of the choice of a black Miss Italy).

To some degree, Chalá's selection in 1995 could be rationalized as a fluke, a one-time deal. Many people, in fact, claimed that, because the Miss Universe Pageant was being held in South Africa, a black Miss Ecuador would have a better chance. The choice of Soraya Hogonaga in 1997 could not be argued away with such simplistic explanations, however. This choice clearly marks, not necessarily a trend, but a clear "fault line" on which the nation has ambiguously secured its national identity. What was merely visible in 1995 became more apparent in 1997: that blackness was far from invisible and not an essentialized static marker of the ambiguous production of Ecuadorianness. A racial fault line is readily apparent in the description of both women on the pageant's Web site: "[Elected] Miss Ecuador for 1996, born in Quito, [Mónica Chalá] was the first black woman to be elected as National Beauty Queen [Reina Nacional de Belleza]. Criticized by many, when she was 22 years old [*sic*]. Admired for her courage, loved by her race, Mónica gave a courageous lesson of what it means to be human without judging her race, ethnicity, identity or social class" (*Nuestras Bellezas* 2000b). Soraya Hogonaga is described in similar terms: "[Elected] Miss Ecuador for 1998, she is one of the most beautiful queens that Ecuador has ever had. She is 1.78 m. tall, an innate elegance, spectacular silhouette, sexy and exotic, in her you have the marvelous mixing of a Latin and African race that make this proud mulatta woman a symbol of *Ecuador's plurinational and multiethnic country*" (*Nuestras Bellezas* 2000a; emphasis mine).

A similar fault line was opened up in the late 1980s, when a black Guayaquilean was selected as the queen of the city for the festivities to celebrate the city's founding. There was concern about an Afro-Ecuadorian woman's representing the cultural and sexual ethos of the city. This particular choice was further complicated by the election's apparently having been rigged by the controversial mayor, Abdalá Bucaram (who became president of the country in 1996, only to be ousted a year later). He manipulated the choice of queen to his political advantage and championed the Afro-Ecuadorian woman's victory as a nearly direct attack against the city's white elite. Abdalá managed to use a powerful global sense of political correctness and a human-rights agenda based on race to further his political image as champion of the poor and underrepresented, even though (or perhaps because) he ruled the city as a populist autocrat and a fascist. This same outlandish political style would prove to be one of the major elements in his downfall after being elected president in the mid-1990s (see Rodríguez Vicéns 1997).

The level of complicit involvement of blackness in the nation's psyche had already been evidenced, if not by the selection of the first black Miss Ecuador, then by the discussion her selection generated. The discussion about the appropriateness of a black woman representing the national social body was tempered by concern for the dictates of race, gender, class, and nationhood, which were never localized but emphasized Ecuador's position in the larger global economic and cultural market. The range of discussion, reaction, and analysis (including this one) exemplifies the nation's ambiguous construction of itself as a nonblack, Western entity. Thus, both the selection of two black women as Miss Ecuador and the ensuing debate express the dynamic, complex, and fragile construction of Ecuador's hegemonic national identity (see Sayer 1994).

Most visible during the debates about racial representation were those who claimed that both selections were a national travesty. The argument was quite simple: blackness is not quantifiably or qualitatively representative of the nation (see "Miss Ecuador 1995" 1995; "Encuesta sobre Miss Ecuador" 1996). For these commentators, blackness did not capture the true emotional embodiment of what the Ecuadorian nation stood for. In many respects, these viewpoints were the most obviously racially prejudiced, but by no means were they unique in this respect. If anything, it is instructive to assess how the discussion's field of force (Roseberry 1994) is pervaded by an explicit understanding of the moral and representational inferiority of a black identity.

At the other extreme, a writer hailed the new Miss Ecuador as "a beauty made of jet ebony" ("La nueva Miss Ecuador" 1995). What is intriguing about this opinion is the singling out of this "beauty" from less-worthy representatives of her race. The black Miss Ecuador, the writer continues, is a worthy representative of the national fold because, first and foremost, she is a true and pure representative of her own downtrodden race. It is her complete racial purity, untouched by "other" races—not only Indian but also white—that allows her to claim to be an authentic representative of racial beauty and national pride.

In this argument, whiteness (for a change) takes on the explicit role of the "other," and it is blackness that becomes the powerful image of national representation (see "La nueva Miss Ecuador" 1995). It is easy to recognize in this approach constraints similar to those imposed by the World Bank and the International Monetary Fund to force the Ecuadorian government to give greater respect and recognition to indigenous communities (see Benavides 2004b).

Yet another interesting implication of the argument that defended the selection on grounds of political correctness and human-rights issues is the implicit relationship, legitimated by this argument, between local identities and global representation (see "Miss Ecuador 1995" 1995). None of these "progressive" journalists and scholars espousing this view ever explicitly argued that blackness actually embodied the national ideal; they conceded that serving as a national representative was out of the realm of possibility for black women, although they never questioned the possibility for other racial groups. Two of Ecuador's presidents between 1995 and 2005 have been of Arabic descent.

But, they argued, Miss Ecuador's constitution as a "minority" is by itself no reason to deny her a chance at serving as a national representative. Rather, allowing its minorities a place in the national sphere was a necessary condition, almost a precondition, of Ecuador's inclusion in the field of modern nations and contemporary globalizations (see *El Hoy* 1995a, 1995b, 1995c). Global struggles for civil rights in places like the United States and South Africa had not gone unnoticed by a significant group of Ecuadorians. But like all global events, these struggles took on a localized meaning that was clearly expressed in the debates over Miss Ecuador. The international struggles over equal rights for minority groups, especially oppressed black populations, were taken to signify the changing dynamics of the global nature of nation-states. Therefore, it was not only not right but passé to discredit people because of race or, even worse, to deny them a chance at the national spotlight in a global event celebrating beauty, friendship, and international solidarity (at least in theory). This particular chance to be modern, to align the nation with what was perceived to be modernity as experienced abroad (a postcolonial syndrome if ever there was one), was not to be lost, and worst of all, to the traditional conservative groups that have historically controlled the nation's sources of wealth and cultural resources.

At the same time, a nation like Ecuador, in difficult economic straits and on a bumpy path to modernization (exemplified in the shift to the dollar as its national currency), could not afford to give to the world such an awkward image of itself and its racial order—a position that, one could argue, has paid off since the 2004 Miss Universe Pageant was held in Quito. The cultural impact and power of U.S. images being exported throughout the Americas, such as MTV and Hollywood films, also should not be ignored (Judy Kreid, personal communication).

As Muteba Rahier (1998) rightly points out, the fact that the leading "democratic empire" in the world presents gyrating black bodies on music videos as the norm and seems to cherish its black bodies at least in sport and entertainment could only provide for different ways to renegotiate blackness at the local and regional levels.

This dynamic global racial renegotiation, although locally reinterpreted, is never disconnected from its global counterpart, even when it is not really produced by either side exclusively. Muteba Rahier's analysis of the selection of Mónica Chalá as Miss Ecuador and the racialized order is by far one of the most sophisticated attempts to understand the production of Ecuadorian blackness within the new age of the free market. What is particularly stunning, however, is the similarity of his analysis to the debates in the Ecuadorian press, even though Muteba Rahier's article appeared in the best-known anthropology journal in the United States. Even though some Ecuadorian voices ("La nueva Miss Ecuador" 1995) and Muteba Rahier seem to support the propriety of a black woman's serving as Miss Ecuador and representing the nation, they seem to disagree about the degree and necessity of her representation of Ecuadorian blackness.

Unlike the Ecuadorian commentators who hail Miss Ecuador's right to serve as a national representative purely on the basis of race, Muteba Rahier criticizes Mónica Chalá for her failure to represent the real Ecuadorian black community or even to attempt to do so. Muteba Rahier's position is particularly problematical, since, by questioning her racial representativeness, he seems to be implying that Miss Ecuador is not black enough, which makes it easier to understand why she was selected in the first place. He seems to be precluding any form of Ecuadorian blackness other than the traditional ones expressed in the regional and class configuration of Esmeraldas and the Chota valley, thereby not allowing for different forms of class embodiment of blackness, such as urban and upwardly mobile.

Muteba Rahier's understanding of Ecuador's racial reality belies his more restricted assessment of the nation's national identity as little more than an explicitly racially prejudiced ideology. As I argue throughout this chapter, of the racist nature of Ecuadorian society there is little doubt or lack of evidence, but the negotiation of the country's national identity (and that of all postcolonial nation-states) is anything but straightforward. Rather, Ecuador's national identity takes on complex forms that not only efface oppressed racial identities but that actually insert them in a dual image of representation in which the national identity distances itself from and becomes the other at the same time. In this respect, the selection of two black Misses Ecuador does not really serve as an exception to either of the two norms. On one level, their selection does not mean only an exclusion of reinforcing and explicit forms of black oppression; rather, it is a much more complex manner of its actual articulation. On another level, the ambiguous relationship with the other as distant and self is far from new, but has been inherited from a Western form of representation that has attempted to digest (anthropomorphically) and incorporate the other into its differing national colonizer entities.

The selection of the two black Misses Ecuador highlights the fact that in neither the heated public discussion about their selection in Ecuador nor in the scholarly analyses has the argument been presented that both women might have been the best candidates for the position. By no means am I presenting this as the "right" position; I simply want to highlight the impossibility of the position's being maintained. The selection of two black Misses Ecuador could only have brought about a national debate on the appropriate racial order of the nation. The qualifications of each woman to hold the crown are denied, belittled, or reified, but never taken into account as a contribution by a worthy individual. This blindness or denial, perhaps much more painfully, defines the difficulty and impossibility of claiming hegemonic national identities when they are clearly based on the exclusion of the human attributes of all those involved. As some would argue, the denial of human experience as nonexistent or irrelevant without a racial discourse to accompany it is one of the most serious limitations on Ecuador's (or any nation-state's) postcolonial existence in the world (see Kureishi 1998).

The Hegemonic Implications of a Black
Christ: Oral History and the Other

The Ecuadorian nation's need to reidentify with the oppressed other is ever-present in the historical record. Neither of the cases discussed above, one occurring at the beginning of the twentieth century, the other in the late 1990s, is an exception but, rather, part of a much longer-lived and more complex form of identification that has allowed the nation to maintain itself and appear socially relevant. I shall now discuss the wooden effigy of a crucified Christ that has been venerated over the centuries in Daule (a coastal city an hour's drive from Guayaquil) and in the port city of Guayaquil. My discussion of this black Christ (El Señor de los Milagros) begs the question of what has been called the structure of coloniality in the contemporary context of Latin American nation-state formation (Quijano 1995). At the same time, this example, more than the other two, addresses the problem of national historical production (see Benavides 2004a). Roland Barthes (1982), among others (Alonso 1988; Foucault 1998), has pointed to the need to take into account both how contemporary discourse structures all historical narratives and the interpretive weight of contemporary symbolic reality on the narratives themselves.

The following story was told to me several times as part of my enculturation as I was growing up in Ecuador. I have also visited the church and icon in Daule several times and wondered about this site's role in black Christian representations throughout Latin America and the Iberian peninsula. In the recounting of the black Christ's story, the origin of the effigy is never clearly elaborated. Instead, two points are highlighted in the versions of this oral history. The first point explains how the image became black in the first place; the second compares the sinful ways of the urban metropolis of Guayaquil with the devotion of the populace and the protection offered Christ's image in the City of Daule.

According to the oral accounts (Pino Roca 1973), the Christ figure was originally white and was situated during colonial times in Daule's major church. Because of the increasing brutality of the white/European (and male) plantation owners, however, the oppressed blacks (former slaves) and Indians (servants) prayed to the Christian God for protection and justice. Because the petitioners were so persistent and because one black slave claimed that the Christian God was a white God and not a real God to all, the effigy turned itself into a black Christ. The tradition tells how, the morning after the slave's irate prayer, as people filed into church, they were faced with the incredible fact that the effigy was now the black El Señor de los Milagros.

Guayaquil's sinfulness is elaborated in the following manner. From colonial times through the early republican period (the late 1800s), the effigy was taken on a yearly pilgrimage down the river to the City of

Guayaquil. This pilgrimage supposedly was established as a result of the effigy's reputation as miraculous (hence its name). Every year on the same date, the effigy was placed on a wooden raft to make its way to Guayaquil. This tradition is present in different narratives about Guayaquil Antiguo, including in the biographies of famous Catholics from the 1800s such as Narcisa de Jesús and Mercedes Molina (both already beatified in the process of becoming saints). Guayaquileans, the narratives tell us, seemed to have forgotten the importance of this tradition, and one year there was nobody to receive the figure at the port. The narrative notes that, seeing that nobody was at the port to receive it, slowly and on its own, the effigy made its way back to Daule. The miracle on this occasion is highlighted by the figure's not only making its way back alone but doing so against the tide, which is usually a difficult task even with several men at the oars (Pino Roca 1973).

In this second part of the narrative, it is clear that an important relationship was established between Daule and the major economic center, Guayaquil. Therefore, the initial pilgrimage of the Christ image to Guayaquil seems an extension of the strong and dependent economic relationship of the agro-export system in place on Ecuador's coast (Hurtado 1981; Quintero and Silva 1991). The religious reconfiguration of geographical associations could be seen as solidifying economic relationships and very much "coloring" these relationships to resignify a much more equitable exchange, including the cultural meanings or, perhaps most important, making them much more relevant. It is also the failure of this cultural resignification that marks the collapse of the religious association, symbolized by the miraculous return of the black Christ to Daule on its own.

This rupture of association is exemplified by the Guayaquilean community's symbolic rejection of the "pious" ways. It is not only that Daule and Guayaquil no longer shared the same interests and spirituality but that the people from Guayaquil had reemphasized their urban (i.e., evil) ways. The miracle of the second "return" reemphasizes the initial "racial" return, but this time the miracle is symbolized not by the fact that the effigy became black but that it returned to its own community, that is, home. In this sense, it is the differentiation between a good, rural population and an ungrateful, urban one that the effigy's black markers and obvious racialization ambivalently highlight. The association of the Christ image, through the pilgrimage, with Guayaquil and then not, as well as the initial association of the effigy with the patriarchal plantation owners and then not, exemplify both an adherence to and a critique of the coast's capitalist system of exploitation (see Quintero and Silva 1991).

Thus, the Christ image exemplifies global practices that have had important political and cultural impacts on the colonial and postcolonial world of Latin America for centuries.

Once again, the use of a racialized blackness to embody these global articulations is not devoid of regional and national meanings. This particular religious myth is rich in plausible interpretations and merits much more in-depth ethnographic analysis to understand its oral tradition fully. My initial exploration, however, points to interesting and insightful contradictions concerning how blackness is blanketed to resignify a series of normative national cultural elements.

The first contradiction lies in the dichotomous construction of urban versus rural identity. As several scholars have pointed out (e.g., R. Williams 1973), the division between rural and urban landscape has less to do with "factual reality" than with economic and cultural significations of our Western socioeconomic experience. Unlike racialized geographical distinctions that present a backward, rural black/Indian population and a sophisticated, white, urban populace, though, this myth looks to invert these cultural meanings: it is a pious rural community that must defend itself versus the impiety of the urban landscape. The geography is the same; the racial landscape is different. The image of a black Christ does violence to the myth of the benevolent white plantation owner of which Ecuadorian historiography from the first part of the twentieth century is full (e.g., Cevallos García 1960; Efrén Reyes 1967; Pareja Diezcanseco 1990). More important, it questions the legitimacy of order and the legality of a colonial system and social relationships of production that were inherited by the early republic.

Even more poignantly, the black Christ, which can still be visited in Daule, points to contemporary exploitative social structures that are maintained by Ecuador's economic relationships at all levels: regional, national, and global. The intimate interrelatedness of these three levels of economic identification only makes their resignification that much more powerful. Therefore, the black Christ of Daule seems to be a double slap in the face: to the exploitative economic relationships that connect Daule to Guayaquil, and to Europe and the global market, including the knowledge of a Middle Eastern God via Europe, through fluvial exports and symbolic trade. As a result, it does not seem that the effigy's miracle voyage upriver, against the current, is coincidental, since all the while the tradition critiques local exploitative social relationships in which the indigenous and African population was unethically "used" to maintain a tyrannical rural elite.

It also could be argued that the myth of El Señor de los Milagros carries within it an ambivalent identification of Christian resignation, for example, all we can do is pray and accept the will of God, however unjust. This reading, albeit perhaps accurate, fails to explicate significant elements of a national racialized contradiction. To say that a black Christ is merely and exclusively a mechanism of control would fail to see the multiple levels of resignification that such an identification with blackness gives to the symbolic Christ metaphor. If it is merely a question of exploitation, or of improving forms of oppression, a white Christ would do, as it has done in most other instances of Ecuadorian cultural religiosity. If, on the other hand, the argument is that a black Christ is much more economical in this regard, that is, that it is much more effective in doing what a white Christ had already been doing for centuries, then one must accept that, even unconsciously, there is more here than meets the eye, literally.

Even as an exploitative tool, "coloring" God to be like the oppressed populations has ambivalent meanings that could only be rearticulated to mark and solidify resistance in productive ways. This Christ metaphor seems to elaborate the use of blackness to further "nationalizing" representations. However, it also must be noted that this does not necessarily mean that these racial reidentifications either worked in exactly the same ways or produced the same power effects (Foucault 1980). This is particularly true since, until the 1830s, what is today Ecuador was still a colony of Spain and had not achieved any nation-state configuration, while the black Christ of Daule has been able to evolve from colonial to republican to modern times.

A comparative religious cultural process can also be seen in the development of other religious icons in the Latin American continent, such as the Virgin of Guadalupe in Mexico (Berkhart 2001; Brading 2001; Castillo 2000). The miraculous appearance of Christ's mother on American/Mexican soil is full of unresolved meanings beyond an initial reading of foreign religious domination—starting with the Virgin Mary's appearance on the sacred hill of a female Nahuatl deity which was still venerated by faithful Aztecs in colonial times, to the Virgin's self-revelation to an Indian peasant who was scorned and ridiculed by the established white/European church hierarchy. This syndrome is not lost on those who question the existence of Juan Diego (to whom the Virgin appeared), whom the Roman Catholic Church expediently canonized not so long ago. Just as in Daule, God and his mother are not on the side of the colonizers in Mexico but on that of the colonized. In this resignification, God and his mother are not white, or at least they are darker shades at significant times (the Virgin of Guadalupe is referred to as "la Virgen Morena" [the Dark Virgin]), and that racialization is not devoid of national importance. There is absolutely no way it could be.

Local/Global Forms of Blackness and Whiteness

Whiteness is a metaphor for safety.
(James Baldwin, *Nobody Knows My Name*)

This chapter assesses the problematic articulation of blackness in three Guayaquilean-Ecuadorian cultural contexts. Far from imposing an interpretation on these examples, I am using them to broaden the analytical realm traditionally afforded racial representation, especially within postcolonial contexts. I am particularly responding to scholarly analysis that provides evidence of the inherent and pervasive racism of postcolonial societies but does little to elaborate on the complex and ambivalent articulation of racial signifiers for the local population and national imaginary (see Benavides 2004b). By not furthering our understanding of the intricate manner in which racial knowledge both structures and is structured by all the groups involved, we will only continue to have a simplified and therefore unreal understanding of the way in which racial markers are played in the national imagination. As White states (2001: 24), when it comes to race and sex, "the silences that we refuse to tell, do matter."

As I argue, Kincaid (1990, 1996, 1997) has been particularly insightful in this regard by providing continual assessment of a postcolonial reality which can no longer be explained or fully understood from the perspective of the colonizer or even from a critique of the colonizer's history. Kincaid manages to uncover several of the layers of postcolonial domination which have as much to do with internal colonialism as with foreign cultural and economic occupation. She follows the lead of many other postcolonial writers and thinkers, many of them involved in the struggle for national liberation, who imagined a utopian panacea for their individual and communal problems. Writers (and fighters) like Baldwin (1984, 1998), Cabral (1974a, 1974b), Fanon (1965, 1967, 1970), and Freire (1992) believed that critical analysis, particularly racial analysis, was essential for the political liberation of all former and neocolonial possessions. It is this line of thought that Kincaid uses to reinterpret from a postcolonial perspective "sacred" realms previously untouched by social analysis, such as kin relationships and family structures. In the process, Kincaid questions the strict division or dichotomies between colonizer and colonized that seem to have permeated not only the political analysis of the world but so much of social science analysis directed at understanding that same global order. In this manner, far from creating separate and contrasting entities, Kincaid has managed to start unraveling a much more complex organization of racialization that does not fit neatly into dichotomous categories or that is even singular in its social signification.

It is in this same fashion that I understand the constitution of blackness in the three Ecuadorian examples discussed above. By no means do I present these as the only instance of racial ideology's ambivalent role in the constitution of Ecuador's national identity; rather, I consider them to be three salient and provocative cases. In each case, I believe the initial reading of a simplified racist state looking to distance the national imaginary from a constituted racial other fails to incorporate the multiple elements of each of these instances. In each of these cases, the supposed black other is not only accepted into the national fold but is actually used to represent the nation to itself (Silva) and to foreign others (Miss Ecuador), and to resignify both identities (as in the case of the black Christ).

This particular type of reconfiguration of racial politics in the differing constitution of Ecuadorian blackness belies a much more complex racial structure than initially articulated for postcolonial societies and especially as provided by Ecuadorian social scientists (e.g., Acosta et al. 1997; Ayala Mora 1983). These three instances mark not exceptions but a more pervasive racial structure that has ambivalently used blackness to constitute the nation as one and the other at the same time. Thus, blackness has served not only as a form of "otherizing" that allows identification but also as a means of self-identification that is not very far removed from the repressed desire of fetishized dark bodies (Julien 1997). It is in this negation of desire and its consequent constitution as repressed ideology that the form of self-identification betrays itself: by becoming that which it really wants and yet fails fully to be (see Butler 1993, 1997a, 1997b).

The constituting identity of repressed/failed desire is essential in a postcolonial subject marked by what it does not have. It is, as Oscar Wilde (1964: 71) pointed out from his colonial British prison, absence that defines one's existence. In either case, sex and the body form an essential element of repressed desire and identification that figures centrally in the racial remappings of the nation. In all three cases discussed, gender and sexual dynamics are clearly expressed and actually allow the full articulation of racial reconfigurations. Perhaps this is most succinctly captured in the Miss Ecuador Pageant, where, for the nation's delight, half-dressed women parade themselves in a faraway theater and other international events.

It is not only in the case of Miss Ecuador that gender and the body play a central role in teaching racial lessons to the social body. It is not a coincidence that Spanish pedagogy is based on the philosophy of "la letra con sangre entra" (reading and writing are taught with blood, or, figuratively, spare the rod, spoil the child). In each of the three instances I have discussed, this theory is being employed: the body is being used to imply a racial knowledge that is of ultimate relevance to the nation. From Silva's concern with an implicit and repressed sexuality that, precisely because of its absence, serves as a center of meaning viable for identification over the decades, to an effigy of Christ that is not only in a state of undress but also of physical torment (see Foucault 1980: 39). In each of these instances, we see the centrality of the body in its sexual expression and repression, both of which are concerned with the constitution of gender, which seems to be the main way in which race and racial knowledge are deployed and mark the construction of the nation's ambivalent homogeneous identity (see Kaminsky 1994; Morrison 1993; Stoler 1996, 2002).

As central to the role of gender and sex in the articulation of race is the racial discourse imposed on this gendered embodiment. Even though in all three cases I discuss I use examples of black racialization or blackness, there is another, silent, script playing a constitutive role: whiteness and its articulation in a global setting. Key in this regard is whiteness' difficulty in defining itself, since, clearly, one of its characteristics is its invisibility, or "unracialization." In a global context, we are almost always aware of whiteness as a race in spite of its not defining itself as such (Rosaldo 1989).

In a local, Ecuadorian, response, blackness is never an isolated sociocultural phenomenon. Rather, as we have seen in these three examples, it is blackness that confronts the least oppressed national identity: whiteness. It is not a coincidence that this normative form of national identification is also the one that most allows Ecuador to identify with an always competitive international market. Thus, localized forms of blackness are never purely local but, rather, are dramatically conflated against supranational forms of identification that structure the nation's body and racial ordering.

Just as blackness is not a purely local phenomenon, however, neither is whiteness a global one. Both racial identities are complex discourses that represent particular orderings of social phenomena at both the global and the local levels. It is this social process that allows the global order to restructure supranational spheres into, for example, the European Community and the North American Free Trade Agreement, including the U.S./Andean pact discussed in Guayaquil in November 2004. At the same time, localized social movements struggle more than ever. This process is clearly visible in Ecuador's Indian movement, represented by the Confederación de Nacionalidades Indígenas del Ecuador (Confederation of Indigenous Nationalities of Ecuador, CONAIE), which since 1990 has become the country's third-largest political party. Significantly, it has ousted the democratically elected president, Jamil Mahuad, was instrumental in having Lucio Gutiérrez elected to the presidency in 2002, slowed down the International Monetary Fund's restructuring policies, and has become the most important social movement in the country (Benavides 2004b; CONAIE 1998).

Just like its Indian counterpart, the black community in Ecuador has some effect on the global scene. The country's reoccurring need to represent itself within a black identity is a clear marker of its dynamic rearticulation of global and local racial identities and of the nonstatic character of racial discourses. It also speaks to a racial ordering that attempts to reify global regulation even when the national reality is not an otherly/ orderly one: whiteness and blackness (along with other racial identities) switch places as the nation-state sees fit.

But the reality is that, as with the local other, there is nothing settled about the global order. It is this complex reality which points to the dynamic reconfiguration of racial discourses and the impossibility of claiming that racial othering/ordering has one, and only one, predictable signification.

Conclusion
Guayaquilean Modernity and the
Historical Power of Sentiment

If history possesses a privilege, it would be, rather, insofar as it would
play the role of an internal ethnology of our culture and our rationality,
and consequently would embody the very possibility of any ethnology.

—MICHEL FOUCAULT, ON THE WAYS OF WRITING HISTORY

Sentiments and Hegemony

My book is a pure and simple fiction: it is a novel, but it is not I who
invented it, it is the relationship of our age and its epistemological
configuration with that whole mass of statements. So the subject is,
in fact, present in the whole book, but it is the anonymous "one"
who speaks today in everything that is said. (Michel Foucault,
On the Ways of Writing History)

In *Gramsci, Culture, and Anthropology* (2002), Crehan states that anthropology's understanding of hegemony has been highly influenced by
Raymond Williams' interpretation of Gramsci's work. For Crehan, hegemony's entering the discipline through Williams' *Marxism and Liter-*
ature (1977) is controversial. Although I agree with Crehan's historical
description, I am less convinced of the representational problematic of
hegemony's evolution in anthropology. Thus, my analysis of the political
production of sentiment in Guayaquil over the twentieth century not only
uses Williams' contribution to the notion of hegemony but also argues
the problematic nature of all representations, theoretical or otherwise. As
Crehan (2002; also see Barthes 1982) argues, I do not believe there to be
a completely right or truthful interpretation of Gramsci (or of any other
work, for that matter). One can have a more or less truthful interpretation
using different forms of empirical constraints and scientific regulations
(Wylie 1995), both of which, because of one's level of anthropological

awareness, are highly culture- and context-specific manifestations. It is mainly due to this fundamental representational ambiguity that I believe that the question of Gramsci's and Williams' contributions to anthropology is less concerned with origin than with articulation.

I am perhaps less convinced than most social scientists about the nature of any representational project, precisely because there is always a translation (Barthes 1972). It is this element of translation that, although denied at times to pretend some scientific objectivity, is inherent in any act of representation. Thus, in Crehan's (2002) case, for example, no matter her painstaking labor, we are still being offered her interpretation of Gramsci, and not Gramsci in the "original." And this is the catch: the "original" is accessible only as a translation and therefore is open to dispute. At the same time, the controversial aspect of the original's shortcoming becomes the most authentic form of representation to which we can aspire. Even if one reads Gramsci in the original Italian or translated into English, there is no way to know that we comprehend what he is saying or trying to get at, since our understanding is contingent on both individual variations and spatial and temporal differences.

I start this conclusion with a discussion of the nature of failed representational projects because I believe it to be essential to the current analysis of Medardo Ángel Silva and Guayaquil Antiguo and to developing a more acute understanding of the workings of postcolonial hegemony. It is this failed project of representation that is at the heart of the postcolonial debate in the humanities and the social sciences and that, in my judgment, offers a provocative way out of the currently conservative politics of academia (see Anzaldúa 1987; Kincaid 1988; McClintock, Mufti, and Shohat 1997; Mignolo 2000; and Spivak 1999 for critiques of conservative academic epistemologies). It is, however, also essential to realize that, even though no original moment, idea, image, or sentiment can be completely brought back (re-presented) in its original reality, they are still continually represented with even more effusive results and consequences.

It is the process of constant and productive re-presentation that provides an effusive production of realities (effects of power, in Foucauldian terms), which is even more fertile than the original idea or sentiment ever was or could ever be. It is thus that the representation of that which cannot be completely represented produces even more failed representational projects than could ever have been initially imagined.

This process of effusive representational production has strong structural similarities to the manner in which hegemony appears to be articulated and with the way in which Lacan's notion of the Real produces unending contexts of social reality without ever exhausting the Real itself (see Žižek 2002). In other words, it is the impossibility of representation which provides, in the first place, the process of representation its fecund context of productive ambiguity and possibility.

The hegemonic implications of the historical representations of sentiment are as paradoxical as they are productive. As I have noted in previous chapters, the constant preoccupation, initially Silva's and later his compatriots', with reproducing an effect that would express feelings in their purest form has fashioned a corpus of realities constrained by the social context in which they were formed and yet not completely limited by it. It is this process that I believe Williams most succinctly expresses as "structures of feeling." Silva, like his contemporaries, was not working in a vacuum but lived in a postcolonial setting in which notions of class, race, and sexuality were essential not only to one's day-to-day life but also to one's unconscious understanding of oneself as part of that livelihood.

Again, it is in this intimate level of self-identification and identity production that hegemony is at its most pervasive, and in which historical creation is essential. This is also where the metonymic invention of a Guayaquil Antiguo is most readily understandable. Guayaquileans' having spent almost a century producing particular structures of feeling that are only later expressible in an explicit form goes hand in hand with this historical imagining. This hermeneutical process also relates to the fact that the imagining of this original period may not fit empirical constraints but suits the sentiments being represented during this whole period. It is in this sense that the historical reality or truthfulness of Guayaquil Antiguo is less relevant than the question of what is it about the imagining of this particular period that produces such a depth of identification, both self and social, for generations of Guayaquileans.

Just like the pervasive imaginary of an ancient Kingdom of Quito (which never existed; see Salazar 1995), the image of Guayaquil Antiguo speaks to the productive structures of feeling of the city's inhabitants. This particular historical imaginary contains the love-filled, love-torn poems written by Silva, immortalized in *pasillos* sung by Julio Jaramillo, and later expressed in the growing conflict created by Guayaquileans having to exile themselves, for socioeconomic, sexual, and cultural reasons, to the United States since the 1960s. In all of these cultural products of effusive sentiment there are underlying structures of feeling richly textured with emotion and realities that are not only mutually understandable but also continually represented and passed down from one generation to the next.

Medardo Ángel Silva, I would argue, was single-handedly able to register an enormous level of discomfort and misrepresentation of what it felt like to be Guayaquilean during his lifetime. His descriptions of deeply heartfelt and vivid emotions made their way into popular poems and journalistic pieces that slowly came to represent a myriad of misplaced feelings that otherwise could not be (and had not been) named.

The overidentification with Silva's poetry and pain-filled images was productive in more ways than one. For example, the pain, solitude, isolation, abandonment, displacement, loneliness, and alienation (the list is inexhaustible) expressed in Silva's work and life must have been enormously resonant. There also must have been an immediate recognition of the medium in which Silva was working: a lone cultural icon without any social support for his lonely struggle. Silva's transmittal of emotions that are socially meaningful and relevant not only to his contemporaries but for generations of Guayaquileans also had enormous repercussions. It is this individualistic element, reified in the literary and historical criticism of his work and lived by Guayaquileans throughout the twentieth century, that, along with the content of his work, is most pertinent to the enculturation of a particular form of being Guayaquilean and to achieving a kind of modernity for the city.

The productive and hegemonic ambiguity of Silva's work and its usefulness in assessing modern Guayaquilean identity is many-stranded. One thread is the setting for the overidentification felt by tens of thousands of Guayaquileans, both during and after Silva's life. Obviously, not everybody has felt what Silva describes, being deserted by one's love, depressed by the thought of becoming twenty-one, or seeing the specter of "the yellow death" (malaria/yellow fever) spread over the city. Yet it is clear from the effusive production of the response to his work that the majority of the city's inhabitants must have lived similar situations, which produced, if not the same feelings, at least sentiments structurally close to those captured in Silva's work. It is because so many people can identify with Silva's work even when it does not exactly represent their feelings that an even greater level of effusive representation is possible. In other words, the constant trying-out, if you will, of those feelings closest to one's own without their being one's own, in many ways, fueled the continuous structures of feeling of postcolonial misidentification so central to Guayaquil's social identity, albeit always depicted in individual terms. It is this same failed representational project later engaged by the continual representation of Silva's oeuvre (including in this book) and the musical tradition of the *pasillo* which is central to the Guayaquilean production of popular culture (see next section).

Another strand of these structures of feeling concerns how the politics of misidentification, that is, of continuous cultural representation, is the most viable sign of modernity for Guayaquileans and their historical production of the city. Once again, the imaginary of Guayaquil Antiguo surfaces to reshape itself according to the needs of the growing and sprawling metropolis that Guayaquil became during the twentieth century. It is precisely the imaginary of Ancient Guayaquil, even though it was less than a hundred years old, that could be used as a mirror image of alterity for the city's contemporary negative identification.

Therefore, while the city entered into a conflict-ridden era of social upheaval and the dawning era of world wars, it no longer needed to define itself, or merely be trapped, within its contemporary existence. Instead, the historical recourse of an imaginary past, an essential for all national communities (see Anderson 1991; Renan 1990), allowed an identification approaching that which the city never had, or, more accurately, had supposedly lost. Thus, the city's inhabitants being able to come up with lost traditions, histories, and identities (even though these had never existed) could only mean that a transition had taken place, even though the transition was more a result of contemporary wishful thinking than of any profound empirical recognition of change. The change had occurred, of that there was no doubt, but the fact that it had to be marked by costumes and festivals such as *verbenas* and *chivas* rather than by the memory of massacre of hundreds of the city's workers, the exploitative migration pull of the city, and, ultimately, the reinscription of the population in new global forms of capitalist exploitation marks the fragile and transgressive nature of this historical change.

Modernity, in its intrusion into an overdetermined global-local marketplace and local-global production of culture (i.e., of lost traditions), was central in Guayaquilean identity throughout the twentieth century. The historical reality of Guayaquilean modernity has never been in question; rather, the actual representation of this modernity carries all the transgressive weight looked to be avoided and denied. Thus, the invention of traditions that never existed and represent only an elite minority was the safest way in which to denote a transition fraught with enormous conflict, particularly for those most affected—the migrants and poorer racialized segment of the city's population.

It is also striking that Ecuador's largest city, with an enormous population still living in utter poverty, would spend so much energy on traditions and investing itself in dynamic forms of popular cultural productions (see next section). Any assessment of this investment of energy must recognize the city's pains to protect the most fragile of productions: its own tenuous identity, one that had been so painstakingly constructed by Guayaquileans and yet continuously denied historically through their own efforts of self-identification. It is also out of this particular cultural paradox that Silva's poetry, and the metonymic device that Guayaquil Antiguo came to be at the same time, that the individuation of feelings enabled by the *pasillo* became central to the postcolonial politics of misidentification and the ultimate production of the city's Real.

I have hinted at a generalization of the politics of misidentification as a characteristic of postcolonial identity. I strongly agree with the interest in the aftermath of colonialism that since 1980 has edged out an area of research, defined as postcolonial studies, which aims to identify the centrality of this misidentification. I would, however, also like to use the politics of misidentification as the fuel for the hegemonic project I have sketched out in this work. Far from being a solid and monolithic apparatus, hegemony is most akin to the productive ambiguity of cultural representation and misidentification.

As I have argued, hegemony is articulated through the popular production and representations of Guayaquileans living their daily life in the most coherent ways possible. It also results from different cultural practices created and put into motion by the wish to hide the unending postcolonial desire for self-denial, which is at the center of misidentification. In other words, the colonial legacy of exclusion was not eliminated with the end of colonialism but merely internalized to serve the mechanism of power of the new political production of the nation-state. Therefore, race and sexuality come to play the hegemonic game in new and provocative ways once class hierarchy is dynamically set into place and articulated through sexual and racial differences.

Hegemony never was nor could it be a top-down mechanism, or one that was put into place exclusively by the ruling elite. This way of understanding political domination, and the central place of culture in its social reproduction, has been amply developed in the scenario of Latin America (Joseph and Nugent 1994; Silverblatt 1987) and furthered by the provocative theoretical scenarios of Michel Foucault's work (1990, 1996). I believe this book corroborates many of these findings by using a Foucauldian approach to better assess the subtle intricacies of hegemonic articulation. The establishment of a Guayaquilean identity and the representation of the city's modernity have never been an exclusive device of the city's white/mestizo ruling elite. As Hall (1997a, 1997b) has noted for other postcolonial scenarios, something always escapes the political realm, and it is in that escape that hegemony is secured in its most fragile constitution (Sayer 1994).

This is why identification as a Guayaquilean is supported by most Guayaquileans' forbidden and unfulfilled desires rather than by official definitions of what should or should not be wanted. This prohibited longing was present in Silva's life and is present in his literary production. It exists in the overwhelming response of the city's population to his work even when his racial and sexual background had to be silenced, although his lower-class background was not.

Again, it is in the historical production of the past (not only in visual representations but in the pride in the nonexistent past, the musical reconversion of the *pasillo,* and the black racialization of effigies of a black Christ and of beauty queens) that a form of power more grounded in culture was being articulated through and not outside of Guayaquilean identity and citizenship.

It is in this manner that continuous yet new forms of power are actively deployed within contemporary cultural practices that define what it means, both historically and in terms of daily life, to be from Guayaquil. At the same time, these cultural practices are not developed in a vacuum but within inherently exploitative capitalist relations bequeathed by colonialism but rearticulated within the postcolonial turn of events. It is also the escape from one's postcolonial alienation—inherent in the poems, music, historical images, and racialized descriptions of Guayaquil over the twentieth century—which further secures newer forms of hegemonic articulation and redistribution of power.

It is in this sense that Williams' reworking of Gramsci's concept of hegemony and the proposed structures of feeling make more sense. As in the articulation of dominance, the truthfulness of the concept is less relevant than the fact that it appears truthful even when, and many times precisely because, it is not. Williams' interpretation of hegemony has become a popular tool for anthropological assessment, and thus it is less a question of accuracy than of usefulness. Does Williams' proposal enable or limit our understanding of hegemony? Does this particular literary reading of Gramsci further our assessment of the production of culture within the wheels of power? I would hope that this book provides provocative answers to these questions and that it elicits a positive problematization of any and all initial answers.

Sentiment and Popular Culture

It's true that history holds a privileged position in my inquiry. The fact is that in our culture, at least for several centuries now, discourses are

> linked in a historical fashion: we acknowledge things that were said as coming from a past in which they were succeeded, opposed, influenced, replaced, engendered, and accumulated by others . . . in a culture like ours, every discourse appears against a background where every event vanishes. (Foucault, *On the Ways of Writing History*)

The decades since the 1980s have seen an enormous interest in the production of popular culture, particularly within in the context of Latin America (Monsiváis 1997; Rowe and Schelling 1991; Yudice, Franco, and Flores 1992). In many respects, this study is also a result of an interest in the inquiry into the production of popular culture and power in Latin America. One of my main concerns in this book has been to understand the production of popular culture within a postcolonial setting, and how its creation is related to larger questions of hegemonic domination and the social reproduction of culture/power in general. It is not surprising, therefore, that culture was of such profound interest to Antonio Gramsci and demanded so much of his time and thought while he was in prison (see Crehan 2002).

My objective has been to assess the problematics of the production of popular culture within the context of Guayaquilean identity and to strive to understand how these different popular expressions came to play essential historical roles in the city's development of hegemonic domination. It is in this respect that Medardo Ángel Silva's ambiguous poetic legacy can be better understood, not as a purely individual finished literary project but as one full of ambivalence and plausible redeterminations. It is on this unfinished cultural project and with poetic license to express despair over a painful existence that the *pasillo* form, Julio Jaramillo's musical legacy, and myriads of Guayaquileans are most comfortable in imprinting their emotional identification. It is also in the playful politics of racial and emotional reidentification that one can understand the pivotal place of popular culture in both expressing and channeling Guayaquil's postcolonial existence.

This is why popular culture has a central place in the hegemonic project of the city's national ethos as well as in the larger national and state context of Ecuador. The different ways in which popular culture is practiced allows for a continual process of identification that is never completely limited by the greater, failed, class projects of the city's white/mestizo elite and allows the incorporation of the majority population's own scheme of self-identification. It is also important to point out that these agency-filled cultural practices are constant emblems of resignification, and therefore are filled with effusive forms of social escape (see Hall 1997a).

It is also precisely because of this agency and escape, however, that these cultural practices both attain such popular and widespread appeal and serve as the ultimate devices for the city's domination. In other words, the cultural projects of the politics of self-identification are intimately tied to specific historical forms of social and economic domination. To some degree, this is easier to grasp in its initial context, in which Guayaquil's population, like that of all communities, must use those historical elements that are afforded to them at the moment of birth and must use them throughout their lifetimes. Once again, however, not even this historical specificity limits their cultural production but, rather, merely provides for an initial stage from which to continue their historical identification and social reproduction.

History, as a result of its hermeneutical constraints, is an ambiguous cultural project, or, as Foucault says (1993: 139), "Genealogy is gray, meticulous, and patiently documentary. It operates on a field of entangled and confused parchments, on documents that have been scratched over and recopied many times." Therefore, the reconstruction of the past provides not only the perfect scenario for self-construction or identification but also the adhesive, as it were, with which to bind the resulting discourses or cultural practices in what would aspire to be homogeneous and coherent identities. It is at this moment that cultural practices, particularly those recognized today as popular culture, articulate this greater hegemonic project as enabled by the historical discourses within and through which they are manifested.

Popular-culture practices, in many respects, correct for the failed project of representation. It is the ambiguity not the clarity that provides for or, rather, allows for the effusive identification afforded by Silva's pain-filled existence as expressed in his literary production. It is specifically the ambiguous production itself, the attempt to grasp an emotional reality that is beyond description, that most clarifies the successful discourse of Silva's words and postcolonial reality. It is the fact that Silva and the later continuous representations, in both non- and official explorations of his work, successfully fail to represent an unrepresentable Real and to which the city's population is clearly reacting, which mark these cultural productions as the powerful and hegemonic structures of feeling that they are.

One is left with differing effects of power, including an enormous ambiguity in the instance of cultural production itself; that is, the success of a particular popular expression is not defined by its being right or wrong but by its being closer to and more precisely articulating that which could not be articulated before. Thus, there is never an actual description of the absolute (see Bataille 1988), and perhaps not even a better approximation of it, but, rather, historically specific scenarios that are more and less accurately portrayed by those actually involved in their self-identifying production. This particular problematic articulation of the Real interrogates the central place of sentiments within the production of popular culture and, through that interrogation, that of the larger hegemonic project always in place before, during, and after the production of popular culture.

The sentimental nature of popular culture is also one of the larger issues engaged in this book. I have attempted to present, if not explain, a plausible scenario of processual resolution. I propose that feelings cannot be recognized as mere individual realities devoid of any social context. Thus, most scholars concerned with the social production of knowledge have been clearly willing to accept the individualistic nature of sentiment (since otherwise they would not function as feelings) but see it as grounded in very specific ways in the particular historical and social contexts in which it is produced (McCarthy and Franks 1989). It is also in this intersection that the greatest problem occurs: How do we understand sentiments as both individual and social at one and the same time? And how de we explain their continuous, almost obsessive, definition as individualistic responses?

Perhaps a brief assessment of Silva's poetic discourse will answer these questions. The popular response to his pain-filled poetics reflects structures of feeling similar to those he was expressing and that he consistently struggled with, as evidenced in his probable suicide. As previously stated, however, this does not mean that Guayaquileans' reaction supports the existence of the same issues Silva enunciated; rather, there is a generalized constraint that makes self-identification with the ethos plausible. This check, which I argue derives from a postcolonial legacy of misidentification, is what was expressed by Silva in the most economical form possible. This is also what I would describe as the nature of the Real within Guayaquilean identity politics—a problematic colonial legacy constantly repressed and denied, resulting in an effusive production of emotional and lived-in realities (see Žižek 2002).

Silva never actually accesses the Real (in the Lacanian sense—a Real which is described as the impossible by Bataille [1988] and even as the absolute in some of Foucault's own writing [see 1996]), since, because of its very nature, access is impossible. Rather, what Silva is able to do, by remaining truthful to his experience of the Real in the multiple and almost boundless realities he lived in his very short life, is describe the Real's symptoms and effects. Therefore, by remaining truthful to the disparaging postcolonial legacy as expressed in the areas circumscribed by racial, sexual, and class concerns (to mention those most readily defined and translatable), Silva was able to produce a popular cultural practice that surpassed his initial objectives, and would have surprised even him.

It is the fact that Silva was emotionally able to touch on these postcolonial discourses of race, class, and sexuality, that enabled Guayaquileans' identification with him throughout the twentieth century. They were also affected by and reacted to a postcolonial Real, even when their individual creations (or sentiments) might have been quite dissimilar to Silva's effusive sentimental production. I would thus argue that feelings are profoundly individual reactions, even if highly tempered by responses to specific historical setting and discourses and the greater cultural context. Sentiments are also, in this sense, individual reactions to a Real that avoids categorization and definition yet needs to be constantly defined and categorized if one is to survive. And it is a closer approximation to the truthfulness of this impossible representation that marks a successful project of popular culture, at least until it is no longer able to carry the burden of its own impossibility of representation.

This immediately brings us to another problem: the fact that structures of feeling are a continuous process that can be identified only in hindsight, when other structures of feeling are already unconsciously in place (R. Williams 1977). This more general issue also defines the ambiguous nature of sentimental representation, like all representation, in its most intimate expression. Popular culture is thereby able to more profoundly express, in its most successful projects, the countless ambiguous productions contained within the inexpressible nature of sentimental representation. It is this same ambiguity that allowed the popular-culture projects described in this book to articulate themselves differently over the twentieth century. At the same time, it is this ambiguous essence that allows Silva's work and the *pasillo* to continue to represent the ambiguity that Guayaquileans feel and perceive as essential to their and the city's current identification.

This is why the emotional portent of these projects of popular culture represents the feelings of Guayaquileans in New York City (as analyzed in Chapter 4) as an extension of the same feelings of exile inherent in Guayaquileans who still live within the physical confines of Guayaquil, that is, in-xiles. This process of self-identification also allows us, almost a century after Silva was writing, to see these particular structures of feeling expressed in all their power-filled productive ambiguity. These two elements, however—the successful contemporary representation of cultural projects and their visibility—also express the unending process of hegemonic articulation within the production of structures of feeling. Therefore, even though I discuss almost exclusively the particular modus operandi of Silva's, Guayaquil Antiguo's, and even the *pasillo's* nationally productive ambiguity, what is at work is the larger hegemonic project in which popular culture and historical production themselves are only part of the process in its full expression.

I hope that this book has successfully assessed the continuous nature of hegemonic articulation as enabled by continuously unconscious structures of feeling and the role that popular culture plays in this process. I strongly believe that this is Williams' insight with regard to understanding political domination, in general, and Gramsci's assessment of culture in its contribution to this cohesive political project, in particular. Thus, my study is a plausible case study, as requested by Williams, that can be used to empirically assess the workings of structures of feeling in the contemporary hegemonic project of the West. This is also why exhaustive and precise definitions are not prudent, or even possible, as argued by my analysis.

What I hope I have afforded is a way of looking at popular culture from a vantage point that is more inclusive of its contribution to the political project of the period and the irrelevance of the project once it can be seen and verbalized by the majority of the population. I believe my study expresses the particular forms assumed by cultural practices such as literary production, musical genres, historical imaginary, and racial configuration in producing a discursive ethos that most readily expresses the hidden meanings and sentiments in Guayaquil's postcolonial legacy. I also hope that this historical ethnography contributes to an understanding of the historical exigencies of the period and its hermeneutical transformation over the greater part of the last century. As with all representational projects, however, a somewhat accurate description is also a vivid depiction of the project's demise.

This book points to the myriad of structures of feeling operating in the project that is Guayaquil's politics of identity. Many of these are potent precisely because they are unconsciously articulated. Therefore, it helps to define some of these structures of feeling to gain a better understanding of the major social discourses that are being reworked. But in this respect, the book's theoretical contribution is of even greater importance. I would argue that it qualifies our perceptions of popular culture and their implications within the greater projects of identity politics and hegemonic domination. Rather than reifying the sterile debate of popular culture, as either authentic popular expression or mere popular capitalist consumption, it demands that we reassess the contribution of popular culture hidden in this Manichean division.

I would propose that the case studies I present support the argument that Silva's effusive production of sentiment allowed any number of Guayaquileans to survive the embattled postcolonial cultural field of their daily lives. At the same time that these cultural practices afforded a sense of survival they also provided a national identity that gave Guayaquileans the illusion of belonging, which was their painful point of departure in the first place. Enabled by the knowledge that their pain was not devoid of social ripples, even when it could be only individually felt and expressed, Guayaquileans found a space for solace and identification, no matter how fragile or unsettled. It is in that fantasy-filled identification of themselves as belonging that Guayaquileans' connection with Silva's sentimental project created strong hegemonic influences while securing its popular success—and this in spite of their acute postcolonial knowledge that fitting in was a virtual impossibility.

We might wonder whether his recognition of the inescapable conflict that he lived and experienced is what led Silva to suicide (if suicide it was). The irreparable sense of the Real made for the construction of the tragic sign of the modern that so many Guayaquileans have adopted with unparalleled zeal and that also made its presence felt in Julio Jaramillo's life, in the evolution of the coastal *pasillo,* and among the generation of Guayaquileans who sought an identity by drinking themselves into oblivion through this popular cultural project. But it is also in this artificial identification (because all identifications are always artificially authentic; see Baldwin 1990) that Guayaquileans have seen their most intimate desires betrayed.

The effusive sentiment of the *pasillo* and Silva's poetry has allowed for the freezing of the larger quest for the Real that still haunts the production of the city and its national ethos. This is why any contemporary ethnography of the city is haunted by productive specters of race, class, and sexuality. This is also why other structures of feeling are unconsciously being articulated to take care of the desire for the Real which has not been, and never can or will be, totally addressed. In this manner, the multiple tragic identifications under the influence of alcohol and lyrical signification are most productive in their negative or inverse reformulations. It is not so much in the accurate representation of pain that a postcolonial legacy has been embedded in our identity as in what constantly escapes that representation. Once again, a tragic constitution raises its head to resignify our point of departure: melancholy, internal alienation, and the impossibility of resolution.

It is also in this sense that Guayaquilean modernity is most easily read as the sign of the tragic, because a postcolonial legacy is always indebted to a culture's failure to give meaning to the initial division (in all possible categorizations) which also forms the constitutive nature of one's identity. This is the same conflict rearticulated since Caliban's time, as so deftly expressed by William Shakespeare and his perception of language and projects of popular culture as modes of representation (1994: 39): "You taught me language, and my profit on 't; Is I know how to curse." It is this same conflict expressed by Jamaica Kincaid (1997) in her critique of the impossibility of postcolonial language: having to use the same language of the colonizer to name oneself and to define one's hatred for those who imposed their language (and with it their culture and identity) on us.

Perhaps popular culture is one of those devices that best serves to rearticulate the failed representational project that postcolonial citizenship and nationalism inherently espouse. For this, Silva's historical structures of feeling are enormously successful by giving new meaning to a tragic oblivion and thereby escaping its hegemonic devices for brief moments, only to be rearticulated in old/new (see Hall 1997a) productive ways. It is this never-ending project of cultural hegemony that allows not a repetitive circular motion but an elliptical one, always landing us back where we started but in a different place (see Butler 1997b). Therefore, it is through the enabling of practices of popular culture that Guayaquilean identity was afforded throughout the twentieth century, albeit in slightly different similar ways.

Sentiments, Life, and the Limitations of the Real

A nightmare has haunted me since childhood: I am looking at a text that I can't read, or only a tiny part of it is decipherable. I pretend to read it, aware that I'm inventing; then suddenly the text is completely scrambled, I can no longer read anything or even invent it, my throat tightens and I wake up. (Foucault, *On the Ways of Writing History*)

The motivation for writing this book and carrying out this research came out of a *chupa* on a memorable New York night in 1998. At that moment and again as I write these last pages, a question about life as expressed in its complete, chaotic beauty returns as the central subject. Questions of identity, sentiment, hegemony, and popular culture are totally dependent on the subject of life; everything else is absolutely irrelevant.

Paradoxically, it has not been easy to keep life (in its broadest and most mysterious sense) the central concern of my research and this book. There are several reasons for this; some relate to life itself, and others to the nature of social science research within the postmodern context of our western academy. Ultimately, it is my belief, and hope, that, even though I do not explicitly address "life" until this last section, it is constantly implied and reworked in every part of the book and the research on which it is based.

An enormous problem with using such a generalized category as "life" is that, in many ways, I am going against the very nature of anthropology's (and, I would argue, the other social sciences') need to tackle specific areas of life in general. At its worst, anthropology's approach has produced a compartmentalized idea which does violence to the integrated aspect of culture and life; however, at its best, this narrow cultural focus rightfully expresses the need for clarity and understanding within a manageable landscape rather than a gigantic void, in which it is easy to lose one's grounding.

My research has therefore been particularly rewarded by a rereading of excerpts from two thinkers who, in their own way, emphasize the central tension of life as the subject of research and literary endeavor. The first quotation is from Antonio Gramsci's *Letters from Prison, II,* in which he states (in Crehan 2002: 13), "It seems to me that it is not difficult to find splendid formulas for life, but it is difficult to live." This insight, written in prison no less and coming from the initial proponent of hegemony (the theoretical fuel of my work) reminded me of the ultimate importance of life in the nature of all human endeavor.

The second quotation had a similar effect. In *Brown,* Richard Rodríguez, while assessing his racial concern of Latino literary production, states (2004: 12), "Literature cannot by this impulse betray the grandeur of its subject—there is only one subject: What it feels like to be alive. Nothing is irrelevant. Nothing is typical."

Both of these quotations were useful in reminding me of why I had embarked on this research project and not another. They also reminded me of the central place of life and being alive in any research concerned with hegemonic articulation as it is spelled out in people's lives through poetry, music, and the historical reproduction of literary and racial images. There is no doubt that remembering Silva, listening to *pasillos,* lamenting not having been part of the pageantry of Guayaquil Antiguo are all nostalgic devices constrained by enormous levels of hegemonic self-domination. But at the same time, they are quite sincere and agent-filled responses to life's folly, and a successful mechanism (if not, they would not be as popular) through which to support the pain, alienation, and daily oblivion that a Guayaquilean postcolonial existence entails.

The effusive sets of sentiment produced throughout the twentieth century, conveniently captured as structures of feeling, are also understandable as a coping mechanism for sustaining daily life. Once again, it is not a question of the truthfulness or even the authenticity of the sentiments but, rather, that the sentiments individually produced were able to embellish a particular political project: the creation and maintenance of a Guayaquilean identity. Thus, the production of these sentiments, and their being right, wrong, or accurate, is irrelevant to the larger reality of their survival, usefulness for self-identification, and maintenance for some semblance of normality—normality that is denied by the impossibility of life's being typical in any fashion (as Rodríguez' quotation reminds us).

In a truly paradoxical fashion, however, it is also in this artificial production of sentiment that a new tradition is constructed, and in which new forms of authenticity are being created to expand the existing sense of identity. I have described these forms as artificial to point out the arbitrariness of sentiment itself and even its hegemonic success in the development of cultural practices that maintain their historical consistency. I think it is quite clear that any sentiment would do, and that any cultural practice would serve to maintain that feeling. In this historical ethnography, I have defined certain sentiments of grief and painful existence and cultural practices that nostalgically reify these sentiments in a national historical account, but I could as easily have had to describe other sentiments and other cultural practices.

So despite the beauty, pain, and life contained within both sentiments and cultural practice, my primary objective has been to point out these discourses' centrality, that is, that there will always be sentiments and cultural practices within any form of nationalizing hegemonic enterprise. It is impossible to disregard both emotions and specific cultural practices when we want to understand the political project of domination that we and our society are so invested in and intricately involved with. The task, therefore, is to define what these sentiments are, how are they expressed (and repressed) within particular cultural practices even as they are incorporated into specific historical discourses that struggle for their own survival. It is at that point that some hope is offered when culture and emotion are not disregarded in the social project that comprises our society and, more important, when a bridge is built between research and the life that fuels it and on which it is based.

Finally, I want to return to the notion of the Real. I have used Lacan's notion of the Real to describe the underlying principle that seems to motivate the production of social realities without its ever being existentially exhausted in its own right. This particular theoretical construct, however, must also incorporate the nature of the Real's transformation, in the sense that, like everything else that it is affecting, it cannot remain still or be static under any circumstances. Instead, what you have is an indefinable Real that, by its very nature, is constantly changing and transforming itself to adapt to life's shifting concerns as reflected in people's reaction to the hegemonic national transformations.

This constant shifting, even under implied and hidden circumstances, is also a powerful purveyor of an attachment to new cultural practices and their transformation into tradition. The powerful and constant movement of the Real, in a profound way, allows for the possibility of accommodation to the introduction of new cultural practices that more powerfully reflect the changing times. At the same time, this movement is what allows these new transformations to be incorporated as tradition even though they have never existed (e.g., the fictitious Guayaquil Antiguo), continue to produce an enormous effect of sentiments (as in the notion of a Guayaquil Antiguo), and, ultimately, permit the "invention of tradition" (see Hobsbawm and Ranger 1983). It is this same transformative nature that enables the introduction and reification of cultural practice as tradition. That tradition is also highly connected with a sense of postcolonial nostalgia and intimately linked to one's production of oneself and a concurring national identity.

The century-long evolution of Silva's life and *pasillos* is testament to the even longer historical production of Guayaquilean identification and hegemonic articulation. If anything, this book has tried to portray a very brief moment in the production of that identity and hegemony, but, because of the book's descriptive nature, it betrays its almost passé existence. As Williams succinctly states, these particular structures can be described only in hindsight, in historical perspective, once they no longer play the central role of hegemonic identifier within which they were produced and served as central fixtures.

It is also because of the very transformative nature of the Real that it is with no little nostalgia that I end this part of the research, conscious as

I am that Silva, the *pasillo*, and the mythical notion of Guayaquil Antiguo no longer serve the purpose that they served during the last decades of the twentieth century. What hegemonic and identification purposes they will serve, if any, is once again a question of genealogy and the production of popular culture. This hegemonic process also belies the fact that there are other, stronger, forms of sentimental structures being affected, developing strong forms of hegemonic articulation that will, and can, be described only in decades to come.

It is in this sense that I speak of a limitation of the Real, because it always leaves us wanting yet unable to fully articulate that which we carry in our hearts and life. As it would be futile to describe the Real, it also would be pointless to describe structures of feeling in the present, since their very expression is enabled by our own historical perspective and existence. Instead, what we have is the path of genealogy and popular culture (see Foucault's quotation at beginning of this chapter) by which to assess the transformative nature of hegemonic domination and the frustrating and limiting productive effect of the Real. I cannot resist, ending the book, and the larger part of my research with lines from Silva's poem "Medianoche de ausencia" (Midnight of Absence), with all its hegemonic implications (1964: 14):

> A veces en la noche, al sonar doce campanadas (la hora de los aparecidos! . . .) un inefable perfume, el inefable perfume de tus rosas vaga por mi habitación . . . Oigo unos dulces pasos . . . Y un aliento de lirios aroma el éxtasis . . . Vuelvo los ojos, y sólo contemplo, inexorable, inmóvil sobre la cornisa, el cuervo de Poe . . . E inclino la cabeza, y sigo burilando aquellos dulces poemas que, acaso, tú no leerás nunca![1]

Hopefully, these ambiguous poetic sentiments better express the ambivalent project of identity and hegemonic production contained within the unending creation of life, in Guayaquil and other postcolonial settings. And as the city continues to re-create romanticized representations of Silva ("Compilación de obra de Medardo Ángel Silva" 2004) and of Guayaquil Antiguo in a historical park (*Parque Histórico Guayaquil;* see Figures 9 and 10), one must wonder both about the productive nature of these obsessive ideological attachments and their fragile hold on hegemonic reformulation within the postmodern parameters of a new century.

Notes

Introduction

Epigraph, "El alma en los labios" (With the Soul on My Lips [Silva N.d.: 133]; all translations are mine):

> I apologize for not having words with which
> to declare the unutterable passion that devours me;
> to express my love I can only, my beloved,
> pierce my chest and in your silken hands,
> leave my beating heart that adores you!

1. "Lo tardío" (That Which Is Too Late):

> Mother: the sickly and sad life you have given me
> is not worth all the pain it has cost you;
> it is not worth, Mother, your supreme suffering,
> this source of mourning and melancholy.

2. "Aniversario" (Birthday):

> But, who paid any attention to the explanations?
> There is so much to observe in the black corners!
> And besides, it is better to contemplate the pigeons
> on the lines; to follow the lighted path
> of a ray of sun or the excited twirling
> of an insect dressed all in yellow silk or a
> fly of golden hair and wings the color of the moon.
>
> The sun is the best friend of childhood!
> It tells us so many beautiful lies from a distance!
> It has a shine as remarkable as that of a new ounce!

Delivering its gold so well that nobody is left without its own!
And it was because of him that we didn't pay
attention to the explanations;
Aladdin the sorcerer evoked so many visions
of a Thousand and One Nights, of one thousand fantasies,
and intoxicated with dreams, our simple souls, without
thinking, extended their desirous hands
like one who seeks at night a handful of diamonds.

3. This phrase—"Do you understand?" ("¿Entiendes?")—may have ambiguous sexual meanings. A recent volume edited by Bergmann and Smith (1995) on queer Latin/o American identities uses this same phrase as its suggestive title: *¿Entiendes?: Queer Readings, Hispanic Writings*.

4. *Mariposear* is commonly used to refer to queer men in a somewhat demeaning manner. For example, a gay man may be referred to as butterflylike (*mariposón*). Without necessarily "reading" anything into the text, both the use of this phrase and the visual fascination with the boy being described have, at the very least, quite explicit homoerotic undertones.

Chapter 1

Epigraph, "La fuente triste: II" (The Sad Fountain [Silva 2000: 301]):

You say my sadness has no reason,
I cry even when the sadness is not mine . . .
Ay, but that is my beauty:
To cry for those who drop no tear.

1. "Velada del sábado" (Saturday Night [Silva 2000: 98]):

The tragic moon marches between gaseous clouds . . .
Without being touched the doors have closed . . .
Fear, like a wolf, paces through the house . . .
The names of people long dead are pronounced . . .

The grandfather, for the eighth time, lights the lamps . . .
All of a sudden, shocked profiles are illuminated . . .
It is when the dwarfish devil crosses the bedrooms
And awakens, in tears, the sleeping children.

2. "De la vieja Francia" (From Ancient France [Silva 2000: 51]):

To you the bowing of wigs,
As the white fans open,
Over the silky surface of the white nape;

Because your name tastes like honey and roses,
And to say it is to recall the rich
Atlases of sumptuous feasts.

3. "A una danzarina" (To a Ballerina [Silva 2000: 47–48]):

Your eyes—perverse magicians—
Are like two black lakes
In whose calm depths,
With Islamic purity,
Cruelty and sadness
Sleep in safe asylum . . .

Your mouth—purple lily—
Flower of slumber and delirium,
Is an Oriental flower,
In whose fragile bosom,
Next to the honey, the patient
Drinks from the poison too.

4. "Estancias: XXV" (Silva 2000: 109):

My spirit is a treasure chest for which you have the keys
Oh, mysterious Loved One, my passion and my muse.
It is futile to wait for your grave sweet eyes
As I feel that the Intruder's shadow falls over me.

But my soul continues without paying attention
To the anxiety of time and the pain of living,
It will wait for you, just as an attentive virgin,
With the devout lamp of her love lit.

5. "Lo tardío" (That Which Is Too Late [Silva N.d.: 88]):

Mother . . .
Why is it that, as I dreamed my childish dreams,
In my crib, surrounded by soft cloths,
From a corner of the room a serpent did not appear
That, when tightening itself against my innocent neck,
With the flexible grace of a beloved woman,
Would have liberated me from life's horrors? . . .

Not to live would be preferable to this life of tears,
This daily massaging with hardship the bread of our songs,
The slow labor of this exquisite pain
Of a soul intoxicated by light and sick of the infinite.

6. "Estancias: XX":

How distant that timid and sweet adolescent
From this pale morbid subject, saddened for having sinned . . .
He took from the bad tree the voluptuous flower
And his heart has been poisoned.

7. "Aniversario" (Birthday [Silva N.d.: 106–108]):

Today I will be twenty years old: anguish without name
Of no longer being a child and becoming a man,
To reason with Logic and proceed
According to the august professors of Common Sense.

My years are hard, and they are barely twenty;
We now age so prematurely,
We live so fast, quickly, we go so far,
Facing the shadows, with our backs to the Sunrise,
And alone with the Sphinx always inquisitive.
. . . . . .
Today, it is no longer an adolescent gaze and naïve smile
But, rather, the tired gesture of an early anguish,
And there is the soul, once a white dove,
Sad from so many dreams and so many readings.

8. "No alegra la sabiduría" (Wisdom Gives No Joy [Silva 2000: 309]):

Wisdom does not help,
Because to know is pain,
And causes melancholy,
Our only reason for existing.

The task of analyzing
Has lost us,
And the hurricane of longing
Threw our ship to the unknown
Sea.

9. "Estancias: XII" (Silva 2000: 97):

Wherever she went tragedy struck,
She had the beauty of somebody who has been predestined,
And on a feverish autumn night she appeared
Pictured in her immense dark eyes . . .

And it was under the auspices of Saturn
That I threw away my flowery youth at her feet . . .
Since then I suffer this taciturn state
That makes my adolescence an eternal night.

10. "La fuente triste: XIII" (The Sad Fountain [Silva 2000: 305]):

The illness I have
Only my heart knows:
Since my heart will never say it,
Nobody will ever know.

11. I use "homosexual" in its most descriptive form, to mean same-sex attraction, in contrast to "gay" and "queer," which have more specific cultural and generational connotations.

12. "En la actitud del que ya nada espera" (One Who No Longer Expects Anything [Silva 2000: 310]):

In the attitude of someone who no longer waits
We are intoxicated by abstract theories,
Dreaming to make spring erupt
From the infection of our own wounds! . . .

Lord, against your law we have sinned
And, instead of the sweet soul you gave us,
On our final day we offer you
A leper's heart, old and sad!

13. "Canción del tedio" (Song of Boredom [Silva N.d.: 89–90]):

Oh, futile life, sad life
that we don't know what to do with!
Everything that exists tires us
Because it is known and common!

Frivolous female lips
Provide us the fatal trap!
Dammed those who heard in the Sirens
The voice of mortal sin!

And with that cool calmness
Of those who initially do not see,
I will go to search for my dark peace,
It matters not where . . . But I will go!

Chapter 2

Epigraph, "Mi ciudad" (My City [Silva 2000: 239; emphasis mine]):

> My city is surrounded by hills
> And, if above these hills the curved moon shines,
> *In the yards the dogs sadly howl,*
> *At the homeless specter of the yellow death.*
>
> *Its streets have provincial memories,*
> *Childish happiness its wooden houses,*
> Familial sweetness its simple mornings,
> And its delicate spring is always a lie.
>
> Oh, city of Santiago, city both small and mine,
> That harbors my joy and melancholy
> And the lyrical universe that inside my chest I carry!
>
> Image of my soul so many times betrayed,
> That triumphs more beautiful, every day more fulfilled,
> With a purer rhythm and a new ideal.

1. "La ronda de noche" (The Night Flight [Silva 2000: 243; emphasis mine]):

> (The Neighborhood of San Alejo)
> It rolls, like a teardrop in the smooth air,
> The voice of the ancient bells: one . . .
> And its echo passes, light as a marine bird,
> Over the white roofs of moon sparkle.
>
> It fakes being a spear, the ancient tower of San Alejo,
> At whose distance shine, trembling, a little star . . .
> Damp side streets . . . *Houses from older times,*
> With windows that the wind, as a thief, shakes . . .
>
> An unfortunate poem trembles in the pure air . . .
> A streetlight twinkles: its wink reflects on the wall
> *And makes even greater the sadness of the dirty yards . . .*
>
> The flight of the night is lost in the street
> And the rumor of the arms, in the shadows, leaves
> *Epic memories of colonial days.*

2. It is worth mentioning that this volume, originally published in the 1930s, revamped national literature and introduced a new period of politically infused magical realism, which would see its greatest success throughout the continent in the decades to come.

3. "Calle Villamil" (Villamil Street [Silva 2000: 241; emphasis mine]):

From the voluminous trees falls, onto the street,
A long, wet shadow over the heavy air,
An oppressive sadness, a melancholy
Against which the cloistered sun can do nothing.

And it is more painful, at midday,
To look at the sky and muddy streets,
And to see, as if through slim blinds,
A brief glimpse of the luminous heavens.

Ah, but in the blue nights of fluorescent
Moon, *what lyricism in the dark street*
And in the homes that pretend to be reclining elders!

What legends are evoked from the half-lit yards,
Made visible by the reflection of a street lamp, projecting on the wall
The shadows of somebody who is walking away!

4. "En el bar" (In the Bar [Silva 2000: 245; emphasis mine]):

In between so many individuals who talk, drink, and smoke,
The poet feels strange. The fog
Of the tobacco flies through the air, and disappears
With a certain voluptuous female fragility.

The tired forehead to dream is inclined
And one longs for the enchantment of that woman,
Soft, as in a Sèvres crystal cup
The swift explosion of the pale bubbles.

To dream, dream . . . ? What are happiness and sadness worth,
Like a goblet of beer foam,
That lasts what as footprints last in the sea . . .

The lie is worth more, lasting illusion,
of the certain eternity of the impossible dream
and the remote star which we will never reach.

Chapter 3

Epigraph, "Nuestro juramento" (Our Agreement [Jaramillo 1997]):

If I die first, it is your promise
that over my cadaver you will let fall,

all the tears that stem from your sadness
so that everybody finds out about our love.

1. "Nuestro juramento":

If you die first I promise
that I will write the history of our love
with my whole soul full of feeling
I will write it with blood, with ink blood from my heart.

2. "Nuestro juramento":

We have promised to love each other until death
And if the dead love,
After death love each other even more.

3. "Un disco más" (One More Song; the gender markers in the song imply
a man referring to a woman):

If you remember this melody
You will also remember you were mine
When you kissed me in a frenzy
Swearing to love me forever.

4. "Fatalidad" (Fatality):

Fatality, cruel sign
That in my life took away my most precious jewel
Which your love offered me
The constant warmth of your tenderness
Which, impatient as a child, I longed for from you
Woman, why did you go away?

5. "Fatalidad":

Evening of shocking sky
Your enchantment I remember every time
Romance of a moment I once lived
With my soul illuminated by your gaze
A love that nobody had for me
Although blind destiny parted our ways
And stricken, I lost you forever.

Chapter 4

1. "I am somebody here, over there I was nobody, you add and you lie: Johnnie the Man" (p. 42).

2. "Just put in the head, they asked, and you responded libidinously: which head because the bird [slang for penis] does not have shoulders."

3. "You were lost . . . to eat [slang for fucking] a faggot not only brings bad luck but also is a stigma."

4. "I am lost, you gravely judge, because you know that pretty soon you will again be Johnnie the Donkey, with a respectable woman as a wife and a lucrative business in response to the dog's life you led."

5. "Your brow is furrowed and wasted as a result of the decision to go back and never return, at least for a long while, you correct yourself, as you respond to your family's questions, as they are not weary of admiring your shirt and hairstyle; you are a dream, Johnnie."

6. "They have not forgotten it, this world has stopped being yours, it does not belong to you, and, even though many years have passed, you continue to be a juvenile delinquent, faggot fucker ['chachero de maricones']".

7. "You laugh, you are a son of a bitch, Johnnie, and you admit it while you prepare the papers to return to Los Angeles in search of your identity and core."

Conclusion

1. Sometimes at night, when it chimes twelve (the hour of the apparitions! . . .) a delicate perfume, the delicate perfume of your roses travels through my room . . . I hear some sweet steps . . . And a breath of lilies surmounts the ecstasy . . . I glance back, and I see only, unflinching, standing still over the heading, Poe's crow . . . And I incline my head, and keep laboring these sweet poems that, perhaps, you will never read!

Bibliography

Abrams, Phillip. 1988. "Notes on the Difficulty of Studying the State (1977)." *Journal of Historical Sociology* 1(1): 58–89.

Abu El-Haj, Nadia. 2001. *Facts on the Ground: Archaeological Practice and Territorial Self-Fashioning in Israeli Society.* Chicago: University of Chicago Press.

Acosta, Alberto, et al. 1997. *Identidad nacional y globalización.* Quito: Banco Central del Ecuador and Corporación Editora Nacional.

Adoum, Jorge Enrique. 1983. *entre Marx y una mujer desnuda: Texto con personajes.* Quito: Editorial El Conejo.

———. 1995. *Ciudad sin ángel.* Mexico City: Siglo Veintiún Editores.

Aguilera Malta, Demetrio. 1970. *Siete lunas y siete serpientes.* Guayaquil: Hispanoamérica.

———. 1977. *Canal Zone.* Mexico City: J. Mortiz.

———. 1980. *Don Goyo.* Translated by John Brushwood and Carolyn Brushwood. Clifton, N.J.: Humana Press.

Allen, Catherine. 1988. *The Hold Life Has: Coca and Cultural Identity in an Andean Community.* Washington, D.C.: Smithsonian Institution Press.

Allende, Isabel. 2003. *Mi país inventado: Un paseo nostálgico por Chile.* New York: Rayo.

Alonso, Ana María. 1988. "The Effects of Truth: Re-Presentation of the Past and the Imagining of a Community." *Journal of Historical Sociology* 1(1): 58–89.

———. 1995. *Thread of Blood: Colonialism, Revolution, and Gender on Mexico's Northern Frontier.* Tucson: University of Arizona Press.

Althusser, Louis. 1971. *Lenin and Philosophy, and Other Essays.* London: New Left Books.

Álvarez, Silvia. 1989. *Tecnología pre-hispánica, naturaleza y organización cooperativa en la cuenca del Guayas.* Guayaquil: CEAA-ESPOL.

Anderson, Benedict. 1991. *Imagined Communities: Reflections on the Origin and Spread of Nationalism*. London: Verso.

Andrade, Xavier. 1995. "Pancho Jaime: Masculinidad, violencia, imágenes y textos de una narrativa popular." *Ecuador Debate* (Quito) (December).

———. 1997. "Carnaval de masculinidades." *ICONOS* (Quito) 2: 71–84.

———, and Gioconda Herrera (editors). 2001. *Masculinidades en Ecuador*. Quito: FLACSO and UNFPA.

Anzaldúa, Gloria. 1987. *Borderlands/La Frontera: The New Mestiza*. San Francisco: Aunt Lute Books.

Archivo Histórico del Guayas. N.d. http://www. guayaquilhistorico.org.ec/webpages/fundacion.htm.

Arias, Arturo. 2001. *The Rigoberta Menchú Controversy*. Minneapolis: University of Minnesota Press.

"El arte se junta con la medicina." 2001. *El Universo* (May 31).

Austerlitz, Paul. 1992. *Dominican Merengue in Regional, National and International Perspectives*. Ann Arbor, Mich.: University Microfilms.

Ayala Mora, Enrique. 1983. *Nueva historia del Ecuador*. 13 vols. Quito: Corporación Editora Nacional and Ed. Grijalbo.

———. 1993. *Estudios sobre historia ecuatoriana*. Quito: Tehis-Iadap.

———. 1995. "Historia." *Diners Magazine* 16 (March).

Baldwin, James. 1972. *No Name in the Street*. New York: Laurel Books.

———. 1984. *Notes of a Native Son*. Boston: Beacon Press.

———. 1990. *Just above My Head*. New York: Laurel Books.

———. 1998. *Nobody Knows My Name*. New York: Library of America.

Barnes, TaNesha. 2001. *World Trade*. Documentary.

Barthes, Roland. 1972. *Mythologies*. New York: Noonday Press.

———. 1982. *A Barthes Reader*. New York: Hill and Wang.

———. 1992. *Incidents*. Berkeley & Los Angeles: University of California Press.

Bataille, Georges. 1986. *Erotism: Death and Sensuality*. San Francisco: City Lights Books.

———. 1988. *Guilty*. San Francisco: Lapis Press.

Benavides, O. Hugo. 2001. "Torn between Two Lovers: Continuous Approximations." *Jouvert: Journal of Post-Colonial Studies* 6(1–2) (Fall). http://social.chass.ncsu.edu/jouvertv6il/lover.htm].

———. 2002. "The Representation of Guayaquil's Sexual Past: Historicizing the Enchaquirados." *Journal of Latin American Anthropology* 7(1): 68–103.

———. 2003 "Seeing Xica and the Melodramatic Unveiling of Colonial Desire." *Social Text* 76, 21(3): 109–134.

———. 2004a. "Anthropology's Native Conundrum: Uneven Histories and Developments." *Critique of Anthropology* 24(2): 159–178.

———. 2004b. *Making Ecuadorian Histories: Four Centuries of Defining Power.* Austin: University of Texas Press.

Benavides, O. Hugo, and G. Melissa García. 2001. "Medardo Ángel Silva and the City: Video Documentary Project." Video interviews on file with authors.

Bergmann, Emilie, and Paul Julian Smith (editors). 1995. *¿Entiendes? Queer Readings, Hispanic Writings.* Durham, N.C.: Duke University Press.

Berkhart, Luise. 2001. *Before Guadalupe: The Virgin Mary in Early Colonial Nahuatl Literature.* Albany, N.Y.: Institute of Mesoamerican Studies, University of Albany.

Borges, Jorge Luis. 2003 [1944]. *Ficciones.* Madrid: Alianza Editorial.

Brading, David. 2001. *Mexican Phoenix: Our Lady of Guadalupe, Image and Tradition across Five Centuries.* Cambridge: Cambridge University Press.

Butler, Judith. 1993. *Bodies That Matter: On the Discursive Limits of "Sex."* New York: Routledge.

———. 1997a. "Gender Is Burning: Questions of Appropriation and Subversion." In *Dangerous Liaisons: Gender, Nation, and Postcolonial Perspectives,* edited by A. McClintock, A. Mufti, and E. Shohat, pp. 381–395. Minneapolis: University of Minnesota Press.

———. 1997b. *The Psychic Life of Power.* Stanford, Calif.: Stanford University Press.

Cabral, Amilcar. 1974a. *Return to the Source.* New York: Monthly Review Press.

———. 1974b. *Unity and Struggle: Speeches and Writing.* New York: Monthly Review Press.

Calderón Chico, Carlos. 1999. *Medardo Ángel Silva: Crónicas y otros escritos.* Guayaquil: Archivo Histórico del Guayas.

Castañeda, Quetzil. 1995. "'The Progress That Chose a Village': Measuring Zero-Degree Culture and the 'Impact' of Anthropology." *Critique of Anthropology* 15(2): 115–147.

———. 1996. *In the Museum of Maya Culture: Touring Chichén Itzá.* Minneapolis: University of Minnesota Press.

Castillo, Ana (editor). 1996. *Loverboys.* New York: Plume.

———. 2000. *La diosa de las Américas: Escritos sobre la Virgen de Guadalupe.* New York: Vintage Español.

Cervone, Emma, and Freddy Rivera (editors). 1999. *Ecuador racista: Imágenes e identidades.* Quito: FLACSO.

Cevallos García, Gabriel. 1960. *Visión teórica del Ecuador.* Mexico City: J. M. Cajica, Biblioteca Ecuatoriana Mínima.

"Las chivas, una forma diferente de diversión." 2003. *El Universo* (July 9).

Cifuentes, María Ángela. 1999. *El placer de la representación: La imagen femenina ante la moda y el retrato (Quito, 1880–1920).* Quito: Abya-Yala.

"Compilación de obra de Medardo Ángel Silva se presenta hoy." 2004. *El Universo* (July 6).

Confederación de Nacionalidades Indígenas del Ecuador (CONAIE). 1998. *Las nacionalidades indígenas y el estado plurinacional.* Quito: CONAIE.

Coronil, Fernando, and Julie Skurski. 1991. "Dismembering and Remembering the Nation: The Semantics of Political Violence in Venezuela." *Contemporary Study in Society and History* 33: 288–337.

Crehan, Kate. 2002. *Gramsci, Culture, and Anthropology.* Berkeley & Los Angeles: University of California Press.

Cromos. 2001a. 4(369) (October 29).

———. 2001b. 4(371) (November 12).

Cueva, Agustín. 1981. *Entre la ira y la esperanza: Ensayos sobre la cultura nacional.* Cuenca: Casa de la Cultura Ecuatoriana, Núcleo del Azuay.

———. 1986. *Lecturas y rupturas: Diez ensayos sociológicos sobre la literatura del Ecuador.* Quito: Editorial Planeta.

Cypess, Sandra Messinger. 1991. *La Malinche in Mexican Literature: From History to Myth.* Austin: University of Texas Press.

Davis, Angela. 1998. *Blues Legacies and Black Feminism.* New York: Vintage Books.

de la Cadena, Marisol. 2000. *Indigenous Mestizos: The Politics of Race and Culture in Cuzco, Peru, 1919–1991.* Durham, N.C.: Duke University Press.

de la Cuadra, José. 1973. *Los Sangurimas, Hornos y otros relatos.* Guayaquil: Publicaciones Educativas Ariel.

de la Torre, Carlos. 2002. *Afroquiteños, ciudadanía y racismo.* Quito: Centro Andino de Acción Popular.

del Valle, José, and Luis Gabriel-Stheeman. 2002. *The Battle over Spanish between 1800 and 2000: Language Ideologies and Hispanic Intellectuals.* London: Routledge.

Dorfman, Ariel. 1998. *Heading South, Looking North.* New York: Farrar Straus Giroux.

Duras, Marguerite. 1986. *The Malady of Death.* New York: Grove Press.

———. 1997. *The Lover.* New York: Harper and Row.

"Encuesta sobre Miss Ecuador." 1996. *El Hoy* (February 13).

Estupiñan Bass, Nelsón. 1983. *Cuando los guayacanes florecían.* Quito: Editorial El Conejo.

Fanon, Frantz. 1965. *The Wretched of the Earth.* New York: Grove Press.

———. 1967. *A Dying Colonialism.* New York: Grove Press.

———. 1970. *Black Skin, White Mask.* New York: Grove Press.

Feliciano, José. 1991. *El sentimiento, la voz y la guitarra.* CD recording. New York: BMG International.

Ferrándiz, Francisco. 2003. "Malandros, María Lionza and Masculinity in a Venezuela Shantytown." In *Changing Men and Masculinities in Latin America,* edited by M. Guttman, pp. 115–133. Durham: University of North Carolina Press.

———. 2004. "The Body as Wound: Possession, Malandros and Everyday Violence in Venezuela." *Critique of Anthropology* 24(2): 107–133.

Flores, Juan. 1992. "Cortijo's Revenge: New Mappings of Puerto Rican Culture." In *On Edge: The Crisis of Contemporary Latin American Culture,* edited by G. Yudice, J. Franco, and J. Flores, pp. 187–205. Minneapolis: University of Minnesota Press.

Foucault, Michel. 1980. *Power and Knowledge: Selected Interviews and Other Writings 1972–1977.* New York: Pantheon Books.

———. 1988. *Madness and Civilization: A History of Insanity in the Age of Reason.* New York: Viking Books.

———. 1990. *The History of Sexuality.* Vols. 1, 2, and 3. New York: Vintage Books.

———. 1993. "Nietzsche, Genealogy and History." In *Language, Counter-Memory, Practices: Selected Essays and Interviews,* edited by D. Bouchard, pp. 139–164. Ithaca, N.Y.: Cornell University Press.

———. 1994. *The Birth of the Clinic: An Archaeology of Medical Perception.* New York: Vintage Books.

———. 1995. *Discipline and Punish: The Birth of the Prison.* New York: Vintage Books.

———. 1996. "The End of the Monarchy of Sex." In *Foucault Live, Collected Interviews, 1961–1984,* edited by S. Lotringer, pp. 214–225. New York: Semiotext(e).

———. 1998. "On the Ways of Writing History." In *Aesthetics, Method and Epistemology/Essential Works of Foucault, #2,* edited by J. Faubion, pp. 279–295. New York: New Press.

Franco, Jean. 1989. *Plotting Women: Gender and Representation in Mexico.* New York: Columbia University Press.

———. 2002. *The Decline and Fall of the Lettered City: Latin America in the Cold War.* Cambridge, Mass.: Harvard University Press.

Freire, Paulo. 1992. *Pedagogy of the Oppressed.* New York: Continuum.

Fusco, Coco. 1994. "The Other History of Intercultural Performance." *The Drama Review: The Journal of Performance Studies* 38(1): 143–167.

———. 1995. *English Is Broken Here: Notes on Cultural Fusion in the Americas.* New York: New Press.

Galeano, Eduardo. 2002. *El fútbol: A sol y sombra.* Mexico City: Siglo Veintiuno Editores.

Gallegos Lara, Joaquín. 1980 [1944]. *Las cruces sobre el agua.* Guayaquil: Casa de la Cultura, Núcleo del Guayas.

Gallegos Lara, Joaquín; Enrique Gil Gilbert; and Demetrio Aguilera Malta. 1973 [1933]. *Los que se van.* Guayaquil: Publicaciones Educativas Ariel.

García-Canclini, Néstor. 1968. *Cortázar: Una antropología poética*. Buenos Aires: Editorial Nova.

———. 1992. "Cultural Reconversion." In *On Edge: The Crisis of Contemporary Latin American Culture*, edited by G. Yudice, J. Franco, and J. Flores, pp. 29–43. Minneapolis: University of Minnesota Press.

Genet, Jean. 1974. *Querelle*. New York: Grove Press.

Giddens, Anthony. 1992. *The Transformation of Intimacy: Sexuality, Love, and Eroticism in Modern Society*. Stanford, Calif.: Stanford University Press.

Gil Gilbert, Enrique. 1983. *Nuestro pan*. Havana: Casa de las Américas.

Gómez Iturralde, José A. 1998. *Los periódicos guayaquileños en la historia, 1821–1997*. Vol. 2: *1883–1920*. Guayaquil: Archivo Histórico del Guayas.

———. N.d. "La verdadera fucación de Guayaquil (Explicación que acaba con mitos y leyendas)." http://www.guayaquilhistorico.org.ec/webpages/fundacion.htm

Gómez-Peña, Guillermo. 1991. "Border Brujo." In *Being America: Essays on Art, Literature, and Identity from Latin America*, edited by R. Weiss with A. West, pp. 194–231. Fredonia, N.Y.: White Pine Press.

———. 1994. "The Multicultural Paradigm: An Open Letter to the National Arts Community." In *Negotiating Performance: Gender, Sexuality, and Theatricality in Latin/o America*, edited by D. Taylor and J. Villegas, pp. 17–29. Durham, N.C.: Duke University Press.

———. 1996. "The Artist as Criminal." *The Drama Review: The Journal of Performance Studies* 40(1): 112–118.

Gramsci, Antonio. 1971. *Selections from the Prison Notebooks,* edited by Q. Hoare and G. Nowell-Smith. New York: International Publishers.

Gregory, Steven, and Roger Sanjek (editors). 1994. *Race*. New Brunswick, N.J.: Rutgers University Press.

Gutmann, Matthew. 1996. *The Meaning of Macho: Being a Man in Mexico City*. Berkeley & Los Angeles: University of California Press.

Hale, Charles. 1996. "Introduction." *Journal of Latin American Anthropology* 2(1): 2–3.

Hall, Stuart (editor). 1980. "Culture, Media, Language: Working Papers in Cultural Studies 1972–1979." Birmingham, Eng.: Center for Contemporary Cultural Studies, University of Birmingham.

———. 1997a. "The Local and the Global: Globalization and Ethnicity." In *Culture, Globalization and the World-System: Contemporary Conditions for the Representation of Identity*, edited by A. King, pp. 19–39. Minneapolis: University of Minnesota Press.

———. 1997b. "Old and New Identities, Old and New Ethnicities." In *Culture, Globalization and the World-System: Contemporary Conditions for the Representation of Identity*, edited by A. King, pp. 41–68. Minneapolis: University of Minnesota Press.

Handler, Richard, and Eric Gable. 1997. *The New History in an Old Museum: Creating the Past at Colonial Williamsburg.* Durham, N.C.: Duke University Press.

Haraway, Donna. 1989. *Primate Visions: Gender, Race, and Nature in the World of Modern Science.* New York: Routledge.

Hesse, Hermann. 1994. *The Journey to the East.* New York: Noonday Press.

Hobsbawm, Eric, and Terence Ranger (editors). 1983. *The Invention of Tradition.* Cambridge: Cambridge University Press.

El Hoy. 1995a. November 9: 10.

———. 1995b. November 11: 11.

———. 1995c. November 15: 7.

Hurtado, Osvaldo. 1981. *El poder político en el Ecuador.* Barcelona: Editorial Planeta Ariel.

Irigaray, Luce. 1985a. *Speculum of the Other Woman.* Ithaca, N.Y.: Cornell University Press.

———. 1985b. *This Sex Which Is Not One.* Ithaca, N.Y.: Cornell University Press.

———. 1993a. *An Ethics of Sexual Difference.* Ithaca, N.Y.: Cornell University Press.

———. 1993b. *Je, Tu, Nous: Toward a Culture of Difference.* New York: Routledge.

Jaramillo, Julio. 1997. *Un recuerdo de los 80 años de Julio Jaramillo.* CD recording. Guayaquil: FEDISCOS.

Joseph, Gilbert, and Daniel Nugent (editors). 1994. *Everyday Forms of State Formation: Revolution and the Negotiation of Rule in Modern Mexico.* Durham, N.C.: Duke University Press.

Julien, Isaac (director). 1997. *Frantz Fanon: Black Skin, White Masks.* Documentary. Normal Film Production, for BBC and the Arts Council of England.

Kaminsky, Amy. 1994. "Gender, Race, Raza." *Feminist Studies* 20(1): 7–31.

Kincaid, Jamaica. 1988. *A Small Place.* New York City: Farrar Straus Giroux.

———. 1990. *Lucy.* New York: Farrar Straus Giroux.

———. 1996. *The Autobiography of My Mother.* New York: Farrar Straus Giroux.

———. 1997. *My Brother.* New York: Farrar Straus Giroux.

Kohl, Phillip, and Clare Fawcett (editors). 1995. *Nationalism, Politics, and the Practice of Archaeology.* Cambridge: Cambridge University Press.

Kristeva, Julia. 1977. *About Chinese Women.* London: M. Boyars.

———. 1982. *Powers of Horror: An Essay of Abjection.* New York: Columbia University Press.

———. 1986. *The Kristeva Reader,* edited by T. Moi. New York: Columbia University Press.

————. 1987. *Tales of Love*. New York: Columbia University Press.

————. 1989. *Black Sun: Depression and Melancholia*. New York: Columbia University Press.

Kundera, Milan. 1984. *The Unbearable Lightness of Being*. New York: Harper and Row.

Kureishi, Hanif. 1998. *The Buddha of Suburbia*. London: Faber and Faber.

Lacan, Jacques. 1977. *Ecrits: A Selection*. New York: W. W. Norton.

Lancaster, Roger. 1986. *Life Is Hard: Machismo, Danger, and the Intimacy of Power in Nicaragua*. Berkeley & Los Angeles: University of California Press.

Leeming, David. 1994. *James Baldwin*. New York: Alfred A. Knopf.

Lessing, Doris. 1987. *Prisons We Choose to Live Inside*. New York: Harper and Row.

————. 1994. *Under My Skin*. London: Harper Collins.

Luzuriaga, Camilo (director). 1995. *La tigra*. Grupo Cine Production. New York: International Film Circuit, 80'.

Macías, Washington. 1983. *Problemas socio-económicos del Ecuador*. Otavalo: Gallo Capitán.

————. 1986. *Ecuador, de la agro-exportación a la industrialización asociada, 1830–1986*. Guayaquil.

Maiguashca, Juan (editor). 1994. *Historia y región en el Ecuador: 1830–1930*. Quito: FLACSO and Corporación Editora Nacional.

Malkki, Lisa. 1995. *Purity and Exile: Violence, Memory, and National Cosmology among Hutu Refugees in Tanzania*. Chicago: University of Chicago Press.

Mallon, Florencia. 1995. *Peasant and Nation: The Making of Postcolonial Mexico and Peru*. Berkeley & Los Angeles: University of California Press.

————. 1996. "Constructing *Mestizaje* in Latin America: Authenticity, Marginality, and Gender in the Claiming of Ethnic Identities." *Journal of Latin American Anthropology* 2(1): 170–181.

"María Luisa Barrios, una Barbie para el concurso Miss Ecuador." 2004. *El Universo* (February 18).

Martillo Monserrate, Jorge. 1999. *La bohemia en Guayaquil y otras historias crónicas*. Guayaquil: Archivo Histórico del Guayas.

Martínez, Luis A. 1992. *A la costa*. Madrid: Editorial de Cultura Hispánica.

Martínez, Rubén. 1992. *The Other Side: Notes from the New L.A., Mexico City and Beyond*. New York: Vintage Books.

————. 1998. "Technicolor." In *Half and Half: Writers of Growing Up Biracial and Bicultural*, edited by C. O'Hearn, pp. 245–264. New York: Pantheon Books.

McCarthy, E. Doyle, and David Franks (editors). 1989. *The Sociology of Emotions: Original Essays and Research Papers*. Greenwich, Conn.: JAI Press.

McClintock, Anne. 1995. *Imperial Leather: Race, Gender, and Sexuality in the Colonial Contest*. New York: Routledge.

McClintock, Anne; Aamir Mufti; and Ella Shohat. 1997. *Dangerous Liaisons: Gender, Nation and Postcolonial Perspectives*. Minneapolis: University of Minnesota Press.

"Medardo Ángel Silva." 1919. *El Telégrafo* (June 15): 4.

"Medardo A. Silva: Le fueron duros sus años." 1999. *El Hoy*, Internet edition (June 7).

Memmi, Albert. 1991. *The Colonizer and the Colonized*. Boston: Beacon Press.

Menchú, Rigoberta. 1985. *Me llamo Rigoberta Menchú y así me nació la conciencia*, edited by E. Burgos. Mexico City: Siglo Veintiuno Editores.

———. 1998. *Crossing Borders*. New York: Verso.

Merleau-Ponty, Maurice. 1963. *The Structure of Behavior*. Boston: Beacon Press.

Mignolo, Walter. 2000. *Local Histories/Global Designs: Coloniality, Subaltern Knowledges, and Border Thinking*. Princeton, N.J.: Princeton University Press.

Minh-ha, Trinh. 1997. "Not You/Like You: Postcolonial Women and the Interlocking Questions of Identity and Difference." In *Dangerous Liaisons: Gender, Nation, and Postcolonial Perspectives*, edited by A. McClintock, A. Mufti, and E. Shohat, pp. 415–419. Minneapolis: University of Minnesota Press.

"Miss Ecuador 1995." 1995. *Vistazo* 678 (November 16): 101–106.

Mitchell, Timothy. 1988. *Colonising Egypt*. Cambridge: Cambridge University Press.

Monsiváis, Carlos. 1997. *Mexican Postcards*. Translated and introduced by J. Kraniauskas. London: Verso.

Morraga, Cherríe. 1986. "From a Long Line of Vendidas: Chicanas and Feminism." In *Feminist Studies/Critical Studies*, edited by T. de Lauretis. Bloomington: Indiana University Press.

———. 1994. "Art in América con Acento." In *Negotiating Performance: Gender, Sexuality, and Theatricality in Latin/o America*, edited by D. Taylor and J. Villegas, pp. 30–36. Durham, N.C.: Duke University Press.

Morrison, Toni. 1993. *Playing in the Dark: Whiteness in the Literary Imagination*. New York: Vintage Books.

Murray, Timothy. 1997. *Drama Trauma: Specters of Race and Sexuality in Performance, Video, and Art*. London: Routledge.

Muse, Michael. 1991. "Products and Politics of a Milagro Entrepot: Peñon del Río, Guayas Basin, Ecuador." *Research in Economic Anthropology* 13: 269–322.

Muteba Rahier, Jean. 1998. "Blackness, the Racial/Spatial Order, Migrations, and Miss Ecuador 1995-6." *American Anthropologist* 100(2): 421–430.

———. 1999. "Mami, ¿qué es lo que quiere el negro?: Representaciones racistas en la revista *Vistazo*, 1957–1991." In *Ecuador racista: Imágenes e identidades*, edited by E. Cervone and F. Rivera, pp. 73–110. Quito: FLACSO.

Naranjo, Marcelo (editor). 1984. *Temas sobre la continuidad y adaptación cultural ecuatoriana*. Quito: EDUC.

Nelson, Diane. 2001. "Indian Giver or Nobel Savage: Duping, Assumptions of Identity, and Other Double Entendres in Rigoberta Menchú Tum's Stoll/en Past." *American Ethnologist* 28(2): 303–331.

Nuestras Bellezas. 2000a. http://www.geocities.com/fotitos2000/GaleriaSoraya. html.

————. 2000b. http://www.geocities.com/fotitos2000/ GaleriaMonica.html.

"La nueva Miss Ecuador." 1995. *El Comercio* (November 19).

Omi, Michael, and Howard Winant. 1994. *Racial Formation in the United States: From the 1960's to the 1990's.* New York: Routledge.

Ortiz, Adalberto. 1982. *Juyungo.* Washington: Three Continents Press.

————. 1983. *El espejo y la ventana.* Quito: Editorial El Conejo.

Otero Garabís, Miguel. 2000. *Nación y ritmo: "Descargas" desde el Caribe.* San Juan, P.R.: Editorial Callejón.

"Página literaria de 'El Telégrafo.'" 1945. June 10: 6–7.

Palacio, Pablo. 1986. *Obras completas.* Quito: Editorial El Conejo.

Pareja Diezcanseco, Alfredo. 1990. *Breve historia del Ecuador.* Quito: Libreas.

Parque Histórico Guayaquil. http://www.parquehistorico.com/html.

Patterson, Thomas, and Peter Schmidt (editors). 1995. "Introduction: From Constructing to Making Alternative Histories." In *Making Alternative Histories: The Practice of Archaeology and History in Non-Western Settings,* edited by P. R. Schmidt and T. C. Patterson, pp. 1–24. Santa Fe, N.M.: School of American Research Press.

Pérez-Firmat, Gustavo. 1997. *Bilingual Blues.* New York: Bilingual Press/Edición Bilingüe.

Phelan, John L. 1967. *The Kingdom of Quito in the Seventeenth Century: Bureaucratic Politics in the Spanish Empire.* Madison: University of Wisconsin Press.

Pino Roca, Gabriel. 1973. *Leyendas, tradiciones y páginas de historia de Guayaquil.* Vol. 2. Guayaquil: Junta Cívica.

Popular Memory Group. 1982. "Popular Memory: Theory, Politics, and Method." *In Making Histories: Studies in History-Writing and Politics,* edited by R. Johnson, pp. 205–252. London: Hutchinson Press.

Pratt, Mary Louise. 1992. *Imperial Eyes: Travel Writing and Transculturation.* New York: Routledge.

Quijano, Aníbal. 1995. "América Latina en la economía mundial." *Problemas del Desarrollo* 24:5–18.

Quintero, Rafael, and Erika Silva. 1991. *Ecuador: Una nación en ciernes.* Vols. 1, 2, and 3. Quito: FLACSO and Abya-Yala.

Quintero López, Rafael. 1997. "Identidad nacional y estado nacional." In *Identidad Nacional y Globalización,* edited by A. Acosta, pp. 139–164. Quito: ILDIS, FLACSO, and Instituto de Altos Estudios Nacionales.

Quintero Rivera, Ángel G. 1989. *Music, Social Classes and the National Question of Puerto Rico.* Washington, D.C.: Wilson Center.

Renan, Ernst. 1990. "What Is a Nation?" In *Nation and Narration,* edited by H. Bhabha, pp. 19–36. London: Routledge.

Reyes, Óscar Efrén. 1967. *Breve historia general del Ecuador.* 3 vols. Quito: Ed. Fray Jodoco Ricke.

Rhys, Jean. 1982. *Wide Sargasso Sea.* New York: W. W. Norton.

Rivera, Lisandra, and Manolo Sarmiento. 2002. *Problemas personales.* Video documentary, Pequeña Nube Producciones and Cabeza Hueca Producciones.

Rodríguez, Richard. 2004. *Brown: The Last Discovery of America.* New York: Vintage Books.

Rodríguez Vicéns, Antonio. 1997. *La patria boba: Artículos sobre el gobierno de Abdalá Bucaram.* Quito: Artes Gráficas Señal.

———. 2001. *Notas al margen, 1990–1999.* Quito.

Romero Castillo, Abel. 1970. *Medardo Ángel Silva: Una biografía.* Guayaquil: Casa de la Cultura, Núcleo del Guayas.

Rosaldo, Renato. 1989. *Culture and Truth: The Remaking of Social Analysis.* Boston: Beacon Press.

Roseberry, William. 1994. "Hegemony and the Language of Contention." In *Everyday Forms of State Formation: Revolution and the Negotiation of Rule in Modern Mexico,* edited by G. Joseph and D. Nugent, pp. 355–366. Durham, N.C.: Duke University Press.

Rowe, William, and Vivian Schelling. 1991. *Memory and Modernity: Popular Culture in Latin America.* New York: Verso.

Rueda Novoa, Rocío. 2001. *Zambaje y autonomía: Historia de la gente negra de la Provincia de Esmeraldas.* Esmeraldas: Municipalidad de Esmeraldas, TEHIS, Abya-Yala.

Rulfo, Juan. 2002 [1953]. *Pedro Páramo y el llano en llamas.* Madrid: Planeta.

Rushdie, Salman. 1994. *East, West.* London: Jonathan Cape.

———. 2000. *Conversations with Salman Rushdie,* edited by M. Reder. Jackson: University of Mississippi Press.

Said, Edward. 1978. *Orientalism.* New York: Pantheon Books.

———. 1999. *Out of Place: A Memoir.* New York: Random House.

———. 2000. *Reflections on Exile and Other Essays.* Cambridge, Mass.: Harvard University Press.

Salazar, Ernesto. 1995. *Entre mitos y fábulas: El Ecuador aborigen.* Quito: Corporación Editora Nacional.

Salecl, Renata, and Slavoj Žižek. 1996. *Gaze and Voice as Love Objects.* Durham, N.C.: Duke University Press.

Santacruz, Nicomedes. 1995. "Afroamericanos: Presencia y expansión." In *Afroamericanos: Buscando raíces, afirmando identidad.* Aportes para el Debate, no. 4. Quito: Agencia Latinoamericana de Información.

Santiago, Esmeralda, and Joie Davidow (editors). 2000. *Las Mamis: Favorite Latino Authors Remember Their Mothers.* New York: Knopf.

Santos, Daniel. 1995. *Interpreta a Julio Jaramillo*. CD recording. Guayaquil: 3 Jotas.

Sayer, Derek. 1994. "Everyday Forms of State Formation: Some Dissident Remarks on 'Hegemony.'" In *Everyday Forms of State Formation: Revolution and the Negotiation of Rule in Modern Mexico*, edited by G. Joseph and D. Nugent, pp. 367–378. Durham, N.C.: Duke University Press.

Schmidt Camacho, Alicia. 2004. "Body Counts on the Mexico-U.S. Border: Feminicidio, Reification, and the Theft of Mexicana Subjectivity." *Chicana/ Latina Studies: The Journal of Mujeres Activas en Letras y Cambio Social* 4 (Fall): 22–61.

Scott, James. 1985. *Weapons of the Weak: Everyday Forms of Peasant Resistance*. New Haven, Conn.: Yale University Press.

Serrano, Marcela. 1997. *El albergue de las mujeres tristes*. Mexico City: Alfaguara.

Shakespeare, William. 1994 [1612?], *The Tempest*. New York: Washington Square Press.

Shank, Barry. 2000. *A Token of My Affection: Greeting Cards and American Business Culture*. New York: Columbia University Press.

Sider, Gerald, and Gavin Smith. 1997. *Between History and Histories: The Making of Silences and Commemorations*. Toronto: University of Toronto Press.

Silva, Erika. 1995. *Los mitos de la ecuatorianidad: Ensayo sobre la identidad nacional*. Quito: Abya-Yala.

Silva, Medardo Ángel. 1964. *El árbol del bien y del mal*. Guayaquil: Editorial Casa de la Cultura Ecuatoriana, Núcleo del Guayas.

———. 2000. *Obra poética*, edited by Antonio Rodriguez Vicéns. Quito: Artes Gráficas Señal Impreseñal.

———. N.d. *El árbol del bien y del mal*. Clásicos Ariel, no. 33. Guayaquil: Clásicos Ariel.

Silverblatt, Irene. 1987. *Moon, Sun, and Witches: Gender and Class Ideologies in Inca and Colonial Peru*. Princeton, N.J.: Princeton University Press.

———. 1988. "Political Memories and Colonizing Symbols: Santiago and the Mountain Gods of Colonial Peru." In *Rethinking History and Myth: Indigenous South America*, edited by J. Hill, pp. 174–194. Urbana: University of Illinois Press.

Smith, Carol. 1996. "Myths, Intellectuals, and Race/Class/Gender Distinctions in the Formation of Latin American Nations." *Journal of Latin American Anthropology* 2(1): 148–169.

Sosa, Mercedes. 1995. *Oro*. CD recording. New York: Polygram Latino.

Spivak, Gayatri. 1999. *A Critique of Postcolonial Reason*. London: Routledge.

Stoler, Anne Laura. 1996. *Race and the Education of Desire: Foucault's History of Sexuality and the Colonial Order of Things*. Durham, N.C.: Duke University Press.

———. 2002. *Carnal Knowledge and Imperial Power: Race and the Intimate in Colonial Rule.* Berkeley & Los Angeles: University of California Press.

Stoll, David. 1999. *Rigoberta Menchú and the Story of All Poor Guatemalans.* Boulder, Colo.: Westview Press.

Stutzman, Ronald. 1981. "El Mestizaje: An All-Inclusive Ideology of Exclusion." In *Cultural Transformations and Ethnicity in Modern Ecuador,* edited by N. Whitten, pp. 45–93. Urbana: University of Illinois Press.

Taussig, Michael. 1992. "Maleficium: State Fetishism." In *The Nervous System.* New York: Routledge.

Trouillot, Michel-Rolph. 1995. *Silencing the Past: Power and the Production of History.* Boston: Beacon Press.

Ulloa, Edwin. 1992. *Sobre una tumba una rumba: Cuentos.* (Ecuador): Abrapalabra Editores.

Uxandaberro, Roura. N.d. *Guayaquil, folklore y paisaje.* Guayaquil.

Vallejo, Raúl. 1988. *Sólo de palabras.* Quito: Editorial El Conejo.

———. 2003. *El alma en los labios.* Quito: Editorial Planeta.

Vasconcelos, José. 1997. *The Cosmic Race.* Baltimore, Md.: Johns Hopkins University Press.

Vásconez, Javier. 1986. *Las criaturas de la noche.* Quito: El Conejo.

Wade, Peter. 1993. *Blackness and Race Mixture: Dynamics of Racial Identity in Colombia.* Baltimore, Md.: Johns Hopkins University Press.

———. 1994. "Representation and Power: Blacks in Colombia." In *Social Construction of the Past: Representation as Power,* edited by G. Bond and A. Gilliam, pp. 59–73. London: Routledge.

Wexler, Laura. 2000. *Tender Violence: Domestic Visions in an Age of U.S. Imperialism.* Chapel Hill: University of North Carolina Press.

White, E. Frances. 2001. *Dark Continent of Our Bodies: Black Feminism and the Politics of Respectability.* Philadelphia: Temple University Press.

Whitten, Norman. 1984. "Etnocidio ecuatoriano y etnogénesis indígena: Resurgencia amazónica ante la colonización andina." In *Temas sobre la continuidad y adaptación cultural ecuatoriana,* edited by M. Naranjo. Quito: EDUC.

Wilde, Oscar. 1964. *De Profundis.* New York: Avon Books.

Williams, Brackette. 1991. *Stains on My Name, War in My Veins: Guyana and the Politics of Cultural Struggle.* Durham, N.C.: Duke University Press.

Williams, Raymond. 1973. *The Country and the City.* New York: Oxford University Press.

———. 1977. *Marxism and Literature.* Oxford: Oxford University Press.

Wong, Ketty. 1999. "The Polysemous 'Pasillo': The Debate around the Musical Construction of Ecuadorian National Identity." Master's thesis, University of Texas at Austin.

Wylie, Alison. 1992. "The Interplay of Evidential Constraints and Political Interests: Recent Archaeological Research on Gender." *American Antiquity* 57(1): 15–35.

———. 1995. "Alternative Histories: Epistemic Disunity and Political Integrity." In *Making Alternative Histories: The Practice of Archaeology and History in Non-Western Settings,* edited by T. Patterson and P. Schmidt, pp. 255–272. Santa Fe, N.M.: School of American Research Press.

Xavier, Emanuel. N.d. http://www.qvmagazine.con/qv9/ qvtriumphs.thml.

Yánez Cosíos, Alicia. 2000. *Y amarle pude* . . . Quito: Editorial Planeta del Ecuador.

Yudice, George; Jean Franco; and Juan Flores (editors). 1992. *On Edge: The Crisis of Contemporary Latin American Culture.* Minneapolis: University of Minnesota Press.

Žižek, Slavoj. 1989. *The Sublime Object of Ideology.* London: Verso.

———(editor). 1996. " 'I Hear You with My Eyes': Or, the Invisible Master." In *Gaze and Voice as Love Objects,* edited by S. Žižek and R. Salecl, pp. 90–126. Durham, N.C.: Duke University Press.

———. 2002. *Welcome to the Desert of the Real.* London: Verso.

Žižek, Slavoj; Judith Butler; and Ernesto Laclau. 2000. *Contingency, Hegemony, Universality: Contemporary Dialogues on the Left.* London: Verso.

La Zona del Trago. N.d. http://www.geocities.com/NapaValley/1155/index.htm.

Index

Lightning Source UK Ltd.
Milton Keynes UK
UKHW012148050821
387960UK00012B/237